LANGUAGE

Mirror,

Tool,

and Weapon

George W. Kelling

LANGUAGE

Mirror,
Tool,
and Weapon

Nelson-Hall *nh* Chicago

Library of Congress Cataloging in Publication Data

Kelling, George W.
　　Language: mirror, tool, and weapon.

　　Bibliography: p.
　　1. Languages—Psychology. 2. Whorf, Benjamin Lee,
1897-1941. I. Title.
P37.K4　　401'.9　　74-10511
ISBN 0-911012-85-0

Contents

Preface

Historical Introduction

This book deals with the relationship between language on the one hand and, on the other hand, "other things," e.g., behavior, thought, culture, personality, philosophy, and politics. While there are a great many statements of this relationship, many of which are discussed in this book, the strongest statement belongs to Benjamin Lee Whorf. Furthermore, his statement has historical significance. A brief review of it will serve to introduce this book.

His statement, which we will call the Whorfian hypothesis, is that the structure and lexicon (the grammar and vocabulary) of a language dictate the habitual thought and behavior of the speakers of that language. We are, he suggested, at the mercy of the world view forced on us by the language we speak.

His hypothesis puts Whorf in the company of Galileo, Darwin, and Freud, all of whom have reduced the size of man's ego.

But as one moves from Galileo to Darwin to Freud to Whorf, one notices a decreasing acceptance of their ideas, both by the general public and by the scholars in their respective fields. One also notices an increasing implication for the concrete aspects of day-to-day life. Man can live knowing that he is not at the center of the physical universe, since he is at the center of his own universe and is so far at the center of the animate universe. Man can live knowing that he is descended from the apes, since he controls apes and the rest of the species of the world. Freud implied that man is restricted in what he is *likely* to know about himself. But Whorf went further: Man is restricted in what he *can* come to know about himself *and* his universe.

Furthermore, Freud offers a way out. Man can learn the language of psychoanalysis. In order to do this, he must be psychoanalyzed. The purpose of psychoanalysis is to make the unconscious conscious. Man thereby escapes bondage.

But Whorf would have said that psychoanalysis is a language like any other. There is no guarantee that any language allows its speakers an accurate perception of reality. And if a language did allow accurate access to reality, there would be no way for the speakers to know that it was accurate.

So while Whorf's hypothesis is not as frightening as Freud's, it limits man more. Yet Whorf's hypothesis has been poorly treated. Critics have not fully explored the hypothesis and popularizers have been over enthusiastic and sensational. The same was true of Freud's theories. Freud believed this treatment resulted from fear. Fear is probably not an important reason for Whorf's neglect. The theory in its general form is untestable, and what empirical research has been done has not been encouraging. Language is better described as used than spoken: Whorf's major flaw was his implicit assumption that man is passive in the face of his language.

Despite all this, I believe that the Whorfian hypothesis, conceived broadly enough to include other statements of the language –other thing relationship, deserves the close scrutiny it receives in this book. The place in history of the study of man's language is even closer to home than the study of man: Any study of man must be conducted in or eventually presented in language. Therefore, the study of language is the study of the study of man.

Approach of the Book

T. S. Kuhn (1962) presents an alternative to the common view that science proceeds by a process of gradual accrual, i.e., by the addition of this small fact to that small fact until finally a magnificant and significant whole is created. I use *accrual* rather than *accretion,* which commonly follows *gradual* in this context. *Accretion* implies that the small parts grow together to produce a whole, while *accrual* doesn't; and there is no evidence that a large collection of facts will be anything else or more unless someone comes along to integrate them. This is often done by someone who invents a *paradigm,* to use Kuhn's term. A paradigm is a revolutionary way of looking at things. Kuhn suggests that science is a succession of paradigms. After one arrives, much time and energy are spent by lesser men filling in the details and integrating the known facts into the paradigm. To use Kuhn's example, Newton did not work out his laws of motion for more than two bodies; it takes no new laws, but a good deal of intelligent work, to extend the laws, and that was what scientists did while waiting for Einstein.

In the social sciences, a paradigm is more a way of looking at things than a set of laws or principles. Freud's basic principle is that *all* behavior is determined. From that all else proceeds, but the principle is a good deal more vague and philosophical than $E = MC^2$.

For example, Freud's paradigm directed him to look for the causes of behavior. Often a person would not know why he did something, but an outside observer might try to make sense of it by postulating a motive the person was unconscious of. But let us try on a new paradigm: Look at what people are doing, not at why they are doing it. Then unconscious motivation looks like a way of explaining behavior. If P says O is unconsciously motivated, P is trying to do something to O. There are various possibilities: P may be trying to get "one up" on O by showing his superior knowledge. P may believe that if O can be made to admit that he lusts after his own mother, O will lose the glib self-assurance so detrimental to the cure of neurotics. Or P may merely wish to deny that O is doing what O says he is doing. In any event, note that this paradigm, by directing us to what *P* is trying to do to O rather than to why O is behaving as he is, leaves out any reference to the existence *or* lack of existence of unconscious motivations.

It is given to few to invent paradigms. And in the social sciences, as the above examples show, the paradigms do not tend to be as clearly revolutionary or shocking as relativity or evolution. Furthermore, there are many paradigms in the social sciences, while in physics, for example, Einstein's has sole possession of the title. In the social sciences, it is a matter of judgment or opinion who has invented a paradigm and who is merely a disciple. Therefore, the paradigms concerning language and communication I discuss would differ from those others would discuss.

The use of a paradigm in the social sciences is of crucial importance, because by nature the social sciences are more applied to humanity than physics, which is not in and of itself applied at all. No position regarding the morality of the atomic bomb is implied by physics proper; but it is impossible to take a social science paradigm without taking simultaneously and unavoidably a view of mankind (Peter G. Ossorio's paradigm is an exception since it involves, among other things, the psychology of paradigm formation): Freud believed man was driven by sex and aggression or life and death; Whorf believes we see via our language; Skinner implies that we are puppets.

Application of a paradigm in the social sciences is not as straightforward and automatic as applying $E = MC^2$. This is because there are no set rules for working out the details of a paradigm and because experimentation and instrumentation are not accurate and valid in the sense that they are in the physical sciences.

In this book I shall present a variety of paradigms. Furthermore, I shall attempt to integrate the paradigms, as well as the facts, so that the word *accretion* is justified. I will apply several paradigms to various problems in language and society. Finally, I will use them to fill in some holes and, I hope, to give the reader some food for further thought.

The paradigms I will use are those of Wittgenstein, Ossorio, Haley, and Whorf. I also rely heavily on the work of Roger Brown, who has invented some valuable concepts (which is almost like inventing a paradigm).

The references in this book are relatively few, even though I consider it a book that goes somewhere rather than a recapitulation and oversimplification of what others have said better. One reads few influential books in one's lifetime simply because there are relatively few books that are good or original or powerful enough to be influential. The books and articles written by originators of paradigms are usually sufficient for the non-specialist, i.e., for the person who does not plan to do research in the area. The filling in that follows a paradigm in the social sciences often seems to professionals and laymen alike to be meaningless nitpicking. In other cases, especially the case of generative-transformational grammar (inventor, Chomsky), the empirical and conceptual work of the disciples reveal such complexities that many people, laymen and professionals, think the paradigm should be dropped. Ptolemy, who invented all kinds of new motions for the planets, was doing OK—that is, he was keeping up with the new data—but he was inventing so many new motions that his theory brought no aesthetic pleasure to anyone except to one willing to devote his life to the intricate workings of the planets. Fortunately, Ptolemy was eventually dropped.

This book concerns the intersection of language, communication, and interpersonal relationships. The first bibliography provides a reader sufficient raw materials for all the thinking he might wish to do in this area. A second bibliography includes all references cited, and is of some scope. A third bibliography lists a few books similar to this one which cover topics I omit.

A Methodological Note

Psychologists do experiments to establish truth. Many of my observations in this book are, from the point of view of a good hard-headed empirical psychologist, outrageous, pointless, armchair conjecture. Linguists ask people questions to establish truth. Many of my observations in this book are, from the point of view of a good, empirical linguist, perfectly good observations on language, given that only one informant is being employed (myself). If linguists want to know what a language is like, they have to take the word of the speakers. Psychologists distrust what people say, often with good reason. People will cover up, lie, attempt to protect their privacy, act in strange ways around social scientists, and so on. But that comes with the territory. Linguists feel that much of what they ask people is the kind of thing people are and can be honest about. Furthermore, linguists feel that language is a sufficiently common performance that small samples are often sufficient. For example, most people in a certain small town in the Midwest probably say *pen* in an identical manner.

When my observations are more properly classed as psychological rather than linguistic, a larger sample might be needed. However, one should not apply the standards of psychology automatically to this work. People are capable of judging whether a person (in this case myself) has failed to exercise proper caution. Judgment, rather than rigid standards, is always a more appropriate approach to judgment.

Many of my observations are sociological. I therefore lay claim to the well-respected methodological technique of sociology, participant observation. I have been a participant observer of various segments of this society for a good many years; I have talked and listened to others talk in various areas, strata, and occupations of this country.

There are, of course problems with the technique. The observer may be over-involved, in which case he will be biased in certain ways. He may be under-involved, in which case he will be biased in certain other ways. Since we all are capable of judging if an account is over- or under-involved, all I can say is that I have taken all the precautions I know how to take. Any reader can judge my success.

Not all precautions are applicable to all undertakings. I have not sterilized my typewriter. Nor have I made sure never to use the personal pronoun, *I*. Such precautions, along with some other standard ones, are irrelevant to the task at hand—in my judgment.

Acknowledgments

My major debt is to Peter G. Ossorio. He has had an enormous influence on my thinking, only some of which can be directly cited in this book. I cannot vouch for the skill with which I have used his concepts, but he knows that one must learn such skill through doing.

I would also like to thank three other of my teachers, each of whom has had some influence on this book. Keith E. Davis led me to believe that unless one did one's best, one would not be rewarded, and that then one could expect his reward to be voluminous and harsh criticism. William A. Scott exposed me to the true complexities of empirical research and I learned some of them. He and Davis told me strongly and directly when they thought my work was poor, and why. One can ask for little more. Stuart W. Cook taught me the value and techniques of criticism of psychological research and I learned some of that.

These four teachers functioned as intellectual superegos in the writing of this book. That is, they did not personally advise me. Thus any failures in this book are due to my faulty incorporation of their ideas.

LANGUAGE

Mirror,

Tool,

and Weapon

chapter one

Some Significant Concepts

This book makes use of several concepts that are not commonly used in day-to-day language, nor are they particularly common in psychological, linguistic, or sociological discourse. They are not particularly difficult, esoteric, exotic, or technical; they are just not often used. Therefore, though knowing full well a book that begins with a definition of terms gets off on the wrong foot, I will introduce some of my main characters before putting them into action.

In addition, this chapter will serve as an introduction to most of the major paradigms discussed in the book. Because of the importance of concepts in social scientific paradigms, mastery of concepts is necessary for an understanding of the paradigms. Ruth Benedict described Japanese culture by giving definitions of a few Japanese words. The result was a book (1946), not a page from a dictionary. To understand the central concepts of a culture is to go a long way towards understanding the culture. To understand the central concepts of the subject matter of this book is to go a long way towards understanding the subject matter and being able to use it for oneself.

Real Names

This concept was introduced by Roger Brown (1965). The *real name* of an object (or behavior, event, person, state of affairs, situation) is the name we feel belongs to the object. It *sticks* to the object and doesn't seem like an "achievement of the imagination," to use Brown's phrase. For example, *pen* belongs to pens, *watch* belongs to watches, *dime* belongs to dimes. But this dime is also a *1952 dime,* a *1952 dime with tarnish and a chip on the bottom,* a *coin, money,* a *thing,* a *metal thing.* It really is all those things and yet those names don't fit nearly as snugly.

How could we measure what the real name of an object is? We could show it to people and ask them what it was. If a large percentage of the population agreed on one name, we could call that the real name. If half the population called it one name and half called it another, we might be tempted to say it has two real names. We might be similarly tempted if a large percentage gave it two names (we might expect this for a chess or checker board). If many different names are given, we might say that the object has no real name. What would happen, for example, if we asked a representative sample of the population in a representative sample of situations what they called sexual intercourse? We would get a different response from a gang of juveniles lounging on a streetcorner than we would get from people on their way to church. The word used would vary widely according to the type of person interviewed and the situation in which he was interviewed. The analysis of such states of affairs is an important part of Chapter Four.

Brown feels that there will be a real name if the object has one major and highly elaborated function. If not, there will not be a real name. The real name codifies the object at that most common and highly elaborated level of non-linguistic functioning (Brown, 1965). A dime functions most often as a dime. It exists as a dime, not as a coin: There is the famous song with the line, "Buddy, can you spare a dime?"; but *coin* is not a common or important concept in our culture. And a dime functions as a 1952 dime only for coin collectors; almost nobody gets attached enough to dimes to notice their individual features.

An introspective criterion for determining whether or not a name is the real name: See how snugly the word and thing fit in your mind, how sure you are it is *really* an X rather than all the other applicable descriptions. But remember that while it may be a real name for you it may not be for another or for the culture as a whole.

The validity of the concept is attested to by Piaget (1969, p. 243). For children, he says, "names are situated in objects. They form part of things in the same ways as do colour or form. Things have always had their names. It has always been sufficient to look at things in order to know their names." Piaget is not Freud, so the survival of real names into adulthood is no sign of pathology. Quite the contrary: Some (people diagnosed as) schizophrenics complain that objects and their names no longer fit together. To put it crudely, when you start wondering if a pen is really a pen, you are either going crazy or having a bout of philosophy.

Language as Reality

This section will serve as an introduction to the following concepts: *family resemblance, language game, form of life, criterial attribute.*

Let us take the position that we have no prelinguistic access to reality and that it makes no sense (and that there is no point) to talk about a reality that exists separately from our linguistic reactions to it. After all, we would have to describe that reality in language. So while it may in some sense exist, there is no point in talking about it; once we do, it no longer exists separately from our reactions to it.

The Whorfian hypothesis is that our language not only shapes but can distort our perception of (an already existing) reality. Here we take the position that our language couldn't distort reality because there is nothing to distort.

Let us consider anxiety, an important concept in today's society. What is anxiety? The only way to study anxiety is to first identify the subject matter. It makes no sense to study something you can't identify and distinguish from other things.

We make the claim here that the only way to identify the subject matter is to watch what people are talking about and doing when they use the word *anxiety*. What is happening to people when they say they are anxious? What is going on when someone says that someone else is anxious? What happens when we learn that someone is anxious?

We have no other guide. Someone must start the study rolling. But what shall we describe when we find people talking about anxiety? Fred says that he is anxious. Shall we identify anxiety with his physiological state, his facial expression, his fearful thoughts, or with the fact that when he says it he always is just about to ask a favor?

In general, we shall look to the whole situation, and we will find out from people what *they* take to be anxiety (e.g., do they think it's physiological?). Again, that is our only guide—if we want to study anxiety rather than something else. Hence our definition: "Anxiety is what people take to be anxiety."

This is an empty formula and full of problems. For example, Fred may think he's anxious. But Joe thinks that Fred is putting him on. Mary thinks that Fred is really hostile. Dr. Certain thinks he is really in existential terror. (*Really* means in the sense of real names.)

There will be disagreement. Negotiation, to be discussed later, is a way of dealing with disagreement. But with our definition at least we are in the ball park. At least we have a way of starting.

But the problems of disagreement and argument seem enormous, so traditionally the social sciences have attempted to simplify the situation, ignoring completely the fact that most of us walk around with these vague concepts we disagree about and get along very well indeed.

Thus, for example, it has been common to consider physiology basic. Anxiety really is a state of the body. This bodily state has some influence on the mental state. But this is manifestly nonsense. In order to discover the physiological state, someone must say, "Now there's anxiety, measure it." But that might be Fred speaking. Fred would have a good physiological measurement of anxiety. Mary would be on her way to a good physiological approach to hostility. And so on. Always the decision will be made by someone. And we all know to what extent people disagree. So unless we find an ultimate authority, we shall have to live with chaos.

In the scientific enterprise there is no ultimate authority. And just as God watches over every robin, science must watch over every native speaker of English who says *anxiety*. Status and money do not make one a judge of how to use a word.

Fortunately, we have little trouble living in chaos. Even more fortunately, the chaos is not so very chaotic. We share our concepts. That is, I mean pretty much what you mean when I say *anxiety*. Otherwise, you wouldn't know what I was talking about and we couldn't argue whether Fred was anxious or not. In order for *that* argument to take place, we must both know what anxiety is.

And you will know that I don't have the concept of anxiety if I say, "I'm so anxious and relaxed, it's wonderful." Our understanding and use of concepts are checked daily.

But why deny it? There are still serious problems. Fortunately, there are methods of solution. One of them is given by John Wilson in a book called *Thinking With Concepts* (1966). It is a technique for discovering what Bruner, Goodnow, and Austin (1956) would call the *criterial attributes* of concepts, i.e., those attributes or features or aspects of the state of affairs that, when they are present, are sufficient and (sometimes) necessary for us to claim we have a case of the concept. In other words, we can find the essential features of anxiety; they might be physiological arousal, a sense of apprehension, and decreased ability to concentrate. If and (sometimes) only if these attributes are present will we call a person anxious.

This is all very well and good and we will discuss this technique in some detail below. However, to cloud the issue let me introduce Ludwig Wittgenstein, who, many feel, is a real fly in the ointment and a man eminently qualified to cloud almost any issue you want clouded. To further confuse the issue, let me also introduce the concept of *love.*

What is love? Well, let's see how it's used:

1. John: "Mary, I love you."
2. Mary: "John, I love you."
3. Mary: "I love tennis."
4. Mary: "I just love your new dress."
5. John: "I love my parents."
6. Mary: "I love God."

What is the English language coming to when the sacred word love is used not only to other people aside from the deity, but also to games and dresses? And is the love of God and parents to be equated with the sexual love of young people?

In 1, 2, 5, and 6 there may be a criterial attribute: a serious intensity. But 1 and 2 do differ from 5 and 6 in that the latter two may indicate something more like duty without passion. And 3 and 4 are different from both. One can be enthusiastic about tennis and dresses, but it is neither appropriate nor quite sane to feel for either with a serious intensity or a sense of duty.

Wittgenstein talks about "family resemblances." I have my mother's nose and my father's fingers and my aunt's eyes; but my mother doesn't have my father's fingers nor my aunt's eyes, nor does my father have my aunt's eyes, and so on. Yet we are all related and part of the same family (although my mother, father, and I might decide that my aunt wasn't *really* part of the family). It is not even essential that I have any specific parts that are close to or exactly similar to the corresponding specific part of my mother, father, or aunt. As Wittgenstein would say, we are related but different. Sometimes it is more correct to say different but related.

It is very unlikely that we would be able to find a nice neat list of criterial attributes for 1–6, all of which are perfectly valid (i.e., common, understandable, and quite ordinary) uses of *love.*

Wilson would be at a loss and would perhaps deliver a stern admonishment such as the one above concerning the proper uses of *love.* Perhaps he would comment that such bastardization of English will occur if rich and bored females get together.

But rich and bored women are just as much a part of the human race as Romeo and Juliet; Wilson would be attempting to enforce order upon (what would seem to him to be) chaos. This is understandable, but that muddle-headed philosopher Wittgenstein has helped us out with his concept of family resemblance. Loving a dress is not far from loving tennis. It is rather far from loving God, but that is OK—they are more distant relatives. One understands that neither tennis nor dresses are worth dying for but there is a certain intensity or perhaps exclusiveness that renders them related to the other uses of *love.*

But perhaps we are pressing the similarity; perhaps the only similarity is that the word *love* has been used. The situations are similar, perhaps, for that and only that reason.

And when John tells Mary he loves her, what does he mean? What Romeo meant? How could we determine that? And does Joe love God in the same way Fred does? And how could we determine that? Given that people are different, it is unlikely that their loves or their usages of the word *love* will have any more similarity than people have in general.

So perhaps the word seems to be all that is common. The relationship would not seem to be one of blood. Perhaps the relationship is a marriage of convenience or a shotgun wedding. Why not accept the fact that the word doesn't mean anything in and of itself but is being used in an interpersonal context, with a certain intent, usually to indicate strong approval? But no. One can use the word to indicate approval, attraction, or infatuation. One can use the word to attempt to force the recipient to respond in a certain way. And so on. There are no clear commonalities here either. So we are back to an empty kind of similarity: Love exists everywhere someone takes it that it exists or uses the word.

But that is highly unsatisfactory. We do feel some similarity exists between situations in which the same word is used.

So let us say that the situations are related. But we play different games. We play, in Wittgenstein's terms, various *language games*. Associated with different language games are different *forms of life*. And, it appears, in a number of forms of life we single out something as rather special. Our parents hold a rather special position in our relationship with older adults. Tennis holds a rather special position in Mary's life as a player of games. Mary says she loves tennis to set tennis apart from other games. The beloved dress is being compared to other dresses, not to God, parents, Mary, or John.

We don't call out "Checkmate!" when we play a trump in bridge (unless we have some strange message to relate: Chapter Seven). Similarly, we don't respond to, "I just love your dress," with, "I'm sorry, it's already married," unless again we have a strange and interruptive purpose (such as protesting the overuse of the word *love*).

And so we talk about *legality* when in the domain of figuring the lowest possible tax, *criminality* when trying a man for armed robbery, *morality* when talking about adultery, and *manners* when talking about which fork to use. As I will argue in Chapter Four, when a word or family of words exists in many language games, it stands for a concept that is very important in the culture and it indicates a very important form of life. In the case of legality *et al.*, we have different words for the various language games but in each language game an important form of life is signified: picking proper behaviors and improper behaviors. In the case of love, we have but one word for all language games; but love functions in the various language games in ways that resemble each other in a family way.

I conclude this section with an answer to the old question, "What is love?" First, love is what people take to be love. Second, we use the word in many language games, and these usages have a family resemblance to each other. Sometimes the only resemblance is that the same word is used in two different language games. In other words, there are cases, and we can recognize them, where there seems to be no other similarity or resemblance or where we would swear two different families were involved. When we recognize such cases, we may wish to "draw the line." That is fine, but other people may not see it as we do. All decisions as to family resemblances must be made by people. There is no ultimate authority.

Paradigm* Cases and Functions

A paradigm case of a concept has all the criterial attributes of that concept. That is, a paradigm case has all the attributes necessary for saying we have an instance of the concept. A paradigm case of anxiety would perhaps involve physiological arousal, decreased ability to concentrate, and apprehension.

It is important to note, however, that we do not need all such criterial attributes to validly (i.e., understandably and correctly) apply the concept. If someone lives in constant fear of doom but shows no physiological signs of arousal or decreased ability to concentrate, we can still correctly say he is anxious, although we probably require more fear in such a case than we require if the other two criterial attributes are present. Furthermore, in such non-paradigm cases there is a tendency to look for a better description. We may describe this person as exhibiting behavior that is a *function* of anxiety. The number resulting when you apply the function *square the number* is the analogy. The resultant number is produced after you have operated on the input number. We operate on the concept of anxiety to produce different (but usually related) concepts, in this case, perhaps, *very well controlled anxiety*. Is this still anxiety? It is not *anxiety*, no, but it is *very well controlled anxiety*. Of course there are many departures from the paradigm case where we do not apply functions.

The value of a paradigmatic approach to concepts is that many cases other than the paradigmatic case can be described in terms of their deviations or differences (along the lines of parame-

---

*The word *paradigm* is used here in an entirely different way than in the Preface. There is no family resemblance. This is a case of *polyseny*. One word has two or more meanings. A *pen* is an enclosure and a writing instrument.

ters or criterial attributes) from the paradigm case, e.g., in this case, anxiety, but without the two criterial attributes.

There comes a point, however, where it ceases to make sense to describe something in derivative terms. For example, all behavior can be described in terms of deviations from the paradigm case of behavior, deliberate human behavior. A rock falling is like a person jumping except that rocks don't behave intentionally. Since intentionality is an important criterial attribute of human behavior, it seems a little silly to talk about rocks in that fashion. There are many ways in which a behavior can "escape the bounds" of an initial description. Anxiety carried to an extreme intensity becomes something else: i.e., it is pulled into the gravitational field of some other central concept, such as terror or insanity. Thus a behavior may be a paradigm case of one concept and a derivative case (or a function) of another: "That was a paradigm case of terror." "Yep, he had a mighty strong case of anxiety."

Anxiety and terror belong to the same family. But families overlap and are defined as needs be. One family may decide it doesn't want to include anyone but Mom, Dad, and Son. Daughter is to be excluded because she is in a funny farm. Similarly, I may claim that anxiety is not part of the family headed by that despotic tyrant, insanity. I would do this, perhaps, because I sometimes feel anxiety but don't want to be considered insane. I might even want to keep anxiety away from terror, but that would seem to be somewhat defensive on my part.

Many behaviors are not paradigm cases of any concepts. Appropriate functions must be sought. A problem in this area is the desire to place something into a well-known category. Anxiety and terror are both better known than, say, "a strange muted feeling of impending doom but with an accompanying feeling that the feeling isn't quite real." This desire is quite natural: We know (to some extent) what to do with anxiety and terror, but the emotion in quotes is strange. Since we don't know what to do with it, we may try to treat it as something we do know how to deal with, so we may channel our experience into categories that don't quite fit.

Cases: Model, Contrary, Borderline, Related, Invented

A model case is similar to a paradigm case. It is almost correct to say that it is different only in that it is used in a different language game from the one described above. Paradigm cases are useful largely in describing non-paradigm cases. Model cases may be paradigm cases, but they are used in the language game of finding out what the criterial attributes of a concept are, a game called the analysis of concepts, presented well by Wilson (1966).

A model case is a specific, concrete exemplar with which everyone would agree. Consider what attributes exemplars have and you have begun to make a map of the concept. A contrary case is a case everyone agrees is *not* an exemplar. Study a contrary case and you can find out what anxiety is *not*. Related cases are cases in the same family. To find the borders of anxiety it is wise to consider its nearest neighbors, e.g., terror, apprehension, fear. While there may be overlapping, that too can be mapped. A borderline case is a case that is sort of in and sort of out. Borders can be fuzzy, but the fuzziness can be mapped. The debate, "Is it or isn't it?" may be fruitful. Invented cases allow one to test one's ability to deal with the concept. Suppose a man lives in constant physiological arousal, with rapid heartbeat, sweating, and tremor, but denies any apprehension and shows no decrease in concentration. Is he anxious? One of Wilson's examples is good here: If there lived on Mars men who were like us in all respects except they lacked emotions, would they be men?

It must be emphasized that in conceptual analysis we use concrete examples as much as possible. We know how to apply concepts to people and situations we have experienced, because we have already applied them. The examples I have given here are too hypothetical, and are already on a more abstract, conceptual level. Better: "A model case of a crazy man was Hitler." "If anybody isn't anxious, it's Joe." "Is China an underdeveloped nation?"

The analysis of concepts is a language game, and a rather academic one at that. Words are things and are used in the ways other things are, e.g., to threaten in a devious manner: "Please don't go out tonight, you know how anxious I get." The person who says this may in fact experience anxiety, but we would not do well to try to find the essence of anxiety here, as a more complete and accurate description of what is going on could be that the speaker is attempting to keep the other person at home.

Incongruent Messages

Jay Haley is my source here.

Humans can communicate on more than one level. Sarcasm is such a common incongruent message that it is given status as a lexical entry. Sarcasm is saying one thing when you mean the opposite. Why would one use sarcasm? In Chapter Six I argue that one can accomplish by sarcasm something one cannot accomplish by any direct, literal statement.

Another example is the mother who tells her son to come give mommie a big hug but who is stiff as a board when her son hugs her. Why would she do that? Probably because she doesn't have just one feeling about her son; probably she loves him and hates him simultaneously, or perhaps her feeling is some compound of love and hate.

Another example is the woman who tells her husband to dominate her. If he does, he is obeying her. But to obey is not to dominate. If he doesn't dominate her, he is disobeying her. But he is not dominating her. In fact, if he dominates her, he is also disobeying her, because he isn't really dominating her.

Why would the wife do this? Perhaps she had a very dominating father. Perhaps this father quashed much of her spirit, and she hated him and herself for it. But she was used to being dominated by men and didn't know any other way of relating to them. So she wants to be dominated; but then again she doesn't want to be dominated. She so informs her husband.

What can he do? He can walk out on her. But she has the option of claiming that walking out is another symptom of his lack of manliness. A real man, she could claim, would stay and face the situation. While *we* can quarrel with her use of the concept of manhood, it will be harder for him to do so. Furthermore, he has been further insulted and has another reason to stay around and prove he *is* a man.

He can also point out the incongruence in her message and refer her to Jay Haley. In the context of a calm discussion aimed at improving the relationship, this would be a good move. But in the context of an emotional argument, she is not likely to consider this a sufficiently strong response. That is, it is not strong enough to dominate her. Therefore, she may reply that he is as usual passing the buck, which is unmanly. Again, he is correct in pointing out the incongruence, but his move is not likely to be effective in proving *to her* that he is a man.

Finally, he can respond in kind. He could get drunk and beat her up. Then he would be sending her an incongruent message. He is beating her up, and that is a dominant behavior, albeit a bit extreme; but no, he isn't really beating her up. It's the liquor in him.

Incongruence breeds incongruence.

Formally, incongruence is when two messages are sent and they contradict each other.

In this book we will only deal with two-message incongruence, but people can send more than two messages. For example, a schizophrenic might say something, deny he was saying it (e.g., by claiming voices made him say it), but deny the denial (e.g., by saying it sarcastically), fear that the negatives might cancel to produce a congruent message, so make the sarcasm insincere.

In Haley's analysis of schizophrenics, he determined that it is their purpose to avoid relationships with other people, and it is easy to see from this example that it would be hard to put the finger on a person who sent so many messages at once.

But sometimes things that are hard to put a finger on put the finger on perfectly. Haley has written a brilliant essay on the art of being a schizophrenic which elucidates some of the truly artistic maneuvering a schizophrenic must go through to avoid relationships. The trouble with the essay is that it is written in a sardonic and cheerfully morbid tone which is not at all congruent with the seriousness of the situations of schizophrenics (a serious-ness one can tell Haley feels from his other writings); so what is Haley up to? Is he trying to be cute? Or funny?

I think he is (very successfully) trying to say what so few writers in this area of psychopathology are able to say. Haley is saying that there is nobody to blame for mental illness, and that it is pointless to cast around for explanations that are merely ways out of trying to deal personally and directly with the mentally ill. For example, it is of little use to know that the simultaneously warm and cold mother discussed above may produce schizoph-renics if we have no way of stopping mothers from behaving that way (as we don't, nor are there any plans from those who "discov-ered" the "schizophrenogenic" mother as to how we might pro-ceed). So we still need to help the miserable schizophrenic.

So why couldn't Haley have said that? Why couldn't he have written the paragraph I wrote above? Because he wants to be funny?

My paragraph has a rather harmful incongruence in it. I claim nobody is to blame, but on the other hand I clearly blame psy-chotherapists who are too lazy and uppity to deal personally with disgusting schizophrenics who will throw excrement on you as soon as look at you.

So Haley needed the incongruence—his incongruence. By keeping a light tone, he denies there is anything wrong, thus refusing to let the reader find a scapegoat. But the juxtaposition of the light tone with the not very pleasant subject matter only serves to emphasize the seriousness of the situation. There is no better way of saying the very profound thing Haley has said.

Hierarchical Level and Generic Terms

The hierarchical level of a name or description is the size of the class the description implies. For example, *coin* is at a higher hierarchical level than *dime,* which is higher than *1973 dime.* it is not always so easy to place descriptions in order of hierarchical level. Is violence a type of aggression? In other words, does it belong below aggression, along with other types of aggression, such as verbal attack and the silent treatment? Or is aggression a type of violence, along with, perhaps, justified homicide and the motion of the sea during storms?

A generic term is a description (usually a word) that is hier-archically higher than two or more words. *Coin* is a generic term for a class of objects, including pennies, nickels, dimes, and quar-ters. Not all terms that have other terms beneath them in hierarch-ical level qualify as generic terms: *dime* is not the generic term for *1952 dime* and *1973 dime.* It seems that the lower level terms must have some degree of reality (in the sense of real names). In addi-tion, the generic term must also have some reality. *Thing* is not a generic term for *coin.*

Languages don't all have the same generic terms. The Eskimo has no generic term for snow, although he has several words for (what we would call) different kinds of snow. But isn't it all *really* snow? (If the Eskimo knew the word *snow,* wouldn't he agree it fit?) Evidently it isn't all really snow to the Eskimo. Imagine someone from a Central American Indian language group that has one word for snow, sleet, ice, freezing rain, and hail. He says, "But isn't it all really triob?" Another shakes his head. "Apparently not to those dumb Yankees." (There is a language similar to this.)

We do have a generic term for all the above: *precipitation.* But, I feel, it is not real enough to be considered a real generic term. A test: Would there be any or even a few situations where you would be satisfied with the statement, "It's precipitating"? Or do you feel that many essential features of the phenomenon are omitted unless the hierarchically lower term is supplied? Unless you live in a very constant climate you probably need to know what kind of precipitation you are having. Another test is to note that we hardly ever say, "It's precipitating." I've never said it. But we often say, "I lost a coin."

Course of Action and Social Practice

These concepts come from Peter G. Ossorio.

To use one of his examples, playing chess is a social practice; winning at chess is a course of action.

A social practice consists of one or more intentional actions by one or more people. The actions are small scale and large scale, simple and complex. They might be described as the basic building blocks of social behavior. They are the "done things." They are things that *can* (be said to) be done with no further end in view; that is, they are not done to accomplish something else. (What do you accomplish by *playing* chess? Note I did not say *winning* or *losing*.) It is often said of social practices that they are done because they are enjoyed. The test of whether something is a social practice, perhaps, is to ask how much sense it would make to ask a sample of people why they did it.

"Why are you going to the movies?" This question wouldn't raise eyebrows the way, "Why are you eating dinner?" would; but for many people, we recognize, going to the movies is something they do with no further end in view. From their point of view it is not even necessary to say they like it. They simply do it.

However, people may bring their own special motivation to social practices, and we are likely to notice this if there is something excessive about the performance of the social practice. That is, someone who spends most of his life in a movie theater is not *simply* engaged in the social practice of going to the movies. We want a more complete description. But if a person goes to the movies only when he is lonely, and is only lonely now and then, we are not likely to want to say he is doing more than simply engaging in a social practice.

And that is partially because loneliness is one of the motivations it is normative to bring to the social practice of going to the movies. In fact, "going to the movies because one feels a little lonely" is a social practice.

Many of our social practices (earning a living, cleaning the house, going to bed, getting up, reading the newspaper) are far less problematical and much less likely to be considered to involve extraneous motivation than going to the movies.

The importance of the concept of social practice is often overlooked. It is revolutionary, for example, in psychology. Ossorio starts with and accepts social practices. The usual psychological approach is to analyze social practices into their constituent elements, including each person's motivation each time he engages in a social practice. That there are large scale regularities in human behavior that are furthermore accepted as regularities requiring no further explanation (by human beings) seems unsurprising—naturally. But psychology, as well as other social sciences and some philosophies, has refused to allow them and has insisted that they are simply the result of other, more basic, processes.

Why have so many wise men refused to accept the fact that social practices exist? If you were starting a science, wouldn't you want to discover something? It is almost a scientific social practice to refuse to admit social practices exist.

To use the concept of social practice, however, is not to take a position with respect to their ultimate reality (whatever that might mean). I will simply act as if there are social practices, which is no more and no less than we all do all the time.

A course of action is distinguished from a social practice by virtue of the uncertainty of the success of the former. Social practices are not just the done things; they are the things that *can* be done, the things whose accomplishments are of no special interest. Driving to work is a social practice, and ordinarily we do not ask, "How did he drive to work?" Driving to work fifty miles down a mountain in a driving blizzard is less of a social practice and more of a course of action, and we are very tempted to ask about the performative aspects of the action; e.g., "I'm amazed he didn't get stuck." Winning a Grand Prix is a course of action. It is not something anyone knows how to do, although many and various skills enter into winning a Grand Prix.

There are cases that are borderline, but model cases of both social practices and courses of action are common enough that there is little difficulty in using the concepts.

The Significance of Behavior Descriptions

Behavior descriptions should be at the appropriate level of significance. Generally speaking, an inappropriately significant description focuses too much or too little on the performative aspect of the behavior. The behavior of people playing chess could be described as "pushing little pieces of wood around." That is a partial description of how people accomplish "playing chess." But that is not what the people are really (in the sense of real names) doing. The behavior of people playing chess could also be described as, "engaged in the timeless battle for power that stems from man's aggressive instincts." That description pays too little attention to the performative aspects of playing chess.

Questions often arise as to what the significant description is. Put somewhat differently, the proper significance is often questioned as a move in interpersonal relationships because often a great deal hinges on which description is accepted as the appropriately significant one.

Witness, for example, the constant bombardment during football season of banal jokes involving wives who fail to understand why their husbands would want to sit around watching twenty-two men running around a field with lines on it.

We can appreciate that in this case many women neither play nor understand football, and therefore can't consider football a real name. Football can't fit football snugly unless one understands the game. Furthermore, women may not be motivated to understand the game. Most wives do not care to never see their husbands; and the national mania for football television is so extreme that "watching football" may not be the appropriately significant description. Perhaps "drowning out quiet desperation by working oneself up over games the players hardly care about, being so rich due to said quiet desperation" fits better.

In other cases, the less significant description is clearly so: "looking at marks on a piece of paper" is not a description of "reading" that many people would accept (although visitors from another planet observing us for the first time might, if they didn't read, wonder what we were doing looking into a collection of thin sheets of a white substance).

Much humor can be seen as resulting from the giving of a less significant description than is usual. As the above example of football jokes illustrates, there is little humor unless the less significant description has some reality (as usual, in the sense of real names).

In many cases, a less significant description is so because it ignores or is ignorant of the fact that what is going on is a performance that is part of an intentional action that is part of a social practice. Hitting a little white ball from here to there is the performance aspect of making a golf shot ("golf shot" is the appropriately significant description), and golf shots are part of golf. Any social practice can be redescribed by focusing on the performance aspect of behavior and claiming that that is *all* that is going on. "Eating dinner," a model case of a social practice description, can be rendered as "placing little pieces of warmed up dead animals and plants in the mouth, chewing them, and swallowing." This description is (designed to be) somewhat disgusting. Ignoring the social practice a performance belongs to can lead to disgust, humor, argument, and other reactions. Doing so is very common in this culture. Perhaps we should call it a social practice. Doing it successfully (so as to get the desired reactions) is, of course, a course of action.

Thus far we have been concerned with behavior description. There is a certain sort of description of objects which is related to insufficiently significant descriptions of behaviors. I will not give this sort of description a name, but will rather give the classic example, provided by Wittgenstein.

Is a broom *really* a broomstick and a brush? Clearly, the way I have been using the word *really*, it is not. That is, if we ask the population to give a name to the object in a picture of a broom, almost all will call it a broom, and almost none will call it a broomstick attached to a brush.

A broom functions as a broom and rarely as a broomstick and a brush. Speaking with the most rigorous behaviorism, it is treated as a broom most of the time (or, if you will, responded to as a broom). So why would we be tempted to call it really a broomstick and a brush?

We shall take up this question in some detail later. Suffice it to point out for the moment that the natural sciences have gone in this direction, e.g., in discovering what an atom is made of. Some religions and philosophies have gone the opposite direction, giving descriptions that ignore the performative aspects of behavior or the concreteness of objects, e.g., in saying God is everything. In day-to-day life one may downgrade or upgrade a behavior or object by giving descriptions that are either too analytic or insufficiently analytic.

Traits and Excess

Ossorio has discussed traits and trait functions as patterns "of excessive frequency over a substantial period of time." (1969, p. 45) In addition, "an excess of occurrences also implies some degree of inappropriateness of some occurrences." (p. 45) These terms, he points out, are appropriately vague. People have no difficulty in operating with vague concepts—only philosophers and social scientists do—and it is people who use trait functions. In other words, Ossorio is pointing out that we say someone has trait X (say hostility) when his hostility is excessive. Let me examine three varieties of excess (there are other varieties and other ways of cutting excess into varieties).

1. If P manifests hostility that is disproportionate to the situation (and does so several times), we will say he is a hostile person. Ossorio is not making a factual claim, but rather a logical or conceptual claim: What basis could we have for calling a person hostile if he were only as hostile as the situation demanded? What does it mean, anyhow, for a person to be as hostile as the situation demands? That's not hostility. Murder in self-defense is not hostility, it's not even "as much hostility as the situation demands."

2. If P is hostile when the situation doesn't call for hostile behavior, we will call him a hostile person. This is a special case of the excess mentioned above, but it deserves mention, since it is a common situation in which we use trait functions. There are some people, for example, who are hostile and we can't see why. So we say the person is hostile. What else could we say?

"We could reserve judgment and perhaps be decent about it and believe it was something about the situation that caused him to be hostile."

To be sure. That is why Ossorio speaks of a substantial period of time. But what is substantial to me may not be substantial enough to you. Where I won't reserve judgment, perhaps you will. Eventually however, you will give in and admit there are no precipitating circumstances. Unless you are the sort of person to continue reserving judgment, or unless you eventually find something you consider part of the situation (something, say, that I wouldn't allow as part of the situation, but would assign to the person). For example, you find the person had a bad childhood. You say that is part of his situation. I say, "Nonsense, we all have to stop leaning on our childhoods sometime."

That is an illustration of why the concepts *must* be vague. What is excess to me may not be excess to you, so there is no way to give "rigorous operational definitions" of *excessive, inappropriate, substantial, situation,* or *personality.*

3. Finally, if P is hostile too often, we will call him a hostile person. We all face countless situations in life where we could be hostile, in fact where we could be no more hostile than the situation warranted. For people who aren't (called) hostile, often other considerations are operating and the hostile aspects of the situation aren't responded to. For example, most of us are upon occasion in a good mood. So we let a guy nearly run us off the road and smile at him benignly. Or we let a friend get a little hostility off his chest by having a jab at us. Or we may be too busy to be hostile. There are countless reasons not to respond to a provoking situation. The person who ignores too many of these reasons is considered a hostile person. What else could we say about him? And that is precisely the point. The person who manifests hostility, even if warranted on many occasions, isn't showing us anything else.

Or consider happiness. We do not consider a person a happy person unless he is sometimes happy when the situation doesn't call for it (we do say, "That's one happy person," when good things are happening to someone, but we can distinguish between happiness that belongs to a person and happiness that belongs to a person by virtue of the situation).

In conclusion, Ossorio is doing no more and no less than codifying the way we behave when we use trait functions. No claim on the nature of reality or human beings is being made here, except perhaps the claim that humans operate on the basis of what they know, a maxim of Ossorio's which is very much a tautology.

Negotiation

Negotiation is an approach to truth that differs from the usual approach, which assumes there is one truth. The concept of negotiation presented here is based on Ossorio's.

If A and B observe a behavior of S's, they may disagree on the description. A: "S was hostile to Fred." B: "S was extremely upset about his job, and he just was ready to snap at anything."

These two descriptions aren't really contradictory. A is focusing on S's interpersonal achievement (it is not justified hostility to snap at someone just because you are in a bad mood); B is focusing on S's intrapersonal state of mind. Perhaps they could resolve the issue by combination (*not* by compromise); e.g., "S was hostile to Fred because S was extremely upset."

This outcome is a joint description based on a pooling of information and descriptive resources. The final description is not necessarily better, nor is it in any sense more truthful. It does seem more complete.

Consider the following: A: "S was hostile to Fred." B: "S was rather polite under the circumstances. Fred was being very obnoxious."

In this case, A might not have known that Fred had been being obnoxious, and so A might accept B's description. This is another possible outcome of negotiation. One of the parties doesn't have all the relevant information and gets it from the other.

Consider another example. A: "S was hostile to Fred." B: "S good-humoredly joshed at Fred."

Negotiation will not be as easy. It looks like A and B are different sorts of people. A may be more sensitive to and fearful of that kind of behavior which seems to be an admixture of hostility and humor. B may be more used to such semi-joking interchanges.

It is the move from attempts to describe the situation to attempts to describe the personality differences that led to the differential perception and descriptions of the situation that is characteristic of the process of negotiation. The negotiation might end here with A saying (to B or to himself) that B is relatively thick-skinned and insensitive and therefore couldn't see the underlying hostility, and B saying that A is something of a sensitive plant and therefore couldn't see the underlying good humor.

Where is the truth? In Ossorio's approach, we don't strive for truth; we strive for a complete and adequate description of the state of affairs. To isolate one part of that total description, which (so far) has included A's and B's descriptions of S, A's description of B, and B's description of A, and call it the truth would be, to use another of Ossorio's examples, like saying the shape of an ashtray was what it looked like from *this* position and no other.

A common method of resolving a negotiation or ending an argument is to conclude that there is probably truth in both positions. This is not a complete negotiation, i.e., a complete description of the state of affairs. It is rather an avoidance of completion by mutual consent. Of course there is truth in both positions. If there were not, there would have been no negotiation. We cannot negotiate with people who hold positions we believe to be totally untenable, although we can beat them up, shoot them, or ignore them. If we attempt a negotiation, we are trying to reach a mutually satisfactory description of the state of affairs, and to conclude that there is truth in both positions is tacitly to admit that no such description will be forthcoming.

(A parenthetical conclusion: The above disagreement could

be resolved in another way: A and B could get into a discussion of the nature of and relationship between hostility and humor. This would require that A take B's point of view seriously rather than as a source of error, and vice versa. This often happens in close interpersonal relationships, so that often a discussion of the nature of the relationship is implied. Thus one can negotiate about one's own behavior and one's own relationships, and one can also negotiate about negotiations ("You never let me get a word in edgewise." "You move too quickly to personality descriptions.") Logically, one could also negotiate about negotiations about negotiations. But I don't know what that would be.

Word Magic

To use word magic is to attempt to do something verbally that can't be or isn't accomplished (merely) with words.

For example, one cannot be cautious simply by making sure one qualifies all the statements one makes by the disclaimer, *it could be that.* Caution is more than verbal flourishes; we are all aware of the harm that can be done by slurs that take that form. On no evidence people can and often do say, "It could be that P is . . ."

Ossorio has dealt with magical behavior in general (i.e., not merely verbal magic) as a kind of symbolic behavior. P wishes to accomplish something by a certain action. However, that intentional action is not available to P. It may be that P has a stronger reason not to engage in that action; e.g., P may wish to murder his wife, but fears the consequences. Or, to use a psychoanalytic example, S may wish to murder his father, but his father is bigger and stronger than he is.

The person then chooses another action that resembles the desired action in as many relevant respects as possible. S may make a doll of his father and stick pins in it. That doesn't resemble killing his father in a great many relevant respects, or perhaps it is very lacking in a very important relevant respect. We shall be dealing with magical behavior of this more or less harmless variety, but we shall also be dealing with less harmless magical behavior: P may attempt to squash his wife's identity by trying to keep her from doing anything except cleaning the house or by trying to induce her to take on the disease of housewife's alcoholism.

We have dealt with motivational and ability restraints on the person's part. Another possibility is that there is no concrete way of achieving the desired state of affairs. Ossorio's example is excellent: "For example, there might not be anything that could be called literally being at one with God." (1969, p. 147) Thus there are various symbolic approaches to attaining such unity. We usually can distinguish kinds of symbolic behavior that are more or less like the desired behavior. For example, religious ritual is one symbolic way of being at one with God, but it lacks something. Another much more impressive symbolic way of being one with God is attempting to do good works as God would if present.

Another example we shall consider from time to time: There do not appear to be any obvious criteria for determining if a given case of humor-hostility is *really* humorous or *really* hostile. We have words for hostile humor in our lexicon (e.g., badinage, persiflage), but, as I will show in Chapter Four, these words attempt the (magical) function of imposing order on a domain that we can't order. We often need to distinguish between hostility and humor, and we are not comforted by words that attempt to imply that both can be present simultaneously. In fact, I have shown elsewhere (1971) that hostile humor is considered funnier than non-hostile humor. So hostility and humor do go together. But it has to be *really* one or the other before we will be comfortable.

The uncertainty is built into the subject matter. I may attempt a lighthearted comment. But perhaps I am more hostile than I knew, so it doesn't come out as lighthearted, even though I sincerely wanted it to. Or perhaps my target is sensitive, so that while I and others may agree no harm was intended, harm has been done. Was it *really* banter, and without hostility? Am I responsible for my target's reactions? Are not my actions independent of his? From the point of view of truth-seeking, we are blocked here and can go no further without assumptions. For example, we could assume that man does what he really wants to, so that if I wounded someone, I must have wanted to. Obviously the truth follows from the assumption, not from an assessment of the situation. From the descriptive point of view discussed in the section on negotiation, we need only say that my intent that what I said should be taken to be lighthearted banter is not the whole story. Was I *really* cruel? Again, that's not the whole story either. In other words, negotiation is called for. But it does not appear that any simple solution will be arrived at. We may be able to describe the situations I discussed adequately. But we will not be able to say what really happened, nor will we be able to give general criteria for solutions. Furthermore, our resolutions of specific situations will be rather unsatisfactory from the point of view of someone seeking to know what (one thing) happened; e.g., "He meant to be lighthearted, and nobody thought he was cruel, but Jack got very upset, and Jack's not the sort to get upset over nothing." In other words, our resolutions will, like the words in the lexicon, indicate that humor and hostility are both present but in some undetermined mixture.

chapter two

The Whorfian Hypothesis

I will not follow the usual practice of books that deal with the Whorfian hypothesis and attempt to give an unbiased presentation of the hypothesis followed by criticism. Rather I will introduce particular specific instances of evidence and give specific criticisms on the spot.

This chapter presents an approach to criticism of anecdotal evidence for the Whorfian hypothesis and some additional criticisms. Chapter Three deals with research concerning the relationship between cognitive tasks and language. Chapter Four is a speculative proto-theory relating culture and lexicon. Chapter Five concerns the semantic differential. Chapter Six takes up naming behavior. Chapter Seven applies a conception of schizophrenia to the old subject of style. By the time we are through with those chapters, we will have covered a good many of the pieces of evidence for the Whorfian hypothesis in its many forms.

Systematic Criticism of Anecdotes

Much of the evidence for the Whorfian hypothesis is anecdotal. This sort of evidence has been criticized on a general level in several ways. Lenneberg (1953), for example, has commented on Whorf's renderings of Indian languages. As Whorf translates them, it does sound as if the Indians speak in very strange ways. Lenneberg offers a Whorfian style translation of English and lets the ridiculousness speak for itself. Another major criticism is that anecdotal evidence is not susceptible to empirical investigation, or to proof or disproof. Others have remarked on the unsystematic character of the total set of anecdotes. One anecdote relates one linguistic feature to the culture of one language group, while another relates another linguistic feature to a different cultural aspect of another language group.

Valid (although passive) as these criticisms are, the anecdotes linger on. I have no objection to this. But if careful professionals don't take care of their territory, fools will rush in. For example, *Psychology Today* (Kolers, 1969) has published what can only be called a sensationalistic account of the Whorfian hypothesis. Few criticisms are offered, and the empirical literature is hardly mentioned, much less its deficiencies. In addition, the impact of anecdotal evidence for the hypothesis is not necessarily greatly lessened in the scientific community by general criticism. The anecdotes are intriguing and have not been empirically disproved. There seems to be something of a wistful, "What if" attitude, and many writers present several anecdotes as if they were true and then give the general criticisms. It seems that they enjoy relating the anecdotes. And why not?

Whorf, like Freud, has continued to exert an influence on the pessimists, malcontents, and misfits of our society. While I have been so influenced, and while I believe the kind of evidence offered by Whorf can contribute greatly to an adequate description of language and language behavior, a more critical attitude must be taken towards these anecdotes. If the evidence is not raised properly, it won't grow into something good.

Therefore, the first part of this chapter is a method of attacking specific anecdotes. It has the advantage that it does not allow a particularly intriguing anecdote to remain alive on the grounds that it might be an exception, or that it sounds so plausible that it should be granted immunity from empirical test. It also has the advantage that empirical work is not required, which is particularly important in view of the near impossibility of empirical work in this area.

I will not concern myself here with evidence relating the lexicon and culture. Such evidence is not considered to be related to the stronger versions of the Whorfian hypothesis since it is not related to the structure of language. The lexicon and culture are the subject of Chapter Four.

The Questions

This is the usual form of anecdotal evidence for the Whorfian hypothesis: A feature of a language is found that English or other Indo-European languages do not possess. Or the language differs from English on a variable. Some attempt is made to relate the structural differences in the languages to differences in the culture.

The testing method consists of asking questions of an anecdote. Sometimes one question is all that is needed; other times several questions are needed.

1. Is it the case that English does not have the feature of the other language, or that English is different with respect to this feature?

2. Can the difference between English and the other language be reduced to the kind of lexical difference that reflects obvious or gross cultural differences? (For example, that the Eskimo has several words for snow where we have but one indicates simply that snow is more important to the Eskimo since he lives in it.)

3. Is the difference simply the result of bad translation procedures?

4. If it were the case that the other language has the feature, and no others, could the speakers of the language communicate things that must be communicable in any culture?

5. Is the anecdote so vague and/or ambiguous as to have no meaning?

6. Does the anecdote depend on the mistaken belief that the unit of perception of speech is the word or morpheme? (See, for example, Fodor and Bever, 1965; Garrett, Bever, and Fodor, 1966: it appears that the unit of perception is considerably larger. That is, we do not hear one word, then the next, then the next; rather we hear phrases.)

7. Is it possible and likely that a feature of the other language is a feature only for one or two language games, whereas for other language games this feature is not present?

8. Is there a confusion in the anecdote between what is acceptable in grammar books and what is acceptable in speech?

9. Can a case be made that the cultural state of affairs said to be associated with the linguistic feature of the other language is a universal cultural state of affairs, or at least a state of affairs present in America, for exactly *opposite* linguistic reasons?

Application

In this section, groups of related anecdotes will be attacked. The anecdotes have been selected so that each question will be appropriate at least once.

I: Conjugating Verbs   The first type of anecdote has to do with the method of conjugating verbs. Verbs are conjugated in many ways. In English, the tense of the action must be expressed. However, the Hopi language (and Wintu to a greater extent) makes the type of validity of the statement obligatory: "The timeless Hopi verb does not distinguish between the present, past, and future of the event itself, but must always indicate what type of validity the speaker intends the statement to have" (Whorf, 1956, p. 217).

Bolinger (1968, p. 256) says of many such differences, "What one language builds into the broadest layers of its structure another expresses informally and sporadically; but both have it." But English does not express validity either informally or sporadically. So I will begin an attack on this kind of anecdote by asking Question 1, i.e., by demonstrating that the feature of Hopi and Wintu is also a feature of English (but not an informal, sporadic, or potential feature).

In English either the speaker (S) makes it obvious what validity his statement is meant to have, or the hearer (H) requests that such validity be made explicit.

Consider the following incident: Dick and Jane, once childhood sweethearts, have grown up and married others. One night S, a gossip, observes Dick and Jane emerging slightly tipsy from a bar. S immediately concludes they are having an affair. S tells H this. But H is a good friend of Dick and Jane's. H responds, "Ridiculous. I know they aren't. How do you know?" At this point S must admit the evidence. H has a perfectly valid explanation: Dick's wife and Jane's husband came out of the bar two minutes later and H knows because he was there too.

However, a Whorfian might claim that the Hopi would not be able to enjoy such evil gossip. S would have had to specify validity immediately. But there is nothing to stop S from giving the statement a high validity, the kind expressed in, "Dick and Jane are having an affair." The Hopi H's response, if he was a good friend of Dick and Jane's, would not be appreciably different. H might simply repeat S's statement, using S's conjugation, in a questioning and menacing tone. S would then have to admit that this conjugation was not completely appropriate. Here I am answering in the negative a specific example of Question 4: Is it possible that a language exists that does not allow the speakers to lie or flirt with the truth? Clearly there could not be such a language, although there could be a culture where everyone spoke the truth.

If H had not been a good friend of Dick and Jane's and was another gossip, H would have less reason to question S, in Hopi or in English. If H asked how S knew in a conspiratorial whisper, S would then know that the facts which our first H rejected will be sufficient for our gossip H. If a Hopi S used a conjugation indicating uncertainty and little evidence, the gossip H would be displeased, for S would be spoiling the fun.

Nor does tense force truth on English speakers with respect to time. Stories and myths are often told in the present or future tense. Many uses of the future tense have not led to the promised behavior. But one can imagine a hypothetical Hopi Whorfian saying, "English, because it has a future tense, compels its speakers to guarantee many things that we do not have to. When we say something will transpire in the future, we must specify why we think so. In many cases this obligatory specification qualifies the statement so much that nothing is promised. The Americans must be at once optimistic and hard-working." But English speakers, even when they use such direct locutions as "I will do it" or "It will happen" are often guaranteeing nothing; and often this is quite clear to their listeners.

But perhaps the Hopi cannot specify time, at least not with the precision with which we can. (Whorf says that the Hopi have something resembling tense, however; 1956, pp. 57–64.) But tense is but one way of locating an event in time, and an inelegant one at that. English, for example, has the following: "In the past," "On October 18, 1927," "Remember when," or "I predict that." Some are vague; others are much more precise than tense. When such locutions are used, tense is in fact redundant; we don't need it.

Whorf, however, is more concerned with the metaphysical implications of grammatically imposed distinctions than he is with the impossibility of expressing certain concepts. He deduces from the fact that tense is mandatory in English that we are especially concerned with time. While the preceding discussion should make clear that our concern with validity is strong (Brown, 1958, p. 312, has commented in this respect on the scientific community), let us consider our supposed preoccupation with time. Let us assume that preoccupation with time is caused by having to express it via tense at all times. But if we ask Question 9, we can arrive at the opposite position: A language with tense is disinterested in time. Tense is not very specific, as I have pointed out. While the time when an event takes place would seem to necessarily be a central concern to all cultures, at least with respect to the gross distinctions represented by English tense, it is not of particular importance to English speakers; therefore, they codify it in verbs just to "get it out of the way," leaving time to be specific about matters of more importance to them. Similarly, the argument goes, the Hopi are not concerned with validity. They get it out of the way as quickly and as automatically as possible.

In conclusion, it appears that this particular difference in conjugation is of little potential significance. The same approach can be profitably taken with other methods of conjugation, e.g., the Chippewa's obligatory specification of the cause of an event.

II: Parts of Speech The second anecdote falls under the general category of the significance of absence of parts of speech.

Lee (1950) states that the language of the Triobriand Islanders lacks adjectives. Attributes of objects represented in the language by nouns are implicit in the nouns themselves. If an attribute is not present, or if one is lost (e.g., ripe fruit becomes rotten), a new noun, of a different root, describes the object.

This is often the state of affairs in English (Question 1). Consider a chair. It has many attributes, some of them criterial. A chair has a seat, a back, and legs. Without these, it isn't a chair. Other possible or common attributes aren't necessary: arms, upholstery, a mechanism allowing a person to lean back. If any of the criterial attributes are missing, we have something else. If the object has a seat and legs but no back it is a "stool;" i.e., it is described by a noun with a different root.

Consider a tree. If it is chopped down, it is at first a "fallen tree"; i.e., we use an adjective-noun construction. Put somewhat differently, it is no longer a paradigm case of a tree but is described as a derivative case, i.e., as a function of the paradigmatic description, *tree.* But eventually the fallen tree falls into the sphere of influence of other concepts, and it becomes chips, lumber, boards, firewood, wood, newspaper, a house, etc. Consider an orange. When it sits long enough, it becomes a rotten orange. Eventually it becomes garbage.

On the other hand, consider our names for fruits. We do not say *yellow fruit, red fruit,* and *green fruit.* We say *bananas, applies,* and *grapes.* That is, in this domain, when playing this language game, we have no adjectives, and a Triobriander Whorfian might comment on this.

But it does seem that English differs from the Islanders' language in two respects: One, we do often use adjective-noun constructions where there is no noun that would suffice, e.g., *red chair.* We must use functions of words. Two, there often is a transitional state "between nouns" where an adjective-noun construction is used. This fits with the picture suggested in Chapter One of paradigm cases of concepts exerting influence on wandering experience. It would seem that the Islanders' paradigm cases are stronger than ours.

These two differences can be reduced to non-structural differences, i.e., to lexical differences that reflect gross and obvious cultural differences (Question 2). The Islander culture is simpler than ours; and it is more stable (in fact, according to Lee, they do not like history, since history suggests that the cultural state of affairs could have been different, better, or worse). Because it is simpler, they have no need for adjectives. It is of no concern what color a chair is. All chairs have the single function of being used to sit in, while in our culture rooms must be harmonious, chairs must be of the proper period, etc. In fact, it would seem that we have stumbled on another approach to the concept of real names: A name is real to the extent that the culture doesn't need adjectives to qualify the name. *Chair* is no doubt a more real name for the Islanders than it is for us.

Another way of looking at it: The Islanders have fewer objects, and therefore their finite storage capacity is not strained by having a noun for each object, as ours would. We need to use functions. Furthermore, because their culture is more stable, what is done with things that change is institutionalized and constant. While an American who owns a piece of forest may let a tree lie fallen for some time, the Islanders know what must be done with it. There is no transitional period during which the Islanders have to choose from an open class of alternatives what to do with the object. In other words, English often assigns a new noun to an object when the object has changed in its most common and highly elaborated function; so do the Triobrianders, except that because of stability, the new function is apparent immediately and takes hold sooner.

The differences may simply be translation difficulties (Question 3). Lee points out that Malinowski did not share her view, and translated the Triobriander language with adjectives. However, Lee suggests that he did this because Western ears are attuned to adjectives. This description of Malinowski's motives sounds unlikely. In the first place, Western ears do not require adjectives, and simple discourse can be carried on with very few adjectives. In the second place, if the Triobriand culture uses objects which are similar to but not the same as objects in our culture, adjectives would be the only accurate approach to translation.

Finally, generative-transformational grammar would tend to suggest that noun constructions are similar to adjective-noun constructions. In generative-transformational grammar one begins with the sentence. It has the ultimate reality (in the sense of real names). A sentence may be rewritten as a noun phrase and a verb phrase. (But it is primarily a sentence. An analogy, although not a perfect one, is the following: People are human beings. They may be rewritten as mind and body, but they are primarily people.)

Noun phrases may be rewritten. Some noun phrases consist of one noun. Others consist of an adjective and a noun. The fact that it is a noun phrase precedes in importance the various forms it may take. We treat it primarily as a noun phrase; of lesser importance and significance are the constituents. A noun phrase has more psychological and linguistic reality than a decomposed noun phrase. Hence we and the Islanders have noun phrases and that is an important similarity. We have, perhaps, different noun phrases than they do; that dissimilarity is of relatively little importance.

Consider the difference from the point of view of descriptive adequacy. The difference between a "red chair" and a "chair" is not qualitatively different than the difference between either and a "stool." All three descriptions provide the necessary and desirable description of the object in question. It is just that the Triobriand Islanders do not find it necessary or desirable to call a chair by its color. If they did, it would be one of their relatively few important distinctions, and they would use different nouns, just as we do in the domain of fruit.

III: Space and Time This section deals with conceptions of space and time which are presumably forced upon speakers of a language by the language.

Bull (1960) has argued that time, or ways in which man must perceive time, influence all languages to represent time in similar ways. If English is representative here, his statement seems doubtful. English does not codify directly some of the aspects of time most familiar to all of us. For example, time does not (appear to) move at a constant rate. Something in the future we are looking forward to may take much longer to arrive than something we are not looking forward to, like a visit to the dentist. The past is not arranged in a straight line; rather memories come and go for reasons often unrelated to temporal succession. Similarly, distance is not constant. A walk that seems short when one is having a pleasant fantasy seems long when one wishes to get to one's destination. (But what is long, the walk or the time it takes?) And so on. But English does not directly represent these aspects of time and space perception.

Whorf says of Hopi that it cannot refer to space "in such a way as to exclude that element of extension or existence we call time." Similarly, "the element of time is not separated from whatever element of space enters into the operation." Finally, the difficulty of what is being done in space-time is also simultaneously represented. Whorf points out that the Hopi cannot speak of an event in another village as happening in the present, being "frankly pragmatic on that score." (1956, pp. 57–64) Presumably, one has to travel to the other village first, by which time the event will be in the past.

In English, on the other hand, time and space are separate and unconnected dimensions. Time consists of equal intervals, and is linear. (According to Whorf and Lee.) For the Hopi, space and time are confounded. Therefore, Whorf felt, the Hopi are natural Einsteinian physicists.

We do in fact independently represent time and space. We can say, for example, "It will take three hours," or "It's 5348 yards away." However, Question 7 is relevant here. While in some language games we do independently represent time and space, in others we don't. We often imply time by spatial locutions, and vice versa. That temporal terms are metaphorical extensions of spatial terms (e.g., long, short), or vice versa, testifies to our perception of the two as related, and attempts to answer the question I posed above: If a walk seems long, does *long* refer to space or to time? Or to both?

If we are to travel by airplane, we can get information concerning distance by asking for time; or we can get information concerning time by asking for distance. Since we know that jets average around 550 mph, we can use the equation $d = rt$. In fact, if rate is constant, r in the above equation becomes functionally equivalent to a conversion constant (such as one would use to convert yards to meters). That is, $d = t$. Distance and time are the same thing.

Therefore, we may suspect that Whorf failed to take account of the differences in culture (Question 2). The Hopi traveled by foot or horse to places they had probably been before (so that difficulty could also be incorporated). Given a rate-constant culture that goes on well-known routes, only one figure is necessary: a space-time-difficulty figure. We operate similarly. *Long* may refer to space or time (or, in my experience, to difficulty of climbs and hikes in the mountains). Some of our locutions are more closely associated with one dimension, e.g., *five miles* is a distance locution. But it often would be a perfectly understandable answer to a question that we would identify as most closely associated with the temporal dimension; e.g., "How long does it take you to walk to work?" "Well, it's five miles."

We can, of course, focus on one dimension, and we often do. When time is of the essence we will not be satisfied with a simple, "Well, it's another 100 miles." We will want to know how long it will take. But note that we wouldn't be satisfied with a simple, "Well, it's another couple of hours." In other words, when we must depart from the casual language game of day-to-day life, we demand *more precision,* not a specific dimension. We may ask for the figure to be given in one dimension rather than another, but a more significant description is that we are asking for more precision.

And, of course, there are specialized language games where we do not refer to space or where we do not refer to time. Science is a good example of such a language game.

However, a claim might be made that because we *can* refer to space and time independently we are likely to be enslaved. Activities that are unpleasant take longer (or seem to take longer, if you want to use one yardstick rather than another) than activities that are pleasant. "I don't want to mow the lawn. It takes two hours." "Sure, but you don't mind spending two hours watching a baseball game on the television." "But that's different." "Nope. Two hours are two hours."

The last speaker has won, but only because the first speaker was dishonest. If he had rejected the suggestion on the grounds that mowing the lawn was an unpleasant or difficult job, i.e., if he had focused on that aspect of the task, he could not have been beaten, at least not by a statement of the general form, "An X is an X."

But what if the Hopi are the enslaved? Is it possible they can't say, "The corn plot is 50x25 yards"? Here we ask Question 4. The Hopi must be able to express such ideas. If time must be involved in such a statement, the Hopi could focus on the spatial aspects, just as we can focus on the spatial aspects of many temporal statements. It seems likely that Whorf has correctly observed the language of the Hopi, but with respect to but one language game, the game of describing trips in a rate-constant culture.

Lee (1950) has compared our conception of time (linear, with equal units) with that of the Triobriand Islanders, who do not conceive of time as consisting of equal units, and who conceive of it as cyclical.

I have already commented on the question of equal units. Time consists of equal units in various scientific language games, and it is possible that the scientific language games have had an influence on our more ordinary language games. But that results from the fact that science, conceived of as a form of life, has had an influence on our society. Science itself, not the linguistic features of science, has had the influence.

Furthermore, we have a cyclical conception of time. Consider weeks. Each week is of equal length. And a week is followed by another week and so on forever. But a week is a cycle. A week encompasses a psychologically real unit. It is composed of smaller units which are not simply equal interval temporal subdivisions. Fridays are not the same as Mondays. Furthermore, the week as a whole has a rhythm (especially for people with a steady job). Perhaps I could describe it as follows (although it is obviously a description of my experience of a week): The week starts Sunday evening, when Monday is a certainty. There is some mental preparation but also some resentment, although a rather sluggish variety of resentment. On Monday morning arousal is highest, although it stays high until Wednesday night or Thursday morning, when the influence of the weekend begins to be felt. By

Friday night it is time to relax. Saturday and Sunday morning are sort of timeless or "out of time." One is neither relaxing from the week, preparing for it, nor engaged in it.

This simplified description serves to illustrate that we *may* look at weeks as cycles in the sense that various curves (of arousal, for example) repeat their pattern each week and start each week in the same place. Luce (1971) has presented a lucid account of the physiological bases for our perceptions of temporal rhythms and changes in rate.

Thus, significant aspects of our experience of time are not directly codified by our language. Cyclicity seems to be an important part of our experience of time.

Days are cycles in the same sense. Years are not so clearly cyclical in the psychological sense, although there is repetition by year for people in certain occupations, e.g., professional sports, teaching, farming. We talk of the cycle of the seasons and for some of us they have psychological reality; for some of us they don't, especially for those of us who live in climates that don't vary much. But generally, June is more like January than Monday is like Saturday.

Decades, hours, and minutes are not cyclical in the sense of this discussion, although for some people under some circumstances these units may acquire psychological reality. For example, I attempted to help a "patient" stop smoking by insisting that she smoke a cigarette every hour on the hour. She was accustomed to much heavier smoking, so the curve of her desire for a cigarette probably had the same shape each hour and started in the same place.

Weeks do not have psychological reality for all people in this culture, of course. But I have known unemployed people who went through the same kind of cycle employed people tend to go through. And I have observed how difficult it is for people on vacation to forget that it is Monday or Friday.

The preceding discussion should have indicated at least that my concept of cyclicity is somewhat vague; but so is Lee's (Question 5). As far as I can tell, my concept is no different from hers.

IV: Parts of Speech and Metaphysics With reference to English's distinct words and parts of speech, Whorf says, "Thus English and similar tongues lead us to think of the universe as a collection of rather distinct objects and events corresponding to words," whereas "polysynthetic" languages such as Shawnee and Nootka have "no parts of speech; the simplest utterance is a sentence, treating of some event or event-complex." (1956, pp. 240–242)

There are two issues here: one, the psychological reality of parts of speech; two, the unit of perception of speech (Question 6).

Berko (1958) presents evidence that children can, when a nonsense syllable is presented in one form and one situation, produce the appropriate form when the situation is changed, e.g., add a plural ending when two of the objects are presented after the child has learned the name for one of the objects. And there is considerable evidence that adults usually give associations of the same form class (part of speech) as the stimulus word. So let us accept for the moment the notion that the form class of a word is one of its attributes that we are aware of and feel really (in the sense of real names) belongs to it.

On the other hand, as I have indicated, empirical evidence suggests we do not perceive speech word by word. This ruins, for example, Boder's (1940) Whorfian-style claim that the word order adjective-noun indicates more sophistication of thought than the word order noun-adjective. (Presumably, one knows what one is going to say about the referent of a noun before one says the noun in the first case, showing planning, while in the second case one rather mindlessly says the noun and then throws in a couple adjectives that seem to fit as an afterthought.)

It does not appear that we perceive the world as a collection of distinct objects and events. Consider a dog biting a man. If we see a dog biting a man and are asked to break the event down, we can do so, but we will do it along the following lines: 1. The dog approached the man. 2. The dog opened his mouth. 3. The dog put his mouth around the man's leg. And so on. That is, we can break the event down into any number of sub-events (each of which would be described by a complete sentence). Thus the breakdown is not along the lines suggested by the sentence, "The dog bit the man." We do not have first a mental image of a dog in isolation, followed by an idea of an abstract bite, following by a mental image of a man.

The argument in the preceding paragraph suggests that if we do see the world as a collection of distinct objects and events, we do not do so because of the way our language is written, i.e., with words separated by spaces. To go further, while we do see objects and events, it is not clear that they are *distinct,* although it is not clear exactly what that word means in this context (Question 5). A dog biting a man is an event, but it can be broken down into sub-events and it could be part of a larger event. So it isn't distinct unless we decide neither to break it down nor to integrate it into a larger event. The same argument may be applied to objects. They may be broken down into a collection of smaller, constituent objects, or they may be considered to be parts of larger objects.

The important point here is that the breaking down and synthesis are done by people, not by language. Furthermore, we don't have to break down an event or an object or make it part of a larger whole. We often do, and for a wide variety of reasons. And people differ in the breakdowns and syntheses they produce, which would certainly not be the case if they were guided by language.

Turning to Question 4, it is nonsensical to suppose that the Shawnee or Nootka cannot perceive a dog as a distinct object. Surely they can and do point. It is unlikely, however, that they point very often. Nor do we. If a man says "dog," he will not have said anything unless the context supplies the full sentence. And if he says, "dog," often and is always only pointing, he will be considered retarded. Similarly, a Shawnee could utter an isolated morpheme, and he would not be considered to have said anything either.

An important exception here is children. They often produce one word utterances, and it is often not clear from the context what they mean (Brown, 1965, pp. 286–304). We will assume for the moment that they may sometimes be saying nothing, i.e., reflecting their metaphysical view that the universe is composed of distinct objects and events. However, the ability of children to produce complex utterances is limited, probably by storage capacity (Brown and Fraser, 1963). So unless Shawnee children are much more intelligent than American children, they too will produce one morpheme utterances. And therefore they will not be "treating of some event or event-complex." All languages have form classes. Greenberg (1962) states that even Nootka has classes that resemble the noun and the verb. Children, when producing short utterances, usually produce morphemes that carry information, i.e., a noun rather than a connective (Brown, 1965, pp. 286–304). Therefore, it would not be surprising to find Shawnee children reflecting their metaphysical view that the universe is composed of distinct objects and events. More likely, what they are doing is trying to say something. At least this seems a more appropriate description of their behavior. With all due respect to Wordsworth, most metaphysicians are older than five.

Whorf is particularly concerned with English's noun-verb dichotomy, since "we are constantly reading into nature fictional acting entities, simply because our verbs must have substantives in front of them." (1956, p. 243). Whorf is in effect asking whether lightning is anything more than a flash (or vice versa), as in the locution, "lightning flashes." The Hopi render this as a verb, "flash." And in fact it would seem that if an English speaker is asked what lightning does, he may note that it flashes; if he is asked what flashes, he may reply that lightning does, although he might reply that yellow traffic lights do. So perhaps we see two things where the Hopi see only one. While science might not agree with Whorf that lightning was fully described as "one thing," it would seem that the Hopi have an advantage in brevity here, and perhaps lightning does appear to us to be one thing.

But English also has an advantage. While much of the time we simply observe lightning, in which case "lightning flashes" is something of a redundancy, lightning does other things besides flash, e.g., destroys buildings, causes fires. And other "things" besides lightning flash, e.g., neon signs, lightning bugs, yellow caution lights. Perhaps the Hopi society is not so complex (Question 2), so that it doesn't need both words. But it seems unlikely that if lightning did destroy a building, the Hopi would be unable to represent this (Question 4).

Such an advantage is not demonstrable in the case of "it rains." If an English speaker is asked, "What rains?", he may humor the questioner and reply that rain, water, or clouds rain. Each of these locutions sounds as queer as the question (although it would not be surprising if a child asked what rains). The person who says "it rains" is simply speaking grammatically when the grammar is not necessary (just as specification of tense is not necessary if a statement is preceded by "Remember when"). The person has no metaphysical entity on the tip of his tongue.

In face, Whorf apparently believes that nouns are names of persons, places, or things. This is the case, if and only if *things* is given rather broad meaning. Lightning is an event, and *lightning* is the name of that event. Running is an activity, and *running,* which functions as a noun in many cases, is the name of the activity. Why should concrete objects be the only "things" named?

In this section we have examined several pieces of anecdotal evidence for the Whorfian hypothesis and have illustrated an approach for destroying such evidence. I don't think any of the anecdotes I have run across can survive if subjected to such close scrutiny. However, I believe the exercise is worthwhile. As Bolinger has said, "Our first awareness of some peculiarity of our own language frequently comes from trying unsuccessfully to transfer it to another." (1968, p. 293) It may be equally the case that this first awareness will come when we are faced with a supposed peculiarity in another language. Generally, it appears, we will be able to find that peculiarity in our own language.

Further Criticisms

In the following section, I will discuss some other Whorfian claims in a less systematic manner.

1. Whorf (1956, p. 135) claims that we tend to behave less carefully around empty gasoline drums because "empty" has a connotation of safe. Empty gasoline drums are just as dangerous as full drums, so our language deceives us.

But if we simply learn that "empty gasoline drums" are in fact dangerous, there will be no problem. Witness for example our fear at the prospect of facing an "empty street" in many parts of large cities at night. An "empty house" scares many of us. We don't operate on words, but on concepts, which may be expressed with several words.

2. Whorf (1956, p. 139) suggests that we erroneously think of aggregates and cycles as similar. For example, we talk about ten days and also about ten men; but ten days can't be "objectively experienced."

It would have been better if he had used the phrase "objectively present," since while we know ten men can be present simultaneously, it is hard to experience them simultaneously. Given that many men, we are likely to have to think of them as *a* group. And what would it mean to experience ten men simultaneously? Furthermore, who says we can't experience days simultaneously? It would seem, in fact, that it is easier to experience ten days than ten men simultaneously: "The last ten days have been one horrible nightmare to me." Furthermore, ten days are very similar to ten men: One can do things with ten days and with ten men, and the differences in what one can do have to do with the difference between men and days. One also does different things with full whiskey bottles and tennis rackets.

"But a likeness of cyclicity to aggregates is not unmistakably given by experience prior to language, or it would be found in all languages, and it is not," says Whorf. That is too bad for those languages that are not aware of the likeness.

3. In a similar vein, Whorf discusses the problems of mass and count nouns in English. He admits some mass nouns refer to things that "present themselves as unbounded extents": *air, water, rain, snow, sand, rock, dirt, grass.* But others: "We do not encounter *butter, meat, cloth, iron, glass,* or most *materials* in such kind of manifestation, but in bodies small or large with definite outlines. The distinction is somewhat forced upon our description of events by an unavoidable pattern in language. It is so inconvenient in a great many cases that we need some way of individualizing the mass noun by further linguistic device. This is partly done by names of body-types: 'stick of wood, piece of cloth, pane of glass, cake of soap'; also by introducing names of containers though their content be the real issue" (p. 141).

But this is the point. These substances are found in such a variety of containers and forms that it is convenient usually to have them free so that we *can* specify the container or form. Thus I would hypothesize that substances that are found in a variety of forms are more likely to be represented by mass nouns. Similarly with substances that are generally not in any form. Things such as pens and books, which are usually in one container and not susceptible to being formed or reformed, should be represented by count nouns.

That this is the case is partially substantiated by the verbal behavior of some non-native bilinguals of my acquaintance who often "make the mistake" of using a mass noun where a count noun is appropriate. To say, for example, "I'm going to have some pork chop" allows one to have twenty pork chops or half a chop without being explicit, for example, about a hoggish appetite (twenty chops) or a sickly one (one-half chop). Or one can offer pork chops without making the guest feel constrained to have only one or forced to have more than one. Native speakers of English could use (what are ordinarily) count nouns as mass nouns and considerably enrich their communicative powers. We can no doubt accomplish the same things, although without such grace, by more involved locutions ("Have a pork chop or two or as many as you want."); and it doesn't sound right to use count nouns as mass nouns.

The Hopi are much closer to nature in this respect, according to Whorf, having no distinction between mass or count nouns. They make this distinction through the verb or predicate. But they make it. And without the distinction built into their semantics they probably are a little more clumsy than we are in this area of experience.

4. Another problem we noun-verbers face is that we tend to look for *things* when we think of a noun. Thus we are forced to think of institutes as having a location in a building or a building of its own.

There are, of course, institutes that haven't a location set aside for them. For example, I could incorporate myself as *The Institute for Observational Psychology*. I could mimeograph my writings and rightfully claim them as publications of this institute. But I would have no space set aside for the operations of this institute, although if law required I could set aside a few square feet in my house and even put up a sign (say in the unused little closet in the basement). I could list myself on my vita (my professional record as a psychologist) as founder and president of the institute, and I could list all my publications (Kelling, G. W. Breakfast menu for August 14, 1974. Technical Report #46 of the Institute for Observational Psychology. New York: IOP Press, 1974). I would be well published.

The example is silly, of course. But why? Because this *isn't* an institute. Saying it is doesn't make it one. But it is not my lack of a location that disqualifies it. Institutes usually do have a location set aside for themselves, but not all legitimate institutes do. For example, a group of scientists at widely dispersed institutions (such as universities) might decide to set up an institute for the study of a relatively obscure problem they were all interested in; to give some coherence to their efforts and to provide to any other scientist who might be interested a complete record of their work they might publish technical reports in mimeo form. If the work they did was good or at least respectable, the institute would have the normal status of institutes.

But this is not a paradigm case of an institute. A paradigmatic institute *does* have a location. So it is not that the nounness of *institute* forces us to think that institutes have locations; most of those organizations that we are willing to call institutes have locations. The group from widely dispersed institutions might more accurately have called themselves . . . a Group.

A group can be (called) an institute if it produces good work and if there is some joint or cooperative effort or if there is an adequately impressive location. These, let us say, are the criterial attributes. So the IOP doesn't qualify because it doesn't do quality work, it only has one person (though I could make up for that by doing very high quality work), and it doesn't have a quality location—although I could make up for that too.

It is not my intention to give a complete analysis of the concept of institute, but I think it is clear that location is only one of (at least) three criterial attributes, and, I think, the least important of the three discussed here. I say that because the most impressive location will not make up for a total lack of output, but a good deal of output will make up for a total lack of location.

We also have institutions, and they are also in buildings, often many buildings. Marriage is an institution.

Let us first suggest that *institute* and *institution* are not the same concept. That is, they are used in different situations. They are related but different. As I use the words, *institute* is a much more concrete (or nounish) noun than *institution*. The latter applies both to large things like universities, which are so large as to lack the focus of an *institute* and which are said to be more than the sum of their parts; and to such things as having a drink before dinner, baseball, or marriage, which also are said to be more than the sum of their parts, the parts in this case not being buildings but intentional actions and performances that are part of intentional actions. The Harvard Library is more than a collection of books; it attains special significance being part of that great university. Hitting a thrown ball with a stick so that nobody can catch it is a *hit* only because it is an action that takes place in the context of that great institution of baseball.

Thus the two meanings (usages) of *institution* make a good deal of sense. They show a clear family resemblance.

But one of the meanings is very nounish. When I hear of the institution *for* something, I do look for a building or buildings. When I hear of the institution *of* something, I have no tendency to look for buildings. This second usage is much more verbish. Marriage is made up of behaviors. Usually married people live under a roof, but they don't have to. Baseball can be played anywhere.

In conclusion, if we study the usage of words rather carefully we cannot avoid the conclusion that the form class or part of speech of a word is but a rough guide to what we may expect to find. Few nouns refer to concrete objects, and few verbs refer to concrete actions.

Summary and Coup de Grace

By now many of the major pieces of evidence for the Whorfian hypothesis have been presented. Each has been defeated. However, the major criticism is still to come.

Whorf is subject to his own theory.

It is quite possible that a Hopi would arrive at quite different conclusions—due to a metaphysics forced upon him by his own language. The Hopi Whorf might decide, due to the blindness forced upon him by his grammar and lexicon, that all languages were similar and could say the same things almost equally well; and that language was a tool that was used, not a force that used man.

If Whorf's theory is true in any major sense, we can only conclude that we are unable to evaluate its truth. If we think it is true, it is only because it appears to be so when viewed through the prism of our own language. If we think it is false, either it is false or it appears to be false from our own linguistic framework. We have no way of telling which is the case.

In fact, the very fact that the theory itself is interesting may say something about English and related languages. What kind of language would produce such a theory? A language that was too far removed from reality and real objects and thus floundered in foolish metaphysical arguments about how some languages got closer to reality than others? It is hard to say. The fact that I offer this criticism and the fact that it is a legitimate criticism may simply be a function of English—a Hopi bilingual who read Whorf in the original might see the truth of Whorf's theory but reject my criticism. But then *he* might be constrained by his language. And so on, infinite regress. The problem with theories that restrain human beings from being paradigm cases of human beings, as Ossorio has pointed out many times, is that they lead to infinite regress, always because they are subject to their own laws.

chapter three

Empirical Evidence for
the Whorfian Hypothesis

In this chapter we shall examine empirical work that has been designed to test the Whorfian hypothesis. (The work on word association was not designed for this express purpose, but it is quite similar to the other studies reported here.)

Color Names and Memory

A small body of empirical work, initiated by Brown and Lenneberg (1954), investigates the relationship between lexical domain and nonlinguisitc behavior (memory) pertaining to that domain. We will here consider studies concerned with the lexical domain of color terms, the major focus of the body of work, although there have been a few studies concerned with other lexical domains (e.g., facial expressions: Van De Geer, 1960; Van De Geer & Frijda, 1960).

First, what is the lexical domain of color terms? Is it the eight most commonly used color names (red, blue, green, etc.)? Is it an enlarged list, including tan, turquoise, and gold? Does it include such names as gunbarrel blue? Or does it go whole hog and include such "achievements of the imagination" as "that yellowish brown with a hint of dirty grey that one can find on the fifth step of the house on the corner of 5th and Main"?

For the moment I will not attempt to answer this question. It is the failure to deal adequately with it that is the major failure of this body of research.

The general thrust of this research is that there is a correlation between the codability of a color (conceptually defined here as the ease *and* reliability with which a color can be named) and ability to recognize that color in an array of other colors after previous exposure to the color. That is, if you show a person a color and later ask him to pick it out from an array of other colors, he may or may not be able to do so; or, put another way, he may make errors, e.g., pick a slightly lighter blue than the original stimulus color. A color's recognizability is shown to be correlated with that color's codability, i.e., the extent to which that color can be given a real name (to give what I consider the best definition of codability).

Why? Because, it seems logical, the evidence suggests, and the subjects of these experiments suggest, that subjects tend to attempt to store colors in memory by giving them names; when faced with the recognition task they go forth with the name as well as with a more perceptual memory of the color. Thus the quality of a lexical domain of color terms for a given language will have something to do with speakers' ability to recognize those colors.

While all in all this seems rather trivial compared to the vaster implications of Whorf's claims discussed in the previous chapter, there is a good reason for "beginning" with color terms (Lenneberg & Roberts, 1956). Color terms cover a measurable part of the spectrum of light waves. By observing the naming behavior of speakers of English, we can map those wave lengths that are called *red*. What we will find is that as we move from a model case of red (here defined as a color called *red* by nearly 100% of English speakers) up or down the spectrum, colors will have a lesser probability of being called red, i.e., the percentage will be less than 100%. We can map the probability profile of the color name *red* as a curve above the spectrum. This curve will peak at the model case of red. It will overlap, for example, the profile or curve for *purple*. Where there is such overlap, the color associated with the wave length on the bottom or baseline of the map under the overlap will be called *purple* by some people but *red* by others. Here we would say that the color hasn't a very real name. In terms of Chapter Four, we might speak of multiple real names, which are correlated with arguments in the culture. In other words, for colors in this area of the spectrum, some people will say *red* and others will say *purple,* so we might expect an argument.

However, due to the continuity of the spectrum and due to the fact that our perceptions of colors are more culture-free than our perceptions, say, of manners and morals (and also less subject to differences between people), we can and do recognize that colors are not either red or purple. Negotiation should be easy in this area (and should not go to the level of giving personality descriptions). We can settle on *reddish-purple.* Hence we don't really expect arguments; rather, we expect immediate compromise, both inter- and intrapersonally.

Due to our rare flexibility, the color situation can become quite complex, even relative to more involving domains. For example, above the wave length baseline, this relatively simple one-dimensional representation of colors in terms of wave lengths, we may have to map the probability profile of reddish-purple. But if and only if we allow our subjects to use such names. And if we do, we may find the names given in the vast spaces between single-word color names multiplying out of control, e.g., "that pale greyish green that is the color of my typewriter when seen in the bright illumination of my basement." Some situations will call forth such names; others will not. The point is that there is no such thing as *the* map of a lexical domain of a language's color terms. First the color names that meet the criteria for lexical entries must be specified, and this is no easy task, as the experiments show to some extent.

Thus even with a seemingly simple and trivial domain we may expect trouble. But there are many advantages, all stemming from the existence of a standard grid, i.e., a dimension independent of all names which uniquely identifies each color, a dimension that is independent of culture (we could, for example, map the difference in meaning between English *red* and German *rot*) and individual differences in perception. Thus a problem we shall often face (What is it that P and O are talking about that is in some sense the same thing, even though they disagree?) is solved here in terms of wave lengths (What P calls *red* and O calls *purple* is a color of wave length X). We have no such standard grid if P says that Joe was angry but O says that Joe was merely annoyed. We have absolutely no independent basis of comparison, at least none with the authority of a scientific measurement of wave length.

We can now examine the studies. As psychological experiments they are good; their major failure is conceptual, and I shall attempt to remedy some of their flaws here.

The measurement of codability has caused trouble, largely because of inadequate conceptual work. In the first study in this series (Brown & Lenneberg, 1954), five measures of the codability of 24 colors were obtained. These 24 colors contained a model case of each of the eight most common color names in English; the other 16 were relatively equally spread out along the spectrum. Subjects were allowed to look at all the colors they would name and were later shown each color individually and asked to give that color a name. " 'Name' was defined as the word or words one would ordinarily use to describe the color to a friend. The *S*s were urged to be both quick and accurate." I quote because, as I have suggested, the directions should be of significant importance. If you were trying to describe a color to a stranger, wouldn't you perhaps give a more precise name? If you weren't told to be as quick as possible, wouldn't you perhaps give a more precise name? And so on.

Brown and Lenneberg computed the following measures: 1. The average number of syllables per name. 2. The average number of words per name. 3. The time between presentation of the color to beginning of naming (latency). 4. The number of people in the subject pool who gave the most common name minus the number of different names given to the color. 5. For five subjects, the number of times they gave the same name one month later. In the construction of this latter measure, an agreement by a subject who had high ability to agree with himself was given less weight than an agreement by a subject who generally disagreed with his previous name.

I will abbreviate these as follows: 1. Syllables. 2. Words. 3. Latency. 4. Modal. 5. Agreement.

In addition, a measure of discriminability was constructed. This measure reflected the "real" perceptual distance of each color from its neighbors.

The five measures of codability were highly related to each other (for *this* array of colors, for *these* instructions). The lowest of the ten intercorrelations was .36; seven of the ten were statistically significant. The matrix of correlations was subjected to factor analysis, a technique designed to identify the number of dimensions needed to account for the various measures. For example, two highly correlated measures are presumed by the method to reflect one underlying dimension. In this case, a one-dimensional solution was found that was considered adequate. It is not acceptable to conclude that the five measures measured the same thing or the same concept; it is reasonable to assume that the measures do not divide into two or three different camps. Measure 4 (Modal) had the highest correlation with this hypothetical dimension or factor, which had been named "codability," and so Modal was utilized in the experiment as the measure of codability.

Before proceeding with the results, let us consider these measures of codability. They are not obviously conceptually homogeneous. Or, perhaps, they represent different aspects of codability.

Zipf (1935) has found a correlation in a number of languages between frequency of usage of a word and its shortness. While correlational analysis can't establish causality, enough examples of shortening exist that it seems likely that as a concept becomes frequently used it will be represented by a shorter name. *Television* has become *TV* and *automobile* has been replaced (in speech at least) by *car*. These changes have been rather rapid compared with the average rate of linguistic change; but, of course, television, for example, has in thirty years changed from being almost unheard of to one of the major features, if not the major feature, of American culture.

This relationship would appear to be the rationale for Syllable and Word. To the extent that a short, brief name can be given, the color name is probably common. If the name is common, so should be the color. If the color is common, we should have a good deal of experience in transmitting its name and in otherwise dealing with it, and this experience seems to be closely related to codability. As our culture evolves, we should develop easy and accurate ways of dealing with and talking about those things we need to deal with and talk about often.

However, this measure of codability is not a stable property of the lexical domain of color terms, nor is it a stable property of individual colors. Length can be changed by directions, as well as by the array of colors the namer knows he must distinguish the target color from. However, for the directions given, which seem to direct subjects to a relatively common and ordinary language game, brevity of description would seem to be a good operational definition of the concept of codability.

(Because much will hinge on what I mean by the Brown and Lenneberg task being ordinary or common, let me clarify that contention. Usually we use color names in situations where the colors aren't surrounded by many similar ones and usually a common color name will suffice, e.g., "The green chair is mine," "She had pale skin and wore a yellow ribbon," "Bring me the red one."

When dealing with objects of very similar colors we can say, "the darker red," for example, and with both colors available the choice is easy to make. In general, we make every effort in ordinary life to make our hearer's choice easy, and we have many other resources besides clever, long naming. Therefore, a situation where the task is not too difficult is quite close to the ordinary, common tasks we face daily.)

Latency is somewhat different in its approach to the concept of codability. While it is conceptually related to the notion of ease and availability of names, it is also related to the inter- and intrapersonal communication aspect of codability. We assume that the longer it takes someone to organize his thoughts or think up a name, the less easy the communication process will be. Furthermore, we assume that communication that takes time to instigate is less likely to be polished or perfectly accurate. Practice makes perfect; practice also makes quick and automatic. Latency seems to capture codability in both its (not very different) aspects.

Measure 4, Modal, is a good operational definition of the concept of a real name. As I have suggested, we would say an object had a real name if it had a modal name; but we would want the modal name to be quite modal. However, this measure would give a color a very high score if it had two real names, i.e., if all people who didn't give the modal name gave the same other name. This is not a liability in the domain of color terms, since it is unlikely that any colors have two strong real names, at least within a single color-naming language game. While *blue-green* and *turquoise* may be strong real names, the first comes from a less fancy language game than the second; instructions should try to put the subject into one or the other game. Subtracting the variability of the remaining names has the effect of taking codability from a color to the extent that it forces people to give idiosyncratic responses, and this makes good sense: communication is based on communality. This measure, then, seems to capture the concept of codability very well in the domain of color terms. It would not be so good in a domain where multiple real names are present.

Measure 5, Agreement, makes the most sense as a predictor

of recognition. Given the assumption of these studies that memory is "A situation in which an individual communicates to himself through time using the brain as a channel" (Lantz & Stefflre, 1964), this measure is as close an approximation to the experimental situation as one could ask for, except for the fact that in the experimental situations subjects had to remember for at most a few minutes, compared to the month for Agreement. However, this measure does not tap codability directly. Joe may call his wife a "no-good, nagging, haggish grouch with elementary oral overtones" month in and month out, and neither we nor his wife may be expected to know quite what he means. Most important, Joe may not either. In other words, agreement may be purely verbal, as opposed to conceptual.

As we shall see, Lantz and Stefflre (1964) have introduced a measure of communication accuracy that involves one person giving the name (encoding) and another picking out the color with the name as aid (decoding). This measure, which we will call C.A., deals with the problems of Measure 5, Agreement. As can be seen, it insures that the communication be understandable and not idiosyncratic.

In summary, all measures approach the concept of codability, but in sufficiently different ways that we shouldn't conclude that they are conceptually homogeneous. But given the "under normal circumstances" aspects of the situation, it would seem that they measure stable aspects of the color lexicon. Given that the language game is the usual one, we expect brevity to be associated with quickness and agreement; and we consider these properties to be properties of the lexicon. Measure 5, Agreement, is somewhat less satisfactory in this respect. Individuals differ in their ability to make idiosyncratic codings, so that the measure may be less completely a measure of particular colors. However, individual differences in overall ability to encode in the same way on two different occasions are controlled for, so that even this criticism is mitigated somewhat.

However, there are three correlations lower than .40, and the mean correlation is .54. While there is obviously a good deal of communality here, there is sufficient variation remaining that it would have been interesting to see if the four discarded measures worked in the experimental situation as 4, Modal, does, as described below. If it were not for the great respect I have for the two writers, I would accuse them of trying to hide something, for the analysis is obvious. However, psychologists are usually not noted for complicating things, and in this situation, which, again, I call the ordinary language game of color naming, it seems unlikely that any radically different patterns would emerge.

Turning now to the experiment itself: A new set of subjects was selected and assigned to one of four different experimental groups, each of which had, for their recognition task, an orderly arrangement of 120 colors (i.e., greens were close to other greens, which were close to blues, etc.), among which were scattered the 24 colors for which codability data had been obtained. These latter colors we will call the stimulus colors. The four groups were treated as follows:

EG I: One stimulus color was shown to the subject; seven seconds later he tried to select it from the array of 120 colors.

EG II: Four colors shown; recognition began seven seconds later.

EG III: Four colors shown; recognition began thirty seconds later.

EG IV: Four colors shown; recognition began after three minutes, during which subjects were required to do "tasks" which were supposed to distract them from attending to their memories.

The recognition task facing EG IV subjects is more difficult than the one facing EG III subjects, and so on; EG I subjects face a rather easy task.

The recognition score for a color was the sum of correct selections over subjects. Each subject's contribution was weighted by his overall recognition ability. A correct selection by a subject who was generally good at the recognition task was given less weight than a selection by a poorer subject, in order to make the recognition score as much as possible a score for colors.

In general, codability was positively related to recognition. Discriminability was also related to recognition, and to a greater extent than codability. This was true for all four experimental groups. The correlation between codability and recognition was higher the more difficult the experimental situation. This was expected: perceptual memory obviously plays a part (witness the correlation of discriminability of a color with its recognition score), but it was expected that as the tasks became more difficult, verbal memory would become more important, while direct non-verbal perceptual memory would fade. The results support this interpretation. Along these lines, it was expected that discriminability would be most related to recognition for the easier tasks. This was confirmed, but the results were not striking. We shall have more to say on this later.

It is important to note that codability was related to recognition at all levels of discriminability. That is, the results do not reflect a simple artifactual relationship between discriminability and codability. In fact, they were essentially uncorrelated, so that the correlations between recognition and codability, with discriminability parceled out statistically, were almost the same as before parceling. This is not surprising if we remember that discriminability is a property of the array, while codability is more a property of a color—or, more accurately, a property of a color given this normal sort of array.

Lenneberg and Roberts (1953) have done a similar study, using English speakers and Zuni Indians, with a similar basic result. In addition, it was hypothesized that differences in the color lexicons of the two languages would be reflected in differences in codability and recognition. For example, the Zuni do not discriminate in their lexicon (of words) between yellow and orange. They have a single name for this area of the spectrum. Consequently, monolingual Zuni often confused these two colors in the recognition task, while English speakers never made this error. Bilingual Zuni were in between in the frequency with which they made this particular error. This suggests strongly the verbal coding already discussed and makes it clear that where a lexicon is deficient, memory will also be deficient.

A major step forward in this series of studies was the introduction as an important variable of the nature of the array of colors used in the recognition task. For example, consider a model case of blue. It should be highly codable (on Modal). It will be easily recognized in a sparse array such as Brown and Lenneberg's, where there was only one near-model case of blue. So the method of verbally assisted memory will be efficient. However, if the subject has an array of colors that are primarily blues, recognition will be difficult and the verbal label worthless. In fact, one might expect that the more model the case (and the simpler the name) the less recognition would profit from verbal encoding (i.e., codability might be negatively correlated with recognition). If the subject knows a color is not a model one, he may try harder on the name. The color will be less codable than a model case. But the increased precision of the name will allow verbal encoding to be of some service in this array. Model colors will be just as lost in an array of similar, near-model colors, but will have a less precise name.

Lenneberg (1961) showed subjects the color intercepting the blue-green segment of the spectrum (a model case of blue-green). Some were told it was an example of blue, some of green, some blue-green, and some green-blue. The question: Would the verbal encoding *offered* (note the difference from the experiments discussed previously) the subjects affect their ability to select the color from an array almost entirely in the blue-green area of the spectrum, with blue-green in the middle? More specifically, would "blue" subjects be more likely to err in the direction of the blue end of the spectrum when picking the color they had seen earlier? And would "green" subjects tend to pick a greener blue-green?

There were no such systematic errors. Lenneberg concludes that, "this suggests that naming habits with respect to unambiguous material are firmly enough established to resist ephemeral influences." In other words, subjects did not use language to help them remember. In this case, I would suggest, the blue-green color was so clearly not a model case of blue or green that the disjunction between the name and the color would be obvious. Subjects would depend on their perceptual memory.

A similar experiment was performed in 1932 by Carmichael, Hogan, & Walter. Subjects had to learn to reproduce line-drawings. The drawings were slightly ambiguous. Each resembled two common objects. Some of the subjects were told that the drawing resembled one of the objects; the rest that it resembled the other. A few subjects served as a control group; they learned to reproduce the drawing without verbal labels. (Some examples are: eyeglasses–dumb-bells; crescent moon–letter C; ship's wheel–sun; kidney bean–canoe.)

While this study is often called a classic and a delight, it is terribly flawed, and I hesitate to draw conclusions from it; however, I will follow the honorable tradition of psychologists and proceed.

Reproductions tended to resemble the object named, although this was true mainly for reproductions of the fifth (lowest) quality. Thus it would seem that those who were able to remember the figures well enough to reproduce them well didn't need or use the verbal labels. It is impossible to determine this from the data, as the authors present no data as to whether individuals were consistent in the quality of their reproductions.

While about 75% of the low quality reproductions were similar to the resembling object, 45% of the control group's reproductions (it is not clear whether the authors mean only the lowest quality reproductions) resembled one or the other of the objects, suggesting that some of the control group used verbal labels even though unbidden.

Why did these experimenters get positive results when Lenneberg didn't? (Assuming, for analogy's sake, that the original line-drawings were midway between, for example, the letter C and a crescent moon.) It seems plausible to put it this way: Carmichael, *et al.*'s stimulus materials were ambiguous, i.e., they looked somewhat like but not exactly like two common physical objects, while Lenneberg's stimulus color was clearly *not* a model case of blue or green. Thus there would be less tendency for assimilation towards the verbal label. Perhaps Carmichael's experiment is to Lenneberg's as EG IV is to EG I in Brown and Lenneberg's experiment. Verbal storage is used when perceptual memory is not sufficient.

To return to the main thread, it seems obvious that using an array of closely packed colors will give different results from those obtained with an array of widely spaced colors. Lenneberg's study is not directly comparable to Brown and Lenneberg's, so we cannot be more explicit or detailed. However, Lantz and Stefflre (1964) have done an experiment which compares two different arrays. Let us first consider their measure of codability (communication accuracy, C.A.), which they consider superior to Brown and Lenneberg's.

Two arrays were used: The Brown-Lenneberg (BL) array and an array of blues and greens very similar to the one used by Lenneberg (the FM array). The BL array had twenty-four colors; the FM array had twenty. Twenty encoders gave a name to each color in order, they were told, to enable a friend to pick out the color. They had initially, as in the Brown and Lenneberg study, been able to look at the colors they were to name (but not the array the friend—actually the second set of subjects—would have to face with the name). Next, decoders had to pick the color the names best fit, but from much larger arrays. Each name given by an encoder was decoded four times. An index of agreement was calculated from these four decodes and summed over all names for each color. As usual, good decoders' selections received less weight than poor decoders'. In addition, since the colors in the FM array were equidistant perceptually, a mean error score could be calculated (this could have been done for the BL array, using the discriminability data; for some reason it wasn't). For the FM array the mean error score and the agreement score correlated .71. The former was used in the experiment, since it gave a wider variety of scores, while agreement was used for the BL array. Since the crux of the experiment rests on a comparison of performances on the two arrays, the same index should have been used for both arrays; the error is rather serious.

Lantz and Stefflre have stacked the deck in favor of their measure. For the FM array low average naming agreement is to be expected, while naming agreement (N.A.) for the BL array should be more variable: The encoders for the FM array know what a task their friends will face, so they should try harder and produce more precise but less common names (for colors that could also be in the BL array). This will reduce the variance of N.A. for the FM array, which lowers its potential correlation with any other variable. And, as noted, for the FM array the measure of C.A. with the most variance was selected, thus raising its potential correlation with other variables relative to the C.A. variable for the BL array.

Lantz and Stefflre suggest that N.A. and C.A. will not correlate "when the appearance of numerous names simply indicates a proliferation of vocabulary for describing the item, or when there are a number of items in the stimulus array that are all named in the same way."

Let us consider these contentions. The first is clearly accurate. If there were many equally effective names for *blue* there would be low N.A. but high C.A. But in what lexical domains is this the case? Clearly not in the lexical domain of color terms in English. We shall run into some such domains in Chapter Four, e.g., the domain of terms referring to sexual intercourse. Interestingly enough, we shall find that when there are "numerous names . . . for describing the item" there is also guilt associated with the domain, i.e., avoidance behavior, at least on a verbal level. Hence we might expect communication accuracy—but little actual communication. And this would seem to be the case. It is remarkably easy to get across the idea of sex, but we are famous for not talking about it (at least not honestly and when it counts, e.g., with children and spouses).

The second contention is also true. If many items have the same name there will be a high naming agreement but low communication accuracy. However, when we face an array or collection of very similar objects (or colors, or other things), we have two options: either we have naming agreement, e.g., we agree that all dimes are alike, and we agree to treat the objects in the same way; or we attempt to work on developing communication accuracy by developing techniques of differentiation. Then we no longer have a number of items that are all named in the same way. In other words, Lantz and Stefflre are talking about a state of affairs that is either acceptable (we are glad to consider all dimes functionally equivalent) or transitional.

So in general it appears that the tasks involved with dealing with the FM array are rather different from the kind of tasks we face in day-to-day life. That is, Lantz and Stefflre ask their subjects to play rather peculiar language games, ones where we do not expect the regularities of ordinary life to hold up. My contention is that C.A. and N.A. will be correlated (just as Modal and Agreement were correlated in Brown and Lenneberg's study) under ordinary circumstances.

However, C.A. should correlate with recognition no matter what the array. If encoders are shown an obvious blue and so name it, N.A. will be high but C.A. will be low, as will recognition. For less populated arrays, C.A. should still be associated with recognition, since there will still be colors that are not easily encoded and/or decoded (or, of course, therefore, recognized). For such arrays, however, N.A. should be correlated with recognition, but only because N.A. will be correlated with C.A.: Colors people can agree on will be those that are model cases of ordinary language color names, which will be easily communicated, due to their high C.A. *in this array.*

This argument has substantially less force if we consider that C.A. is superior in predicting recognition not because it is a better measure of the concept of codability, but because it is, as I suggested with respect to Brown and Lenneberg's Agreement, adopted precisely for the kind of memory tasks employed in these experiments. There are other cognitive tasks where another measure might be superior.

Going now to the experiment, three different experimental groups were used, differing in difficulty of the memory task. The procedure was similar to that employed by Brown and Lenneberg.

For the FM array, N.A. correlated negatively with recognition in all three recognition situations (it will be recalled that I predicted this on the grounds that verbal encoding would be worthless for model colors); but C.A. correlated positively in all three situations, for both arrays, and especially for the harder recognition tasks. Thus the major hypothesis is confirmed, although I have attempted to show it is partially artifactual.

C.A. correlated .32 with recognition in the FM array and .51 in the BL array for the groups with the easiest recognition task, which was somewhat easier than Brown and Lenneberg's easiest. The .51 correlation is higher than the correlations of N.A. with recognition in the easiest task in both experiments. Apparently C.A. correlated substantially with recognition even when perceptual memory should be efficient and dominant. Recall also in the Brown and Lenneberg experiment, discriminability correlated more highly than N.A. (Modal) in all experimental conditions.

These findings suggest that perceptual memory may be influenced by language, i.e., in this context, that we can better perceive what we can better communicate—without the necessity of postulating a mediating process such as verbal storage. This is only suggested; further research would be needed.

But if it were the case that perceptual memory was more efficient in areas of the color spectrum where the lexicon was more efficient, a much stronger version of the Whorfian hypothesis would receive verification in this area.

An analogous situation is the manner in which we perceive speech sounds. While English speakers are born with no more ability than Japanese speakers to distinguish *r* from *l*, English speakers learn to hear the distinction, but Japanese speakers don't. The distinction is significant in English. That is, *rot* is a different word than *lot*. But the Japanese would not even hear the difference, unless they were trained or asked to focus on it. As is well known, the Japanese have difficulty learning to hear this (to us extremely obvious) distinction.

Perhaps we see the world of colors differently than the Zuni; the implication of this series of studies is that we may use our language in various cognitive tasks, but perception remains relatively untouched. It seems doubtful to me that there is a great deal of differential color perception. Hearing the difference between speech sounds is of great importance in day-to-day life, while usually not much hinges on the difference between, say, *red* and *purple*. Furthermore, when colors are close we have, as I have indicated, other ways than verbal encoding or perceptual memory to pick the proper one. But the studies still hint that color perception is influenced by language.

Communication accuracy and naming agreement correlated —.10 for the FM array and .43 for the BL array, as expected. Thus there is additional evidence that in an ordinary language game measures of a single concept will tend to stick together, but that a rare or difficult language game will destroy the expected regularities of day-to-day life.

These studies are often cited and discussed, usually uncritically. Miller and McNeill (1969), in a discussion often considered definitive, attempt to distinguish between codability and communication accuracy on the basis that the former is a property of colors and the latter a property of messages. They completely ignore the fact that Brown and Lenneberg considered Agreement, which is very similar to C.A., to be a measure of codability; but, then, Brown and Lenneberg were, I suggested, not very conceptual either. I think the discussion thus far has indicated that such a distinction is, at any rate, not worthwhile. Miller and McNeill would prefer to have something be a property of what is out there (colors) and something else a property of what is dealing with what is out there (we and our messages).

Such desires for tidiness are laudatory, but we cannot talk about colors without talking about them in some specific context (and colors don't have properties aside from those we humans give them). I have suggested that Brown and Lenneberg have dealt with a common and ordinary context. Common, ordinary contexts, being, as they are, common and ordinary, do not really seem like contexts (note that here, as in ascribing traits, we require some kind of excess), but they still are, at least in this context.

I have suggested that in such a common, ordinary context all the various approaches to codability will be correlated: those that emphasize the communication aspects of codability, those that emphasize the brevity aspects, and those that emphasize the commonality. Under duress or more exacting conditions this unity may break down. Certainly there are situations where the least brief communication is the most exact and accurate (as in a detailed description of an event that must be analyzed, such as a crime); and there are situations where the least common approach is the best, if not the only way to communicate, as in some poetry. But in ordinary day-to-day contexts we should expect that lexical domains handle some areas of experience more efficiently, briefly, and modally than others, i.e., that we will be most able to deal with those areas of experience where we have a model name—and we will probably have a model name in those areas of experience with which we need to deal most often and effectively and modally. Thus the relationship between Brown and Lenneberg's measures becomes tautologous.

But the experiment of Lantz and Stefflre is valuable in that it deals with naming behavior in areas where we need all our "creative" resources. Naming colors is hardly poetry, although in some periods of history the ability to name colors in original and striking ways would have been considered part of poetic ability. But Lantz and Stefflre put their FM subjects in a difficult situation, one where it is clear that they cannot be constrained or restrained by commonly used vocabulary entries. Correlations between measures break down, but it is not clear why. But this is something future research might possibly look into.

A final note on color-naming behavior: To call an object *red* is not to make a commitment to the "exact" color of the object, but is to treat the object as something that is red (recall the previous discussion of the Triobriand Islanders' lack of adjectives), and to believe that *red* is an adequate name, given the circumstances, for the color. In general, there is no description we give that we can't qualify further if we are called upon to do so.

In conclusion, these studies have demonstrated that we do use verbal encoding in memory. Therefore, the language we speak will influence our memory ability. I have attempted to put these studies in a conceptual framework that would allow future research to proceed in a more fruitful manner. At present, this research tradition is dormant or dead. I don't know why.

Object Sorting Behavior

There have been two studies (Maclay, 1958; Carroll & Casagrande, 1958) that have attempted to deal with Whorf's contention that the grammar of a language has something to do with how we perceive or deal with reality. As with the previous set of studies, these deal with a relationship between a linguistic variable and a cognitive variable. The cognitive variable in this case is sorting behavior rather than memory.

Since it is more likely that readers know a European language than an American Indian language, and since it is more likely that the reader is familiar with the kind of distinctions European languages make, since English makes similar ones, let me first frame the question with an example from those languages.

Is a German likely to see a dog as more similar to a grown man than to a child (of either sex) because the words for dogs and men are of the masculine gender while the word for children is of the neuter gender? The answer seems obvious: of course not. Gender is, for the most part, accident or caprice. The various inflected Indo-European languages do not agree on the gender of various non-sexual objects.

On the other hand, the answer seems equally obvious. Yes: Just because languages differ in the gender they assign to various non-sexual objects (the usual argument against gender having an effect) doesn't mean that gender doesn't have an effect. Perhaps a language in which *moon* is feminine forces its speakers to see the moon differently than speakers of a language in which *moon* is masculine.

On a more trivial but more important level, if you ask a German what is common to dogs and men that isn't common to children, one answer he can give that an American can't is that dogs and men are treated similarly by grammar, while children are treated differently (Analogy: What's the difference between the Queen and the Jack of Spades? The King loves the Queen but has thrown the Jack out of the country. He treats them differently).

This is clearly far from Whorf's metaphysical comments on the noun-verb dichotomy. It is like pointing out that one bird is different from two birds because you have to put an *s* after *bird* when you talk about two of them. Is a bird more similar to a tornado than to two birds because both *bird* and *tornado* are in the singular? Probably not: Grammar gives reasons for grouping things, but they are weak reasons compared to others we can think of.

Therefore, it is not surprising that these studies have not shown strong results. While we are often aware of grammar (or could be made aware of it), when dealing with the world we aren't stupid or maladaptive. "Anyone who hates dogs and children can't be all bad." The similarity is too obvious to miss for Germans or Americans. Dogs and children are small, need affection, act up, etc. Any grammatical dissimilarity is bound to be lost in the shuffle.

There is another problem, already hinted at. While it is clear that a man is masculine and a woman feminine, it is not clear what sex a pen is. And many languages do not (as would be convenient for people trying to learn the language) put inanimate objects into a neuter class. As I have suggested, there is often no obvious basis for the placement. It may be that if something doesn't fit well anywhere, we shove it into the first category that comes to mind.

The problem is more difficult when we deal with nouns, verbs, and other form classes. Why is justice a noun? In what sense is it a person, place, or thing? Clearly if anything it should be a verb, for justice is only accomplished through actions. Again, it appears we pick a form class at random.

Consider Navaho: A verb stem will be fitted by up to twelve different endings, depending on the nature of the predicate noun. Generally, writers talk about how it is the shape of the referent of the predicate noun that determines the stem. Three categories used in the research are: Slender-rigid (e.g., stick), slender-flexible (rope), and flat-flexible (fabric). Imagine what a bother it must be to change the ending of the verb depending on the shape of the predicate noun. But the Navaho handle it without difficulty or complaint, although they are not consciously aware of the basis of classification, lacking (lucky as they are) grammarians. Children of three and four use them correctly and seem to understand the basis of classification, for if you show them an object they haven't seen they will give it the ending appropriate to the shape of the object.

But what is the shape of justice? What is the shape of water? And so on. There is bound to be difficulty with any classification system.

Given this feature of Navaho, it is tempting to ask whether they would use it as a basis for sorting. Consider a blue ruler, a green tape measure, a green candle, and a blue electric cord. They are sitting on a table, and some fool white man wants you to divide them into two groups: "I want you to look them over and as soon as you become familiar with them, place two over here on the right and two over here on the left. You may find that they divide easily into two groups and, if you don't notice a natural pairing, and there may be none, please make a division anyway. There is no right division; I'm interested only in your own personal opinion." (Maclay, 1958)

You know now that the white man is speaking with forked tongue, for there are *three* natural pairings, a possibility not mentioned in the instructions. You can sort on the basis of color (the blue ruler and the blue electric cord vs. the green objects), shape (the ruler and the candle vs. the electric cord and the tape measure) or function (the ruler and tape measure vs. the candle and the cord). Would you, a Navaho, tend to place the ruler with the candle because, in addition to the obvious similarity of shape, you also use a similar verb inflection when talking about rulers and candles? The general answer is that you sometimes would, but not much more than somebody who doesn't speak Navaho.

Notice that this task is really very similar to the tasks used in the color naming experiments. The structure or grammar of the language is not obviously more involved than the lexicon. (That this last statement is puzzling reflects the problems involved in separating what is structure from what is content [lexicon]: By saying that the lexicon is involved I am claiming that verb endings can be considered as semantic aspects of discourse. Why not? Two birds are different from one bird; slender-flexible is different from slender-rigid, and these differences are substantive as much as formal.)

At any rate, think how much more interesting it would have been if these investigators had approached the problem as Brown and Lenneberg did. Do the Navaho, for example, have a greater ability to remember objects that fit snugly into one of their twelve categories than objects that are on the borderline between two categories (e.g., something slender but half-way between rigid and flexible, such as a broom made of hard rubber?) And do the Navaho have more difficulty remembering objects when the array they must pick the stimulus object from consists only of objects of the same shape? More important, do they have this tendency more than do English speakers? In other words, do they perceive such objects as more similar than they really are (to our non-Navaho eyes)? And will the Navaho make fewer errors with objects with modal shapes than English speakers, but more errors in the borderline areas of the shape spectrum? All these questions could have been asked, and it seems somehow more likely that interesting and positive results would have followed.

So it is clear that the relationships investigated in the experiments described below are not clearly structural, as opposed to Brown and Lenneberg's lexical relationships. But the authors shouldn't be faulted for claiming they are investigating structure. For some reason, this kind of relationship is deemed structural. But the distinction between the semantic and the structural aspects of language has never been made to my satisfaction. Except, of course, when dealing with model cases; but that is easy.

Maclay used four sorting tasks (and the instructions quoted above). For each task, the subjects were presented with four objects; the subjects were asked to sort them into two groups. For Type I tasks, either a color, a form, or a function (or material) sort was possible. For Type II tasks, either a function or material sort or a form sort was possible. For Type III tasks the form sort was the only possible one. For Type IV (control) sorts, there was no sensible basis for classification.

As I have indicated, subjects were Navaho Indians (with varying degrees of bilingualism in English); native English-speaking Americans, and Pueblo Indians.

There were six major hypotheses:

1. The three groups of subjects shouldn't differ on Type IV sorts. There is no reason why they should, and if they had we would immediately suspect there was something wrong with the experiment.

2. It should take longer to do Type IV sorts for all groups than other sorts (longer latency). Since there was no sensible basis for classification this seems logical and obvious. However, a case could have been made that Type I sorts, with three competing sensible sorts, should take longer due to decision making time.

3. Navaho Indians should make more form sorts than the other two groups. This follows from the basic premise.

4. The number of form sorts for the Navaho should correlate with the Language Experience Index (L.E.I.), an index of the extent to which the person had spoken the Indian language compared to English, and also, probably, a (negative) indicator of familiarity with Anglo-American culture. Again, this follows straightforwardly from the basic premise. Furthermore, this correlation should not obtain for the Pueblo, for while their L.E.I. should correlate negatively with familiarity with Anglo-American culture, it shouldn't have any relationship to the number of form sorts, since the Pueblo language doesn't have the form feature of grammar. If a correlation between the L.E.I. and form sorts was

found for the Pueblo, it would indicate that Indian culture rather than language was responsible for form sorts.

5. The Navaho should have equal latency for Type I, II, and III sorts; Anglos and Pueblos should take longer on Type III sorts than on Type I and II sorts. This makes no sense. Maclay's logic is that, "The Navaho should have an equally available solution for all three types whereas the other groups should find Type III, with only a form solution, more difficult." But form sorts are quite obvious. As I suggested above, in addition, Type III sorts should be easier for all groups, since there were no competing sensible sorts.

6. Navahos, when making a form sort, should do so more rapidly than Anglos or Pueblos. "This, and the other hypotheses involving latency, are based on the common psychophysical assumption that a difficult task will be associated with a longer response time." But there is no reason to expect that the form sort task is easier for the Navaho. Their grammatical system gives them another reason to make a form sort, perhaps (all else being very equal); but the consideration of this additional reason could (it could be argued) take time and be associated with longer latencies.

The first two hypotheses were confirmed, as they should have been. Hypothesis 3, which must be considered the most sensible and least ambiguous of the hypotheses, as well as the most crucial, was not confirmed. Hypothesis 4, concerning the L.E.I., was confirmed, as the Navaho correlation was .48, quite high and statistically significant, while the Pueblo correlation was .19, low and statistically insignificant. Hypothesis 5 was not confirmed. In fact, all three subject groups showed longer latency for Type III sorts. This tendency was stronger for the Navaho, suggesting my alternative hypothesis concerning latency, advanced above, may be valid. Hypothesis 6 was also not confirmed. For the comparisons involved in testing Hypotheses 3 and 6, Navaho and Anglo groups were very similar and were both different from the Pueblo group.

The results from this experiment may be termed either inconclusive or disconfirmatory of the aspect of the Whorfian hypothesis tested here, although, as I have suggested, it is not really a very fair test of the hypothesis.

Carroll and Casagrande report two similar studies. The first was very much a lexical rather than a structural study. For example, the Hopi, in speaking of things breaking, must use one verb if there is one "fission" and another if there are many. This distinction is analogous to ours between *break* and *shatter*. The Hopi use the same verb for spilling and pouring but a different verb depending on whether what is spilled (or poured) is liquid or not liquid. For the latter example, we would expect the Hopi to group together two pictures showing liquid coming out of a container, where one was obviously (to English speakers) a case of pouring and the other was obviously a case of spilling. They would leave out as separate a picture of "pouring" apples out of a box. But English speakers would group the two pouring pictures and leave out the spilling picture (although I don't speak of *pouring* apples, but rather of dumping them).

In general, there was some tendency for a Hopi group to differ from an English speaking group on several such items, as well as some tendency for the two groups to reflect the distinctions of their language in explaining the basis for their sorting behavior. The effect, however, is weak, and I will not make much of it, since it shouldn't have been so weak.

The second study was very much like Maclay's, although children were used as subjects. Carroll and Casagrande suggest that the Navaho object categorization would force the children to learn to make form distinctions sooner than non-Navahoes. This makes sense, although there is evidence that development of this sort is more a function of age than culture.

The procedures were similar to Maclay's. Navaho dominant Navahoes, English dominant Navahoes, and Anglos from Boston were compared. There is a tendency for form sorts to increase with age for Navaho dominant Navahoes; this tendency is present in

English dominant Navahoes but is less strong at all ages compared to the tendency for Navaho dominant Navahoes.

Unfortunately, the Navaho dominant group's curve relating form sort tendency to age was almost identical in height and shape to that of the Boston Anglo children group. This prompts the authors to suggest that form sorts may be learned either because of the high usage of toys the Anglo children enjoy or because of the category system of Navaho. This explanation is hardly suggested by the data, so I will offer an equally farfetched suggestion:

Children who speak the language of their culture will learn to prefer form sorts. But children who don't speak the language of their culture, or who speak the language of a dominant culture to which they don't really belong, will become alienated. Alienation leads to a preference for non-form sorts. After all, if you are alienated, you don't believe that life has much structure or form, and you may take refuge in the formlessness of pure color.

In conclusion, the results of these rather unsatisfactory studies are not very strong, but they would not have been expected to be. However, such cross-cultural experimental work is interesting and may have further possibilities.

Word Association

In this section we will deal with word association, its relevance to the Whorfian hypothesis, and two interesting studies utilizing the technique.

In word association, the subject is given a word and told to give the first word in response that comes to mind. Freud is considered the originator of free association, as he asked his patients to associate to words, dreams, and slips of the tongue. Jung is more often given credit for developing the technique of word association as a full-fledged clinical tool. The idea was that the therapist could penetrate the subconscious (or, in Jung's case, discover complexes) by examining the words given by the patient to such leading stimulus words as *mother, death, knife,* or *my therapist.* Many people, as we shall see, give rather common and uninteresting associations, even to such loaded words, e.g., respectively, *father, life, fork, you.*

Even the most imaginative psychoanalyst would have trouble reading much into these associations. A nice option is open to the analyst: he can claim the patient is resisting treatment when he gives such common and therefore defensive associations. If the patient can be taught to loosen up his associations, perhaps he will somehow loosen up in other ways. If we think in habitual ways and if our thinking is guided by our responses to the stimulus words in our environment, including those we have just said (as some theorists think), loosening up or changing associations should allow us to change our ways of thinking and our habitual behavior and thus escape our neurosis. William Burroughs (in *The Ticket That Exploded*) has suggested various methods of so doing, e.g., splicing tape recordings randomly.

More commonly, however, a therapist would interpret word associations and thus help a patient discover his own unconscious. Thus if a patient gave the associate, *mother,* to the stimulus word, *moon,* the therapist might wish to explore the possibility that the patient considered his mother to be basically cold and dark and brightened artificially. It would be possible of course that the patient was simply alliterating. That too, in more modern approaches, would indicate disorders of the mind. Or the patient might be said to simply have his mother on the brain so that he would be likely to give *mother* as an associate to any stimulus word. This too would show disorders. Or the patient could be intentionally causing the therapist troubles by giving tantalizing associations. This is not a healthy attitude towards therapy, of course. And so on.

Thus word association behavior has been taken as an *indicator* of non-verbal behavior; and there has been some suggestion that changing the verbal behavior could also change the non-verbal behavior.

What is the status of word association behavior? We do not, after all, usually go around giving associations. Let us consider it another language game. Perhaps it is an artificial one, but then social scientists hope to find out a great deal about human behavior in real life situations by studying their behavior in the artificial situation of the laboratory (psychologists have taken to studying game-playing behavior, although the games they study are very dull indeed); furthermore, artificial situations are nevertheless situations (just as verbal behavior is behavior). So let us consider word association behavior as a (relatively uncommon) language game that may, due to relationships to other language games, shed some light on other behavior—even on other kinds of verbal behavior (other language games).

There is experimental evidence that adults tend to give associates of the same form class (part of speech) as the stimulus word. That gives some evidence of the psychological reality of the form class. On the other hand, people also tend to give opposites (which are, of course, of the same form class), things that belong together (like *table* and *chair, running* and *walking,* also of the same class), and so on, so that the form class tendency may be the result of several smaller, less significant tendencies. However, we shall discuss some additional evidence for this in the next section.

It has been found that tables of associates to stimulus words can be constructed in terms of the frequency with which various associates are given. These tables are quite stable. That is, for example, 65% of most groups of people will give *light* in response to *dark.* Furthermore, if you consider a list of associates to a given stimulus word, arranged from most frequently given to least frequently given, it will be very highly correlated with a list obtained by having single individuals give several associates to the word. In other words, if 65% of most groups of people give *light* to *dark,* 65% of the population will give *light* as their first response to *dark.* This is not surprising; but the word given second most frequently to *dark* will probably be the word most people give second. And so on. In other words, the structure of associations seems to be stable in the population and in the individual; the structures are similar. Put another way, people tend to have similar structures of associations.

Deese (1962) has suggested the possibility, therefore, of a map resembling the storage patterns of words in (presumably) our brains. Such a map, where words would be connected to each other by common associates, so that distance and also the nature of the intervening terrain would be determined, would be a map of lexical structure, something any linguist would like to have. As we shall see, Osgood and his associates have attempted (using another somewhat artificial language game called the semantic differential) to map various words, not so much in relation to each other but in relationship to a standard grid. For both approaches to mapping, of course, the proof would be with the map. That is, unless the map strikes us as corresponding somehow to the reality of lexical structures, we will reject it.

And, of course, the question would arise whether words that are given to each other belong together. Any examination indicates that they do, but the bases for togetherness are heterogeneous; so it is doubtful that one satisfactory map can be constructed.

At any rate, given the notion that the structure of lexical domains has some correspondence to the ways in which we structure reality, the study of word association behavior, even though it may be behavior that results from various and disparate language games, could be very profitable.

Having looked at some of the potential value of word association data, we will now examine two studies concerned with the non-verbal correlates of word association behavior.

Jenkins has done a study entitled, "Commonality of association as an indicator of more general patterns of verbal behavior." His hypotheses are that commonality of association, defined as the extent to which a person gives associates that are frequently given by the general population, should be associated with the person's being near the *mean* (or, to use a slightly more loaded but mathematically equivalent term, the *average*) position on many personality dimensions and other kinds of dimensions; and that it should be associated with the low end of scales designed to measure psychopathology, such as the MMPI clinical scales.

The first hypothesis is based on the questionable but reasonable assumption that the person who is average in one form of behavior will be average in other forms of behavior. It is particularly questionable given the artificiality of word association behavior. However, if one assumes that being average is a general trait and is furthermore associated with degree of socialization to the norms and habitual behavior of society, one could with reason assume that a person who gave habituated, socialized responses to stimulus words would also give habituated, socialized responses to other stimuli.

The second hypothesis is less questionable, particularly since schizophrenia is characterized by strange verbal behavior and since other forms of "mental illness" have been shown to be associated with various departures from normality on a number of indices (although they are not *characterized* by strange verbal behavior). The second rationale suggested above also applies here: The socialized person is not the (at least overtly) crazy person. The person who sees only the usual, socially given connections will be too insensitive to go crazy.

The notion, then, is that people who give common associations are real clods. Before considering the data, let us briefly deal with the biases we are avoiding here. Freud's theory would claim here that people who give unusual associations are in close contact with their unconscious, which is the seat of creativity, not to mention insanity. The more repressed person will keep the old censor busy at all times and won't allow the unconscious wishes even slight release during the harmless word association game. But perhaps the more repressed person is simply smarter. Repression and suppression are closely allied concepts. Perhaps smart people suppress associations that might "give them away."

Hall's theoretical approach would have it that under conditions of high drive the strongest habit will have a much greater tendency to be released than under conditions of low drive. Under high drive the differences between habit strengths of various behaviors are magnified by a multiplicative factor, so that, in a sense, the individual has less choice. If a person is the kind who is suspicious of psychologists or worried about evaluation, he may give common associations. When alone, that same person may give very uncommon responses and be creative and far from average in many respects.

It is also possible that people who give rare associations are simply showing off.

So we have several theoretical possibilities. The person who gives common responses may be a clod, oversocialized and entirely average. Or he may be smart and aware that the price of liberty is eternal vigilance. Or he may be paranoid. Or he may be in a state of high drive due to fear of evaluation. Or he may be a closet creative. Or he may be less of a show-off than the person who gives uncommon associates.

The two studies will not allow us to pick one or two of these possibilities and reject the others. This is largely because the above "theoretical possibilities" are not independent of each other or separate. For example, being the antithesis of a show-off is not independent of being socialized. The "two" possibilities are logically related. For another example, being smart and aware is not a possibility separate from that of being paranoid. Both in a sense refer to the same thing. They differ in their connotations. It is good to be smart and bad to be paranoid. To be paranoid is to be afraid when fear is not appropriate. But who is to judge when fear is appropriate? The reader is invited to read anything by Thomas Szasz or a book called the *Brain Watchers,* by Martin L. Gross (1962), if he wishes a few examples of abuses by psychologists and psychiatrists.

We will now turn to the results. But watch out for hidden biases.

Jenkins found that the tendency to give common responses is stable. That is, people tend to give associates of a pretty constant frequency (i.e., very common, medium common, uncommon) to all stimulus words. Furthermore, this tendency is stable over time. Finally, high-C(ommonality) individuals, as Jenkins calls them, tend to give the same response to a given stimulus word on a retest to a much greater extent than do low-C individuals. (So high-C individuals are rigid in their word association behavior? Nonsense, it is just that they are faithful. Is the man who stays with his wife for many years to be called *rigid?*)

But with respect to word association behavior, however we care to interpret it, we *are* dealing with a general and stable trait. The question is, is this trait of any greater generality?

There are some positive results. High-C individuals tend to give associates of the same form class as the stimulus word to a greater extent than do low-C individuals. Adults do so, as we have mentioned, to a greater extent than children. This puts the word association finding in a somewhat different light, as we shall see.

We could say that high-C individuals are more socialized and rigid. But given that giving the same form class is an index of adulthood as well as an index of socialization, we could say that high-C individuals are more mature than low-C individuals. Since Jenkins' subjects were college students, this latter interpretation has some point, as maturity is one important dimension along which college students vary. That is, some stay out of trouble and get decent grades, while others don't. From this point of view it is not so bad to be a high-C individual.

High-C individuals tend to score lower on scales of psychopathology than do low-C individuals. This could indicate they are more sane. It could also indicate they had a stronger need to place themselves in a socially desirable light, since some psychologists believe that it is this need that accounts for how people score on such tests as the ones given these subjects (the MMPI clinical scales). (Or we could replace "stronger need," with its connotation of passivity, with "greater desire in the face of well-founded suspicion of psychologists," with its more favorable connotation, and do no greater justice or injustice to the findings).

On a long questionnaire designed to assess interests, likes, and dislikes, no differences were found between the upper quartile on commonality (high-C individuals) and the lower quartile (low-C) except that the low-C individuals tended to spend fewer hours in social activity and more hours alone than did the high-C individuals. This is not strictly consistent with Jenkins' hypotheses. High-C individuals should spend an average number of hours in social activity and alone, while low-C individuals should spend either many more or many less than average. It is, however, consistent with the picture of the high-C individual as socialized (in the sense, however, of being an active part of society rather than the previous sense, which emphasized the high-C's conformity. One can spend all one's time with people and be completely unsocialized, i.e., a real strange one). The general picture that emerges from this questionnaire is that of no difference.

Turning now to what Jenkins calls "more general patterns of verbal behavior," in an essay describing the University of Minnesota, no differences were found between high-C and low-C individuals on the number of sentences, words, words per sentence, syllables per word, type-token ratio (a measure of diversity of word use), number of nouns per first 250 words, or verbs per first 250 words. It is not at all clear why a high-C individual should differ from a low-C individual on any of these measures. If Jenkins had taken the trouble to be more theoretical about his data collection, he would not have had to hypothesize these relationships.

There was one difference between the essays. High-C essays were more easily "clozed," i.e., when words were eliminated from the essays the correct word could be more often guessed for high-C than for low-C essays. This difference is consistent with the picture of the high-C individual as socialized. The high-C individual puts the common word in a given context. Therefore, people, who are, on the average, average, should guess the word correctly. But the relationship is of little significance because of the similarity of the situations. In both cases, the individuals were given the choice of using either a common or an uncommon word.

Again, however, the general picture that emerges from the essays is that of no difference. There were some other, mixed results.

The two groups did not differ in degree of preference for picture rather than verbal responses to words; I can't see why they should, from any of our theoretical vantage points. Nor did they differ in the popularity of names they gave to color chips; it would seem that low-C individuals should give idiosyncratic names to colors. There is no evidence that the high-C individual yields to social pressure (on a paper and pencil test designed to measure this tendency), and, of course, the high-C individual should be more responsive to social pressure, for social pressure is what produces socialized individuals. There are no differences on the Allport-Lindzey scale of values, although we would expect the low-C individual to be higher on the less socialized aesthetic interest and lower on the socialized and conformist economic (money) interest. High-C individuals remained more stable in their interest patterns over time, which is consistent with their consistency in word association behavior as well as with their socialization—or faithfulness and maturity, if you are a high-C individual.

In general, then, Jenkins got mixed results. He got many positive results and many "no difference" results; most favorable to his study, he got few if any results that were clearly contrary to his hypotheses or our theories. It would appear that the picture of the high-C individual as more conforming, sane, mature, consistent, and socialized is valid to some extent. We shall take up the problem of the various evaluative biases operating here later, but let me note now that there are several forms of life. The creative, productive person may be a lousy person. The good person may be a clod. We have need in this society for both types of people. If we say there are two types of people, the creatives and the commons, creatives are crazy from the commons' point of view, and the commons are clods from the creatives' point of view. Perhaps the people we (whoever that is) should feel most sorry for are the many people who are neither creatives nor commons, the people who are borderline cases of both. Such people are disliked by the commons for their somewhat crazy behavior and hate themselves for being too common to be creative.

MacKinnon (1962) reports related findings. He studied a group of the most creative architects in the country. They had been ranked for creativity with great reliability by editors of architectural journals and by members of an architecture department. That is, even though the group was highly select, judges could agree on a rank order in terms of creativity. For comparison, suppose we can agree on the top forty or fifty baseball players ever to play the game. They all will have been great players. Then we select other baseball players, not only who are pretty good but who have a good knowledge of the game. Do you think they would pretty much agree on the rank order of the top forty? Anyone who follows baseball or any other sport will know that they won't. Arguments over who is greater than whom are endless. Furthermore, they are similar to arguments about creativity in that there are no agreed upon criteria. Often intangibles are invoked and the usual criteria (such as batting average or home runs) are discarded. So if a number of architects can agree on a rank order of this sort, it means that creativity is a pretty stable and visible trait in this area.

MacKinnon reports that one of the best predictors of creativity among architects in general was uncommonness of word association behavior. Furthermore, this measure could predict significantly even *within* this highly select group, which is quite something. Intelligence had a slightly negative correlation with creativity within this group, although it has a positive correlation with creativity within the general population. In the terms of the baseball analogy: If we could come up with a stable rank order of the top fifty baseball players of all time, we would be very surprised if we could come up with one index which correlated highly with this rank order. For example, we would be very surprised if batting average were an excellent predictor of rank order among this select fifty. In the first place, most of the fifty would have very high batting averages. So that the determination of position would be made, it would seem, on the basis of many factors, many of them competing. But here, we find one index, word association behavior, that does a very good job of predicting creativity within this select population.

MacKinnon found, furthermore, that predictive ability was increased if associations given by the general population between one and ten percent were given more weight than associations given by the general population less than one percent of the time.

These results may be interpreted as follows: Creativity is

doing or making something (relatively) new, but it must be eventually something someone else appreciates or understands. In this case, the understanding has to have come during the architect's lifetime; otherwise there would have been no creativity rating, and more probably there would be few if any buildings to judge. Architects can't wait around, like poets, for posterity.

Highly idiosyncratic responses are not likely to be appreciated or understood. While an association may come from a single personal experience, it is necessary for the artist to transmute his personal experience into terms others can understand. Perhaps highly idiosyncratic responses come from minds that aren't "in touch with reality" (i.e., that we don't understand). That is, there is a suggestion of undersocialization. Even so, architects who did give highly idiosyncratic responses were rated as more creative than other highly creative architects. But creativity was predicted somewhat better if the slightly less idiosyncratic responses were given more importance.

These two studies suggest that gross measures of word association behavior are associated with rather important non-verbal behavior. In general, it would seem that giving words of low frequency is associated with creativity and with psychopathology: As Barron (1965) has reported in more detail, these architects showed themselves to be highly pathological on the MMPI, the same test Jenkins' used. Thus Jenkins' results are corroborated. However, it is necessary to point out that being pathological on the MMPI may be little more than a willingness to admit to various bodily symptoms most of us have to some extent but which are a little bit shameful. (For example, do you like to think of yourself as the kind of person who goes to the bathroom more often than most? If you don't mind, would you admit it to a *test?*)

People who would willingly admit to such foul and distasteful secrets about themselves would not seem to be the kind of people who would care much about what others thought of them. And in fact, another highly characteristic feature of these architects was an indifference to social approval.

Consider that the creative group studied by MacKinnon consisted of architects. His findings do suggest that it is *necessary* to (be the kind of person who will) give uncommon responses. But these findings may hold only for architects, perhaps for the following reasons:

Architects do not—at least initially—have to display their ideas verbally. In fact, it is possible that socialized verbal behavior could be a hindrance to an architect. It might tend to force his visual behavior into conventional forms, forms codified by and represented in the language, e.g., square. Perhaps more would be revealed about architecture and about creativity if the actual responses given were analyzed in a less gross fashion. Perhaps the architects who gave uncommon responses simply gave highly visual responses.

We cannot tell from the data presented whether the above suggestion has any validity. However, I hope it has been made clear how much care must be exercised in drawing conclusions from data. Too often laymen and just as often so-called professionals do not pay sufficiently close attention to others' work (being so busy doing their own). Hence people get hurt and disturbed by findings that are not really warranted by the data.

Therefore, I reserve a special paragraph for a final important comment:

Insanity and creativity are not the same thing. While it is true that schizophrenics have been reported in several studies to give unusual associations (Pavy, 1968), and while a review of the empirical literature indicates that the theme of pathology in creative people is common and strong (Kelling, 1967), few (people diagnosed or hospitalized as) schizophrenics are creative, at least in any usual usage of the word; and few highly creative individuals are overtly schizophrenic or show the symptoms of other "forms" of mental illness. It may be that it is not appropriate to consider the disturbance of a "schizophrenic" and the disturbance of a creative person exactly the same thing. Clearly they are not functionally similar. In addition, the creative person has, the evidence shows, high "ego strength", i.e., whatever pathology he has (or admits to) he can control and/or use for his creative purposes.

Perhaps we can in a sense duck the question by saying the two "insanities" have a family resemblance. At least describing the state of affairs in that way allows us to duck the temptation to say that insane people are creative or that creative people are crazy. And it could point the way to more careful and detailed analysis of data on this issue. For example, perhaps creatives give different infrequent responses than schizophrenics (the odds are that they do, since infrequent responses are infrequent, after all). A qualitative analysis of the kind of infrequent responses given by creatives compared to the kind given by (people considered) the mentally ill could be instructive.

Nouns and Verbs

There have been a few studies that purport to test Whorf's contention that English and other Indo-European languages, in the words of Flavell (1958), "bifurcate reality into two arbitrary classes of events: static objects labelled by nouns and dynamic events labelled by verbs." Flavell feels that due to this bifurcation an active event in noun form *(storm)* has a static quality, while less active events in verb form *(endure)* take on an active quality.

Flavell does not test *this* directly. He does not deal explicitly with active nouns and inactive verbs. In addition, this hypothesis is suspect in view of Osgood's findings (Chapter Five) that one of the major dimensions of connotative meaning of nouns is "activity." Therefore, nouns vary widely in the activity they connote; so do verbs. It may be that on the average nouns are less active than verbs, but this has yet to be established. And it seems very unlikely that a storm is considered less active than enduring.

Flavell showed subjects what they were told was a title of a picture. Then they were given a very brief exposure to five "pairs" of pictures. The members of each pair were in fact identical. All that differed was the title, one of which was the noun, the other of which was a verb of the same root, e.g., *swim, swimming.* The subject was asked to pick which picture was the most active. Flavell also gave subjects five control pairs, for which the titles were nearly synonymous nouns. The pictures were given short enough exposure that the subjects were not able to tell that they were identical. Half the subjects were given the noun title first; the other half were given the verb title first. No differences were found between these two groups.

Flavell reports that "on the connotation task there is a striking systematic group tendency to associate the verb form with the more active picture." This tendency was significant for all five pairs. However, there are methodological flaws, and even if we accept the results, the implications are trivial. A verb is seen as more active than a noun of the same root. Since verbs deal with actions more often than nouns do, this isn't surprising. But Flavell has not demonstrated that verbs are more active than nouns. Nor has he indicated that nouns denoting active events are in any sense static nor that verbs denoting inactive events are in any sense active. Of most importance, he has not shown that English bifurcates reality: The very fact that English has nouns and verbs of the same root suggests that English does not bifurcate reality. There need not be any difference in denotative or connotative meaning between, "I'm swimming" and "I'm having a swim." It is true that the first statement refers more to the physical activity of swimming, while the second refers more to the social practice of swimming. But then, "I'm going swimming," also refers more to the social practice. Even if there are slight differences in usage, the mutual translatability of many noun-verb pairs suggests that English does not sharply distinguish between the two grammatical classes.

Livant (1963) has done a similar study, using the semantic differential. He matched his noun-verb pairs even more rigorously than did Flavell: They had to be phonemically the same. Livant hypothesized that there should be no differences on the evaluative dimension between verbs and nouns (i.e., that they should be evaluated equally favorably), that nouns should be more potent than verbs, since potency "seems closely allied to the 'concrete' character of objects," and that verbs should be more active than nouns.

The words used were *age, attack, command, dream, doubt, fear, love, plan,* and *want.* This is a very poor sample, given Livant's reasoning that nouns should be more potent because they are related to the concrete character of objects, since none of the words refer to a concrete object. Therefore, it might be suggested that Livant is giving his hypothesis an especially rigorous test. But this suggestion assumes that the hypothesized quality of "nounness" generalizes to all types of nouns.

Subjects did noun and verb ratings for each pair before going on to the next pair. The author points out, correctly, that "forced comparisons may tend to emphasize the noun-verb contrast." In fact, such forced comparisons would tend to emphasize to the subjects that the experimenter expected a difference in ratings. (It is a commonly used tactic in reporting results of studies to admit one's errors freely, as if that were sufficient for forgiveness. Perhaps it is sufficient for forgiveness, but it shouldn't be sufficient for accepting the results, although it often is.)

However, despite this improper push in the proper direction, subjects returned only one significant result: Verbs were rated as more active than nouns.

Two experiments, then, confirm that verbs are perceived as more active than nouns. This is not really surprising, as I have said. Other than that the results have been negative.

Johnson (1967) has reported a related study. Using the semantic differential with nonsense syllables, he found that syllables in the subject position were consistently rated more active and potent than syllables used in the object (predicate) position. (This suggests the generalization of "nounness" and "verbness" to nouns and verbs that are not paradigmatically nouns and verbs, i.e., names of persons, places, and things, but it also indicates that this generalization is due not so much to "part of speech" as to syntactic position.)

It appears that Johnson used sentences where the subject did something to the object. His only example is, "The NIJ hurt the GAQ." It is not surprising that NIJ was judged more active and potent than GAQ; Johnson did not, as far as can be determined, examine such sentences as, "The NIJ knuckled under to the GAQ." Therefore, the results are ambiguous at best; one cannot tell if they reflect the fact that for some subject-verb-predicate sentences, the predicate individual or object is, because of the relationship stated in the sentence, less active and potent than the subject individual, or if in general nouns in the subject position are perceived as being more active and potent than nouns in the predicate position. If he had demonstrated the latter, it would have significant implications for advertising or propaganda.

It is, in general, a waste of time to investigate the effects of grammatical position with nonsense syllables. Words have meanings, which will often wipe out any effects that can be found using nonsense syllables.

This small set of studies has few implications. They are methodologically flawed; their results are trivial; and there exist alternative explanations for any Whorfian interpretations.

I will conclude this chapter by noting that the stronger the version of the Whorfian hypothesis empirical investigation has attacked, the more flawed, ambiguous, and subject to alternative interpretation are the results. In addition, the results tend to be less supportive as the version is stronger. The word association studies give perhaps the best results and have no pretense of being concerned with the Whorfian hypothesis. The relationship between word association behavior and other behavior is not, at least as reported here, presumed to be causal in any way. Next best are the color naming studies, where some causality is involved (we are born into a lexicon which influences memory and perhaps perception); the results there were generally positive and unambiguous. Next are the sorting behavior studies, which have poor results, but which claim to deal with structural aspects of language. Last and least are the studies presented in this section, which presume to deal with the metaphysical implications of nouns and verbs.

What this relationship suggests about the Whorfian hypothesis is not altogether clear. Perhaps the stronger versions are simply not true. But, given that the studies done on the stronger versions are so poor, methodologically speaking, and given that they are not done by really bad social scientists (but by rather good ones), we may conclude that it is going to be more difficult to adequately test these stronger versions and may require a good deal more complexity, in thinking and in experimental design, than is usually provided by social scientists.

There is a parallel here with psychoanalysis. Psychologists have made many attempts to verify psychoanalytic theory; when they fail, as is usually the case, psychoanalysts complain that their concepts have not been adequately operationalized. This complaint has caused considerable merriment among psychologists, who feel that this proves that one cannot operationalize psychoanalytic concepts. About all it proves is that psychologists can't operationalize psychoanalysts' concepts. One value of psychologists is that they are trained to operationalize concepts. Instead of sneering at psychoanalysis, perhaps they should try a little harder. The same attitude might properly be applied to the Whorfian hypothesis.

chapter four

Culture and Lexicon

That the lexicon of a language reflects the culture of the language group is a proposition accepted by most social scientists. A standard example is that the Eskimo have several words for different varieties of snow, while the English have but one. The explanation for this kind of phenomenon has been considered obvious.

Fishman (1960) has presented a "systematization" of the Whorfian hypothesis, with four levels of relationship between language and either culture or behavior. The kind of relationship displayed by the above example is a case of (the lowest) Level I, "linguistic codifiability and cultural reflections." In Fishman's view, such relationships do not constitute strong evidence for the Whorfian hypothesis, since they do not involve a "truly structural analysis of language" nor a "full-blooded analysis of the non-linguistic concomitants or resultants of language structure." Fishman finds such relationships obvious: "In all of these cases, it is not difficult to relate the codifiability differences to gross cultural differences."

Miller and McNeill also offer a systematization of the hypothesis, consisting of a strong and a weak version. Such relationships are not cases of either version, since they do not demonstrate that language exerts constraints and restraints upon man's non-linguistic behavior. They find such relationships equally unremarkable: "Since language is part of culture, it is not unreasonable to expect that correlations exist" (1969, p. 728).

Thus in this chapter we deal with the relationship between language and other things considered most obvious, trivial, and uninteresting. We shall see that all is not as simple as it seems.

Brown is not so nonchalant about these relationships. He offers "what may be a general principle of comparative semantics. Cognitive domains that are close up are more differentiated than are remote domains" (1965, p. 317). He offers two phrases which help to elucidate the concept of "close up": "importance" and "central concerns." This is the most elegant statement of the relationship so far. Snow is close up to the Eskimo in the sense that it has more importance in their day-to-day existence than it has in ours. Another of Brown's examples illustrates this: the Hanunoo of the Philippines have names for ninety-two varieties of rice (1965, p. 317). Rice is a more important food for the Hanunoo than it is for us. Sand and camels are important for the Arabs; hence they have many descriptive terms for sand and camels. And so on. Unfortunately, Brown has dealt largely with our lexical dealings with rather concrete phenomena that are of pragmatic but not psychological importance. In this chapter I present a schema that complicates matters. My schema is based on my observation of American culture, and my presentation is not precise or programmatic. The relationships I explore are not quite clear as yet. To a certain extent, it is better that way: The reader can use the schema without wondering if he is using it "properly."

The schema consists of six different lexical states of affairs (LSAs), each of which is associated with a cultural state of affairs

(CSAs). At present, lexicons of cognitive or linguistic domains are differentiated only on one variable, described as differentiation or codifiability. The present schema further differentiates the domain of lexical states of affairs.

The schema has some resemblance to a theory in that the logic of several LSA-CSA associations is presented. However, there is no general logic covering all LSA-CSA associations.

Definition of a Domain

The delination of what constitutes a lexical or conceptual domain is ambiguous. Because languages differ in the ways in which they cut up experience, what is a domain for language X may not be a domain for language Y. While the Eskimo have several words for different varieties of snow, they have no generic term. Unless "snow" is considered a domain, the Eskimo's snow terms do not constitute a domain (for the Eskimo—and perhaps they don't, for them).

Any domain is someone's or some language's domain. Domains do not have an *a priori* existence. It is just as legitimate to speak of the domain of green color terms as it is to speak of the domain of color terms. Even within a language it is not self-evident to everyone that a set of concepts belong together and are in some important respect separate from other concepts. Therefore, the word "domain" will be used rather loosely.

With similar looseness, I will not make much of a distinction between cognitive and lexical domains. A lexical domain attains its status due to its being a cognitive domain; a cognitive domain may attain its status due to the presence of an associated lexical domain.

Cultures and Sub-cultures

There are many sub-cultures in this society. They vary in size, from one on up (as do sizes of domains). Some sub-cultures are model cases of sub-cultures, e.g., hippies. Other are less model, and are usually referred to as situations or roles. I will adopt a generic term, linguistic sub-communities (LSCs), to refer to sub-cultures, roles, and situations, because a person's usage habits are determined by all three and in the same manner.

An LSC differs from the total culture in an important respect: It is (to a greater or lesser degree) part of the total culture. Because of this connectedness, the schema is most schematic and informative when used to analyze a total culture or an LSC within the context of the total culture. The schema may be used to analyze LSCs separately, but such analysis will probably be false or incomplete. The usage habits of an LSC are significant largely by contrast with the usage habits of the total culture. This is because the LSC chooses its usage habits to define a certain relationship with the total culture.

Plan of the Chapter

I will first present the schema. Next, some inadequacies in the current approach to defining and describing the lexicon will be offered. (These are *ad hoc* and allow the schema to work more fully. There are other lists of such inadequacies, all valid. Given time and money, many improvements desired by one group or another could be made.) As they are introduced and corrected, it will be possible to give examples of the use and utility of the schema. Next, problems of measurement are discussed. Finally, the implications of the schema for empirical research and social change are discussed.

Tables 1 and 2 summarize, respectively, the schema and the inadequacies in the definition of the lexicon.

The Schema

The LSAs and associated CSAs are presented as states of affairs. However, they are states of affairs that vary as a function of cultures and domains. To the quantitative extent that an LSA is present, the associated CSA is hypothesized to be present (and/ or vice-versa, as causality is not at issue here).

However, LSA I constitutes an important qualification of this implied correlation. LSA I is frequency of usage of lexical entries.

TABLE 1

Associated LSA-CSA Pairs

Pair	LSA	CSA
I	Frequency of usage	Commonness in day-to-life
II	Density	Ability to discriminate
III	Multiple names	Fascination
IV	Incomplete diff-erentiation	Uncertainty
V	Multiple real names	Arguments and dis-agreements
VI	Permeation of language	Permeation of culture

Entries that are used infrequently would not be expected to be indications of a pervasive CSA. A certain degree of frequency of usage of domain entries must be present before we would want to make much of other LSAs.

If the words of a domain are used infrequently, and if another LSA is descriptive of the domain words, it is likely that small, isolated, or dead LSCs are responsible. Frequency should be relative to the frequency found in other cultures. Certain words are bound to be rare in all cultures, while others are bound to be common in all cultures. Inadequate frequency should be determined by large deviations from such norms.

Pair I LSA I: Overall frequency of usage of all lexical entries in a domain.

CSA I: Commonness in day-to-day life of the objects, events, or behaviors, referred to by the concepts of the domain.

Brown suggests that where there is higher frequency, "the community has more to say about the one referent or category" than a community with lower frequency of usage (1965, p. 338). This is not necessarily the case. It is probably true, as Brown suggests, that the Hanunoo have much to say about rice. What they do say about rice contributes to the frequency of usage of rice terms. But if hostile words are used frequently, it follows from the schema that hostility is a common part of the day-to-day life of the culture. It does not follow that the members of the culture have anything to say about hostility; if they don't, we might expect that they were afraid of their hostility. If they do, we wouldn't expect this. But both states of affairs are possible.

Pair II   LSA II: Density (degree of differentiation) of the lexicon within the domain.

CSA II: Ability to easily make fine distinctions and discriminations between the objects, events, or behaviors, referred to by the concepts of the domain.

Language can be used to make finer discriminations than there are words, of course, i.e., by phrases and more elaborate constructions. But when a discrimination is codified by a word, it is easily available to the speakers of the language because, "we all have had a lot of transmission training on conventional short meaningful forms, training we have not had for phrase names" (Brown, 1965, p. 339). Obviously we are talking about what we called in Chapter Three the codability of a domain, in this case summed over the whole domain for comparison with other domains in this language and the same domain in others.

Pair III   The following LSA-CSA pair is presented in two parts. Two variables are involved. LSA III(A): CSA III(A) is variable with respect to fascination in the culture but a paradigm case of lack of shame, guilt, or embarrassment concerning that fascination. LSA III(B): CSA III(B) is variable with respect to fascination but a paradigm case of guilt, shame, or embarrassment.

LSA III(A): Multiple names for an object, event, behavior, etc., where all names have the same connotation, can be used in all situations, are on the same hierarchical level, and one of which is the real name.

CSA III(A): Fascination without embarrassment, shame, or guilt about the object, or the fascination itself.

LSA III(B): Multiple names for a single object, etc., where the names vary in connotation, cannot be used in all situations, are all on the same hierarchical level, and none of which is the real name.

CSA III(B): Fascination with embarrassment, shame, or guilt about the object, or the fascination itself.

Fascination is hypothesized to be present as a function of the number of names. Guilt, shame, or embarrassment is hypothesized to be present to the extent that connotations vary, situation specific use is found, and a real name is absent.

Connotation *here* refers to that which can vary across words that describe what is in some sense the same thing. Differences in connotation allow for the emotive conjugations invented by Bertrand Russell, such as, "I am honest, you are blunt, he is tactless." (These words do *not* mean the same thing, but they could be descriptions of the same behavior by three different people, each with a different attitude towards the behavior. Furthermore, this kind of conjugation allows people to hurt each other verbally.)

Typically, the connotations are either polite and denying, rude and assertive, childish, or proudly and aggressively obscure. Most of these types of connotations are found in domains that can be described as a case of LSA III(B). Where one or more types are lacking, the lack is significant.

In a pure case of LSA III(B), all names are euphemisms. But there are different kinds of euphemisms, i.e., the domain of euphemisms is differentiated in this chapter.

Pair IV LSA IV: Incomplete differentiation at a hierarchical level below that of the (somewhat) real name of the object. Lower names are also somewhat real.

CSA IV: Uncertainty in the culture as to the function or nature of the object, event, behavior, etc.; the upper level name does not imply a function or nature that is completely satisfactory or the whole story; the same is true of the lower level names. Word magic is rampant.

Complete differentiation is found in the domain of mammals. Everyone agrees that a monkey is different from a man. However, all mammals are clearly really (in the sense of real names) mammals. While *human being* is the real name of a person, *mammal* is the real name of a person if we are dealing with the genus to which various living things belong. While *mammal* is not man's realest name, it has a certain reality: It is man's real name when we play the language game of assigning living things to their genera.

In domains with incomplete differentiation, there are no clear-cut real names, although often the upper level name operates as a real name (that is, in many cases for many people it is *the* real name; but from the standpoint of the culture as a whole, it doesn't have complete reality).

Consider the domain of terms for comedy. In the first place, there are two similar terms of approximately the same (high) hierarchical level: *wit* and *humor.* None can lay claim to being *the* real name, nor does each sit astride a separate domain.

There are many more specific terms. But they are not clearly real names nor are they clearly the loyal subjects of wit, humor, or comedy. Consider *farce,* for example. While clearly a kind of comedy (in fact a genre in its own right) there is some question as to whether it is "really" comedy (i.e., whether it really belongs to the domain implied by using comedy as a generic term). Farce is sometimes considered too crude. And is *farce* clearly different from *burlesque?* Dictionaries and other sources will make distinctions, but, as Berlyne has pointed out (1969), the diversity of such sets of distinctions is bewildering. Thus, I suggest, it appears that there is no genuine agreement but rather that each authority attempts to mark out his own territory in the interests of making order out of chaos. That the difference is not clear is also indicated by the absence in newspaper and magazine reviews of arguments over the true nature of a movie or play.

But few people would agree that farce and burlesque and parody are "the same," although they would be hard-pressed, I think, to give a distinction, at least a distinction that others would agree upon (i.e., one suspects that if the domain of terms referring to making fun of somebody or something by imitation were employed in a Brown and Lenneberg type of experiment, there would be very low naming agreement (Measure 4, Modal); but this perhaps needs empirical investigation).

So we do not have multiple names. The domain is thickly populated, and it is difficult to tell who lives where.

In such domains the hierarchically higher names codify an ordinary, mundane function. *Soap* is to wash with, *beer* is to drink, a *car* will transport you, and *deodorant* keeps you from smelling bad. The hierarchically lower level names imply functions that are somewhat contradictory. The lower level names in the above examples are brand names, and they usually attempt to change and raise the significance of the substance. Hence a certain brand of beer is not something you drink to get drunk or to relax after a hard day taking orders; drinking it expresses a oneness with the gusto of the universe. Washing with a certain brand of soap becomes an expression of a desire to be close to people. Often commercials establish the connotations of the brand name; sometimes the brand names do the job themselves. If you drive a *Rough & Tough* to work, you are not just driving to work. You are powering your way through and over a difficult obstacle course.

The upper level names cannot be totally unsatisfactory. A car, of whatever brand, is still to some extent really just a car. Thus the upper level name, having some reality, influences the lower level names by decreasing their reality. The driver acting as if he is driving a *Rough & Tough* only (and not a car) can be made to feel, or at least appear, slightly ridiculous. However, the lower level names also have reality and decrease the reality of the upper level names. So we can observe that some people who drink *Snob Scotch* almost feel compelled to dress up and look beautiful.

In short, the influence of the various weak realities tends to produce a degree of uncertainty as to what exactly is going on in these domains. Further examples will clarify and expand this description, but I will conclude for the present with the following on terms for hostile humor: *Parody* is a type of comedy. Comedy is to make people laugh. Parody involves imitation. If a parody is vicious, people are *influenced* to laugh anyhow because parody is comedy. But the laugh won't be whole-hearted because parody isn't always the harmless thing comedy is supposed to be.

Pair V   LSA V: Objects, events, behaviors, etc., in a domain may be named on several (usually hierarchically different) levels; a large proportion of the members of the LSC can vary, according to their needs or feelings of the moment, on which of these they consider to be the real name. And/or the population is sharply divided as to which is the real name (although both must have some reality to all). In other words, we have a case of multiple real names or, perhaps, multiple potential real names. Each can be, at a given moment, very strong, which is not the case with LSA IV.

CSA V: There will be arguments and disagreements among members of the LSC or culture when they are "in" the domain. The more real names, the more arguments or disagreements.

The rationale for this relationship is logical and nearly tautologous. I will give one example:

A family dog is both an *animal* and *Spot.* If the father can't take Spot to where his new job is, he may point out that Spot is but an animal. His wife will argue the point, but the argument will have substance because she will recognize the reality of her husband's description, just as he will recognize the reality of hers. The children will probably not be able to think of Spot as just an animal, so the argument will have no substance for them. That is, they will consider their father's behavior completely arbitrary (they won't see his point of view). It is crucial that most of the culture recognize the reality of the various real names. In negotiation, if the disagreement can't be resolved on a situational level, people move to making personality descriptions. In this example, the children will move immediately to personality description, because they don't perceive an issue on the situational level.

Pair VI   LSA VI: The entries in the domain may take a variety of forms, e.g., suitably modified, they may be used as nouns, verbs, adjectives, and adverbs; they are often metaphorically extended into other domains; they enter into a wide variety of language games and thus have a wide variety of meanings, which are distinct, but which have a family resemblance.

CSA VI: The concepts, and the distinctions the concepts allow, permeate the culture, and constitute central and important concerns of the culture.

The Lexicon and the Use of the Schema

While formally this section discusses inadequacies in the description and definition of the lexicon, it provides a forum for examples of analysis of the culture via the schema.

Table 2 provides a summary of the list of inadequacies.

TABLE 2

Inadequacies in the Definition and
Representation of the Lexicon

A. Some qualifier-qualified constructions should be admitted along with single words.
B. Frequency of usage should be listed.
C. Degree of differentiation of a domain should be specified.
D. The fact of multiple naming should be represented.
E. Brand names should be allowed entry.
F. The extent to which words and word families permeate the language should be measured.

A: Single words are usually the basic entry of the lexicon. Some qualifier-qualified constructions and some even more complex constructions should be admitted.

The Eskimo have several different words, each referring to a different variety of snow. This LSA is granted significance as a lexical state of affairs. English has several "adjective-noun" constructions with *snow* in the noun position. They are not considered to constitute a *lexical* state of affairs.

Thus the lexicon cannot represent *as a variable* the extent to which a domain is differentiated by easily transmitted and reliable concepts.

But to some extent, perhaps, it makes sense to draw the line. Once a concept becomes important or common enough, it should, following Zipf's law, become short. It is not strictly true that we have but one word for snow, for example: skiers now talk of *powder* and *corn* rather than *powder snow* and *corn snow*. Zipf's law provides a convenient criterion; without it we would have to include all adjective-noun combinations, and most of them do not get at a unitary concept, but are more accurately described as creating a shortlived concept by the combination. We want concepts represented in the lexicon that are common, highly codable, easily and reliably transmitted and that have a certain solidity. A red chair is a chair that happens to be red. The redness is added on (as the adjective is). But an armchair is more than just a chair with arms. And a high chair is a good deal more than a chair that happens to be high. It is a very specific kind of chair.

Note that the extent to which you accent the first syllable rises as you move from saying *red chair* to *armchair* to *high chair*. It is characteristic of English nouns that the first syllable is accented. Hence *high chair* should be considered a noun and a lexical entry.

Bolinger offers other criteria for determining whether a phrase should be considered a word (although in fact he is talking about something else): speed of pronunciation, vowel reduction, regularization of inflection, and reluctance to break up the compound. (1968, pp. 106–107) These criteria, like Zipf's law, involve increased speed and decreased effort. Zipf's law should not be granted sole status as a judge at the gate of entry to the lexicon.

B: Estimates of frequency of usage of lexical entries should accompany definitions.

Frequency may be considered the extent to which an entry "belongs to" the lexicon. The importance of frequency can best be illustrated by an example.

Consider the words that refer to "making fun of some state of affairs by mimicry." We shall here take "mimicry" to be the generic term and a (somewhat) real name. Let us assume there are four words below "mimicry," although there are others: spoof, burlesque, satire, and parody.

Suppose that in English each lower level word has a frequency of one per million. For the total domain, English has a frequency of four per million. Language X has one generic term similar to mimicry. For speakers of Language X it is not a generic term but the real name, for there are no lower level names. But this word has a frequency of twenty per million.

Using the usual approach we would have to say that the cognitive domain of "making fun of some state of affairs by mimicry" is more close up in English than in Language X, and is therefore of more importance and a central concern.

But how can it be that this domain is more important to English speakers if they "enter the domain" one-fifth as often as do speakers of Language X? It is not clear that it is—or that it isn't. Nor can we infer that this domain is of any great importance to speakers of Language X. Let me interject another example:

Suppose I use the phrase "my office" twenty times a day. But surely my office itself is not an important aspect of my life (although it *could* be: some people do luxuriate in the quality of their office—a Bigelow on the floor and all that). It might be objected that things of importance and centrality go on in my office— activities concerned with teaching and research—but that begs the question. It could also be that what I do in my office is "just a job" that gives me the money to do what *is* central and important to me. And it could be that I do the job poorly, e.g., stare out the window and doodle. Or perhaps I don't even go to my office because it bores me, but I feel guilty and am therefore always promising to go to my office. It is not safe to draw any inferences from frequency except that my office is a common part of my day-to-day life.

Similarly, we can only infer that the domain of "mimicry" is a more common part of the life of the speakers of Language X, but that English speakers have the (more easily available) ability, though less often used, to make finer distinctions than do speakers of Language X (we are assuming complete differentiation in this example so far). Nothing else. After all, perhaps English speakers hardly ever use the terms because they hardly ever have plays using this sort of humor; but perhaps these plays are the central activity of the culture. It is interesting to note in this respect that one complaint about Christmas is that it starts earlier every year;

while frequency is therefore going up, the (true) importance of Christmas is said, in fact *therefore,* to be going down.

While we are dealing with this example, we will move somewhat away from frequency for a moment.

An extremely common way of "making fun of some state of affairs" is to laugh. If we decide to include laughter in the lexicon, we are in deep trouble, because it is a short step further to include all behavior. Laughter is a borderline case between verbal and non-verbal behavior, and illustrates the problems with a rigid distinction between the two "types" of behavior. When we deal with verbal domains which approach this poorly defined border, inferences from frequency will be problematical.

In most cases, however, such problems are not present to any great extent. A culture could be humorous all the time but never express its humor except by laughter (in which case frequency of humor terms would be low and we would not think it was common). If Language X uses "book" five times more often than does Language Y, however, we would not be in trouble if we assumed speakers of X read more books than speakers of Y. The modal and model behavior with respect to books is to read them. However, the inference cannot proceed directly from LSA I. It would be less problematical if we could determine that books are important and fascinating, since there are some in our society who buy books and don't read them, e.g., status seekers and some students. There would be the possibility that all speakers of X were of this sort.

Some importance in our culture can be inferred from the existence of such semi-metaphorical expressions as "a bookish person" and such variation in meaning or extensions into other language games as "he's only got book learning." In addition *book* has been fused with a large number of other words, producing new language games or forms of life (a bookstore provides a living—to misuse the concept somewhat—for a few people and is not simply a store where you can buy books. Note that the accent is on the first syllable). Finally, *book* may be used as an adjective and as a verb (with suitable modification in form).

It would not appear that our culture has much fascination

with books. There are a few terms, such as *volume* and *tome,* which can be used in place of *book,* but most of the time they have a more specific use. So it doesn't appear from our lexicon that we have a case of multiple naming.

Therefore, books should be central and important but not fascinating. And this seems to be the case. While our culture is highly vulnerable to what is said in books and may be said to be permeated by book-learning, outside of a few collectors and status seekers, there is not much fascination with books. People believe the answer to most questions is some place in the library. But most of us are content to let the answer stay there until it is needed.

It should be reiterated that a major reason for placing a domain on the variable implied by LSA I is to determine if other LSAs that may describe the domain are applicable. LSA II also has this important function, as section C will illustrate.

C: Some measure of degree of differentiation should be employed even though a standard grid does not exist, as it does, e.g., for color terms. There may be several seemingly different entries in a domain which in fact do not make clear distinctions.

Let us again consider the words for making fun. I have contended that they are not different from each other in any way that can be clearly mapped by anyone but an authority; and that an authority can make the map only because he believes he can; and that authorities disagree with each other.

That the words are not uncommonly used indicates that this type of comedy is common in our culture. But it would not seem appropriate to describe the domain as a case of the differentiated end of the variable implied by LSA II. The domain is not highly differentiated; it is merely highly populated.

Nor does this domain display LSA III, multiple names. We all know the various words don't mean the same thing.

The domain is best described as a case of LSA IV. LSA IV involves incomplete differentiation, rather than total lack of differentiation. I do not claim, for example, that we cannot distinguish irony from burlesque—if we are limited to calling a play either ironic or a burlesque. But surrouding each of these terms is a host of similar terms that do not always have a place to call their own. Recall from Chapter One that we can map fuzziness. But unless a concept can have a model case that would not be the model case of any other concept, we claim incomplete differentiation.

I have already discussed the uncertainty surrounding humor. I will here give a longer and somewhat different discussion, since I am claiming that the whole domain is a case of CSA IV.

There are questions of motive in humor. Several are possible and more than one may be operating. Hostility may be "underlying." "Good fun" is recognized as a motive. Man may have a "natural" and often irrepressible urge to mimic (as monkeys seem to). Humor may be directed to a more serious purpose. A person may use humor to show he is relaxed or to make people pay attention to him. Humor sometimes comes as a mood. No wonder there is some uncertainty here.

Similarly, humor has many effects. It can simply make you laugh; but it can make you laugh when you shouldn't (for example, if someone can make you laugh at a joke that is really in very bad taste, he may gain an advantage over you). Humor may be intended to insult you, but it is hard to tell, since you can't deny that it is really not an insult but a joke. Someone without hostile intent may turn out to be hostile in his joke. I don't mean to be paranoid, but you can tell a good deal about a person by noting what he laughs at, so someone may say something to see if you laugh and if you do in his mind you are an idiot. Again, given that several of the effects may occur simultaneously (e.g., when we laugh at a painful joke at our expense), it is not surprising that uncertainty surrounds humor.

Much of the uncertainty is removed by transplanting humor from day-to-day life to the screen and stage. We then can laugh heartily and single-mindedly, since we are not involved. However, who can a comic laugh at anymore? All the old butts (blacks, wives, homosexuals, funeral homes, insane people) are gone. Only the drunk remains, largely because he is incapable of forming a liberation group. So uncertainty is following at our heels. Is it right to laugh at the misfortunes of a drunk? Why would you do such a thing? Isn't it because of your insecurities and your need to think you're better than someone else? Any attempt made to categorize and distinguish kinds of humor is an attempt to find order in chaos.

In summary, the lower level names may be seen as attempts to divide the domain so that we may have some certainty. If we have a word for a laugh at an unfortunate that helps build the ego of the laugher, then if we laugh we can *say* afterwards that we did not (to make up a word) sark, no, we laughed. But if we examine our motives carefully after a good hearty belly laugh, or especially if we analyze the motives of someone we don't like after he has had a good hearty uncomplicated laugh, it may look rather more like a sark. All laughter sounds pretty much alike. And saying we didn't sark doesn't make it so. But it may make us feel better.

D: There are multiple names for some objects, events, behaviors, etc., that are *exactly* synonymous. (Most synonyms do not mean exactly the same thing, e.g., *angry; irritated, enraged.*)

(However, if we take Wittgenstein's position that the meaning of a word is its use in the language, we will find that *fuck* has a much different use than *sexual intercourse*. In this case we will accept this, but will plead the now discredited but still useful referential theory of meaning, and will on that theory claim that *fuck* and *sexual intercourse* refer to the same thing.)

That many objects, etc., have multiple names is not really denied by the dictionary approach to the lexicon. But most of the names are labeled slang or vulgar, or they are not entered.

I will discuss this phenomenon by beginning with the most difficult example of multiple names I can think of, names for evaluation.

The youth culture uses many words to evaluate or respond to music and everything else: *heavy, groovy, far out,* etc. Fashions change rapidly as youth attempts to keep one step ahead of adults trying to be "in" again. (These evaluative terms were "in" when I first wrote this; they are no longer as "in." By the time this book is published, they may be in again, or they may be as out as *cool.* Except that *cool* seems to be coming in. If you find your sensibilities jarred, try to think back—or into the future.)

Despite the fairly rapid rise and fall in the acceptability of individual words, there are always several that are acceptable. No differentiation of experience is apparent. However, there is some attempt to distinguish degrees of goodness. These attempts are unsuccessful: *fantastic* has been used so often that it now may indicate simple, modest approval. Therefore, LSA IV is suggested, and it seems that CSA IV is present. There are no clear and accepted cultural criteria for deciding the goodness and badness of human beings, music, experience, books, or much of anything that is important. Nor is it clear what we should do with something once we have evaluated it (recall the discussion of the fallen tree; one would like to be a Triobriand Islander with respect to trees and the Queen of Hearts with human beings).

LSA VI is also strongly suggested. Everything can be and is evaluated; evaluative terms are present in all substantive form classes; evaluation is part of almost any language game you could name. And there is no doubt that evaluation is a central concern of humanity (CSA VI), as the work with the semantic differential (Chapter Five) indicates.

While LSA IV and VI are clearly present in this domain, it is also possible to analyze it as a case of LSA III. I shall attempt to do so.

An observer of our culture using the old approach to the relationship between language and culture, i.e., that a dense vocabulary indicated a very close and differentiated domain, might be compelled to note that youth have several words for describing music, people, and experiences, and that the same words are used for all domains. Therefore something should be close up. But it is not clear what, and it is clear that there is not much cognitive differentiation. So the old approach flounders.

Let us consider these several names as multiple names for the same thing (positive and negative reactions and evaluations). They have similar connotations. There is no real name in the youth LSC, but, with some *deus ex machina*tions, one may be located. Perhaps in the early stages of the development of language there was a sound that signified a positive reaction, e.g., a grunt. This could be considered the real name. Or the real name could be said to be the mediating response between stimulus presentation and the response (the evaluative word). Or, it may be "evaluative behavior." Here again we are faced with the border between verbal and non-verbal behavior. Evaluative behavior is real enough. It is a dominant form of human and animal behavior. Most organisms can be described in terms of approaching some things and avoiding others. But there is no one name for evaluation that fits. Yet we feel there should be one, since evaluation as a behavior is such a simple, solid, unambiguous notion.

So let us accept for the moment the notion that here we must lower the artificial boundary between verbal and non-verbal behavior and accept as valid the notion that evaluative behavior is the real name for evaluative behavior.

If we do, we may say that the youth culture's language for evaluation can be described as a case of LSA III(A). Evaluative behavior does not clearly differ in connotation from "far out" (especially since saying "far out" is evaluative behavior). In fact, it doesn't make much sense to talk about behavior having a connotation. Evaluative behavior is on the same hierarchical level as "far out." (It doesn't, however, make much sense to talk about behavior having a hierarchical level.) So, while it seems a little strange, LSA III(A) seems the most appropriate diagnosis.

Turning to the culture, it seems reasonable to say that American youth are fascinated with evaluation. It is said of youth that they want to try everything. And they do not appear to be ashamed of this. Why should they be?

But this analysis has gotten us nowhere in particular. We can conclude that youth is fascinated with evaluation; but so is everyone else. Other LSCs in this culture have multiple names for evaluation, e.g., *good, grand, fine, wonderful, great.*

The lack of an obvious real name proves significant here. Consider the lexical state of affairs with respect to evaluation from the context of the total culture (as I have said, the schema is most informative when used from that perspective).

The youth LSC has its evaluation terminology; the "establishment" has its own, different terminology. Connotations vary when the total culture is considered. A youth might offer the following emotive conjugation: "I am heavy, you are groovy, he is wonderful." Or: "I say *heavy*, you say *groovy*, he says *wonderful*." (At the time this was first written, *heavy* was clearly in and *groovy* was quite out for the very in but not quite out for the less establishment youth in small towns all over America.)

A member of the establishment might say, "I say *wonderful*, you say *groovy*, he says *heavy*." (These examples assume that *groovy* is already nearly obsolete.)

Thus while youth and the establishment are both evaluating, they do not recognize, and in fact (attempt to, word magically) reject the notion that the opposing LSC is "doing the same thing." Therefore, while the real name may be located by saying it is an abstract, non-verbal behavior, and while this real name is the same for both youth and adults, the youth are attempting to add attributes to produce a concept that is different, but they are failing. This again suggests LSA IV. But the better description is LSA III(B): One, *far out* is not clearly an attempt to add attributes. Two, for LSA IV to be present, the influence must come from the upper level term; here the influence is from other terms on the same level, mainly the establishment's words. Third, the hypothetical real name in this domain is so hypothetical and ambiguous that it seems best to drop it, giving us a clear case of LSA III(B). There is no real name; there are different connotations; and there is situation specific use.

Therefore, we should find the accompanying fascination with shame, guilt, or embarrassment. And it seems to exist. Any adult who has attempted to use the words of youth has felt some embarrassment, especially in the presence of youth, who report they can tell who is "in" by the way they say their jargon words. No wonder. The person who is "out" feels very uncomfortable using someone else's words. The fascination is most apparent in the youth worship of today. Television and national magazines move in on the language of youth, who then must and do move on. Older people who use youth jargon with aplomb are much admired by other older people who would like to try but are afraid.

On the other side of the coin, a young person who likes his parents and still enjoys doing some of the old things with them might use the word "wonderful." He would probably be very embarrassed to be overheard by his friends.

To some extent, there is differentiation of experience here. "Wonderful" will not be used to refer to the same things as "far out" because adults and young people often like different things. It sounds ludicrous or depraved to describe Sunday's sermon as "heavy." It is more comic coming from a young person and more disgusting from an adult. Similarly, it is ludicrous to describe hard rock as "beautiful." Thus it would appear that the two generations are (among other things) attempting to deny that there is a generation gap. Rather than face the fact that values are changing, youth develop a new vocabulary. Thus they do not have to implicitly reject their parents by using their parents' words in praise of things their parents would condemn. I know that this analysis is at odds with the contention that youth is attempting to differentiate itself from the establishment, but we cannot forget that the establishment is also one's parents. Thus, it would appear that youth is attempting to differentiate itself without hurting anyone's feelings. But I wouldn't put too much stock in this analysis.

The preceding example is a difficult test of the schema. Many other domains have LSA III. The need to tinker with the schema is much less. I will now discuss some of these domains.

Consider the words that refer to what I shall for convenience call sexual intercourse. There are words that are not used in polite company and which have rude and assertive connotations: *fuck, hump, screw, ball, bang,* etc. There are polite terms, model cases of euphemisms, generally used between couples or when talking to friends, which often deny or skirt the issue: *doing it, making love, going to bed, sleeping together.* There are clinical terms, acceptable in polite company or in public: *sexual intercourse, coitus, copulation,* etc.

Each connotation may be identified with one or more Freudian defense mechanisms, respectively displacement of frustration (onto the act of saying the word) or perhaps over-compensation; denial of reality or perhaps repression; and intellectualization. This fit is not surprising, since sexual intercourse is, in Freud's theories, the paradigm case of a behavior man is fascinated with but guilty and shameful about.

Note that, as was the case with words for evaluation, the behavior itself has some reality, but none of the words fit exactly or comfortably.

In many situations in our culture, of course, we are perfectly comfortable with these various words. The hippy on his commune feels free to say *far out;* the college students feel free to say *fuck;* and in these isolated contexts the names have reality. But unless one is a member of a fairly tight knit LSC, it is hard to feel comfortable with any of the words. In polite company, none of the words feel right. One knows full well that *copulation* is a euphemism.

Two terms from Shakespeare illustrate another connotation: *making the beast with two backs,* and *the deed of darkness.* Such terms may be considered aggressively and proudly obscure. Sublimation might be the associated defense mechanism, since when one sublimates one attempts to produce something in the culture that is symbolic of one's neurosis but at the same time socially useful or acceptable. These terms are (word magical) attempts to avoid expressing guilt or the hostility resulting from guilt or frustration, i.e., attempts to rise above the current cultural state of affairs by exaggeration to the point of absurdity. To use these terms is to show that one is above the crowd. However, if such terms are used often, they take on one of the usual connotations, showing how hard it is to rise above the culture. *Beast with two backs* could in the past be said with a smile, as if to say, "I and perhaps you refuse to share in this society's guilt and frustration; we choose a term that illustrates to the poor guilt-ridden masses how fearful of the subject matter they are." Now it has taken on a lewd connotation.

The lexical state of affairs for the excretory functions is similar. There are clinical terms: *urinate, defecate, micturate.* There are rude
and assertive terms: *shit, piss, crap.* There are two varieties of polite
terms. The first type has an unmistakable relationship to the defense mechanism of regression: *wee-wee, pee-pee, tinkle, go potty.* This
is not surprising: In Freud's theories, preoccupation with the excretory functions is a regression. (Note there are no regressive
terms for sexual intercourse, which is a behavior that belongs in
the excessively serious genital phase.) The second type of polite
term is related to denial of reality or displacement of accent.
People do not say they are going to a room where excreting goes
on, but rather to a room where entirely different functions are
performed: bathing, washing, or powdering.

There is a strange term I have heard on rare occasions, usually
with children: *make dirt.* As a Freudian would say, this shows how
we regard our natural excretory function. I don't know what to
make of this term, but I find it quite disgusting. In psychoanalysis,
one way of denying something is to assert it directly. For example,
if a man were to tell me he wished to have sexual intercourse with
his mother I would suspect him of conspiring to cover *something*
up, for one does not entertain that idea with earnest seriousness.
Perhaps *making dirt* serves the same function in this domain. It is
a way of denying what I find, as I said, particularly disgusting.

Turning briefly to the CSA, I am sure no reasonable person
would deny that Americans are somewhat ashamed of the fact
that they must occasionally remove waste products from their
bodies. Paradoxically, the owner of a river-polluting manufatur-
ing company would no doubt be morally outraged if I were to *take
a dump* (the new sublimation term) on his front lawn.

The lexical state of affairs for "liquor" is similar to the
preceding two, but it is closer to LSA III(A). Terms such as *hooch*
and *booze* are assertive in the same sense as, but with much less
intensity, than *fuck* is. *Drinkie* resembles *wee-wee. Drink* is a dead
euphemism (*To have a drink* doesn't sound like a denial these days,
but having a drink is not having a drink of lemonade). *Alcohol* and
liquor resemble clinical terms, and function as such in some profes-

sional groups, but in some segments of society, the most permissive with regard to liquor, they function as real names, as do scotch, bourbon, rum, and gin. Many people feel no discomfort with any of these terms at any time. For them, at worst, we have LSA III(A).

Clinical terms are necessary if everyone in the culture must take part in the behavior. If one wishes to avoid drinking, one may do so. A non-drinker does not need a clinical term to protect himself (nor does he need regressive or assertive or even polite terms to protect himself). He may simply condemn all drinking and drinkers. People who don't drink too much and in whose circles drinking is an accepted part of life don't need a clinical term to protect themselves either; so for them, *alcohol, liquor, gin,* etc., function as perfectly real names. And the drunks are too ashamed of themselves to have the audacity to attempt a clinical term. In the LSC of drunks and heavy drinkers, *hooch* and *booze* and similar terms seem to function as real names, but from the point of view of the total culture their over-assertive and basically defensive nature can be seen. A drunk comes home and tells his wife he's been "boozing it up" at his peril.

Regressive terms seem to be most common among the "better" classes. People who drink, as they say, *a wee bit* too much upon occasion are likely to use slightly regressive terms. To use *booze* and *hooch* would be to admit too much.

Therefore, this is not a paradigm case of LSA III A or B. The domain is somewhere in between, which mirrors the variability in the culture with respect to this behavior. Some people feel intense guilt; others feel mild guilt; others feel none at all.

Yet it is still a case of LSA III, so we must find fascination. And we will, in all segments of society. I have pointed out that drunks are perhaps the only minority group we may still laugh at. Teetotalers are far from indifferent to alcohol and often seem to protest far too much. Many members of the upper middle class drink a good deal and show their fascination in that way. Drunks are more than fascinated.

The domain of money is as pure a case of LSA III(A) as I can think of. *Money* is the real name, but there are countless other terms: *jack, coin, bread, kale, wampum,* etc. While *money* is somewhat more appropriate in polite company, and while the other terms are somewhat assertive, or, perhaps, over-enthusiastic, the differences are minimal.

Americans are, we are told by all kinds of people from other countries, who wouldn't touch the stuff themselves, money mad. And, worst of all, unashamed of this fascination. Some very rich people I know are sometimes slightly embarrassed, but they really don't see how it is their fault they have money (although it sometimes is their doing).

The final example is particularly difficult. I will discuss it here and again in section E.

Consider the words used to refer to people who have brown or black skin. At first glance it appears to be a case of LSA III(B). There are rude and assertive terms: *nigger, spearchucker, junglebunny, coon.* There are terms which have been used as polite euphemisms: *Negra, colored, darkie.* There is something of a clinical term: *of Negroid ancestry.* There is even an analogue to *beast with two backs: nigger* is sometimes used in white company by people who know themselves to be unprejudiced. The hope is that *nigger* will suffer the fate of *fantastic.* And the aim is to dissociate oneself from everyone but particularly from white liberals, who, it is felt, spend more time worrying about what name to use than doing anything about the problem. The word magic fails, however, and the person who uses *nigger* in this way finds not only that other people begin to wonder about his prejudice, but that he himself has doubts.

However, for many there have been real names. *Negro* worked for some time. While it is still somewhat acceptable, an unsuccessful attempt was made to supplant it with *Afro-American.* Then a (so far) successful attempt has been made to substitute *black* or *Black.* This last realish name is somewhat strange. Over the years liberals of both colors have attempted to convince people that color was not of any importance. The most acceptable term now codifies the color difference in very black and white terms: Blacks aren't black any more than I'm white.

That these changes in official name have occurred suggests that none of the real names have been used as comfortably as, say, *dime* has. The clinical name is not used comfortably either. It is so cumbersome and uncommon that we would immediately be suspicious of the person who used it.

So it is not clear that the essential feature of LSA III(A) is present (the real name), and it appears that the clinical term is not accepted as such. So we don't have LSA III(A), and it doesn't look like we have a clear case of LSA III(B). In addition to the absence of clinical terms, the polite terms are not very polite, nor are the assertive terms really assertive. They are better described as terms of abuse, but this is not the whole story.

Therefore, I present the highly speculative description of this state of affairs as a case of LSA IV. The names at the higher hierarchical level, *human being* and *person,* have a good deal of reality and exert influence on the lower level names. The culture has shown a willingness to produce a number of lower level names, and has sometimes attempted to differentiate them ("there's niggers and then there's decent colored folk"). But these attempts have failed.

Because most of us, even bigots, feel that *really* blacks are human beings, the heart has been taken out of the assertive terms (they are mean, small terms used when one is mad in a frustrated, impotent way); the polite terms sound condescending; the clinical term sounds like that of a quack. But the lower level names exert influence also. Even the unprejudiced know that blacks aren't really human beings (or aren't really *simply* human beings). The name, *human being,* doesn't fit snugly. Why? Because it is not a sufficiently significant description. Blacks in this culture have been treated as something besides human beings, and a real name must reflect the true status of the object it names.

Brown and Ford (1961) have reported an analogous phenomenon. Close friends often call each other several names, e.g., nicknames, last names, first names. They do not report whether various names are situation specific, i.e., if first names are used in some situations, and last names in others. It is my impression that they are. A similar phenomenon (not studied by Brown and Ford) is the use by married and other couples of terms of endearment. This may resemble fascination without shame, but, as I will discuss in more detail in Chapter Six, often such terms resemble euphemisms in that they avoid the real name. After all, John Doe is not really "honey."

In many cases new names are produced by a subculture. They then may become part of the general culture. Let us examine some explanations for this process. Perhaps sub-cultures produce a new name where none is needed because they want to give themselves identity and individuality. If they want to do this by naming behavior, it makes sense that the new names would be given to the more fascinating aspects of life. It would not have much impact on the culture at large, nor would it give the sub-culture a great feeling of identity to invent a new name for pens.

Another possibility is suggested by the list of sub-cultures who contribute the majority of slang (Wentworth & Flexner, 1960, p. vii). These sub-cultures may be described as either deviant or "larger than life" or, simply, young. That is, they do things most people would like to do but are afraid, unable, or too busy to do. So in naming their own activities, these sub-cultures will be producing names for activities that fascinate the general culture.

But sub-cultures are not necessary for the production of new names. Roles and specific situations produce them also. And it could be that in many roles and specific situations, people find themselves wanting to rise above the culture, e.g., produce a name for sexual intercourse that will show that they do not suffer from the problems in this area that the general culture suffers from. They find that naming behavior does not do the job in a completely satisfactory manner (as in the case of *Afro-American*), but a new name has been produced. This explanation does not, however, explain why the name should survive.

Another explanation is suggested by Brown and Ford's findings. If one is fascinated with something, one wishes to explore or caress it. Using multiple names for people, while it resembles word magic, is one way of exploration.

The same is true for using multiple names for objects. I recall seeing an excited hold-up man in an old movie saying something like, "Come across with the money, man, the jack, the kale, the coin. Make with the bread, the dough, the sheckles." And still not expressing his excitement. He needed more names and he wanted money.

Probably all of these explanations of multiple naming have some validity. Explanations aside, it does appear that multiple naming exists and is correlated with fascination or high interest.

E: Brand names have not been granted status as lexical entries. Given sufficient frequency of usage, they should be.

Americans have a vast number of terms for varieties of beer. The Eskimo have several words for varieties of snow. How do these words differ from brand names for beer (aside from the fact that snow doesn't fall with a name on it)?

Immediately it is clear why I shall call many brand name domains cases of LSA IV. Most tests show that experts can't tell beers apart without the labels. As is the case with comedy, we label beer in the hopes of producing order where chaos is destined to reign. Differentiation appears to be almost nonexistent.

Snow words represent different kinds of snow. These differences are important for the behavior of the Eskimo, e.g., they would go hunting in one kind of snow but not in another. Surely the differences among beers with different brand names are insignificant compared to the differences among kinds of snow. Perhaps brand names are merely the inevitable result of a wealthy, capitalistic society. A choice of a particular brand is at best a preference, but more likely is a habit.

But let us not overestimate the differences. A degree of difference is judged by an individual. A particularly brave and competent Eskimo might become annoyed at his tribe for refusing to hunt in a certain kind of snow, i.e., he would be essentially saying that there was no real difference among some kinds of snow. An American, renting a car with some friends, might be annoyed by squabbling over which brand of car was best. He would be saying the same thing as the Eskimo. In both cases, one individual belittles a difference which is codified by the lexicon.

Brand names make a difference. A Budweiser drinker will not drink at a bar that does not sell Budweiser, just as an Eskimo will not hunt in a certain kind of snow. Brand names are an extremely important and common part of our culture. They are so common that in some cases Zipf's law has shown itself. One rarely asks for a Budweiser beer or even for a Budweiser. One usually asks for a Bud.

When brand names are sufficiently "in" the lexicon (i.e., have sufficient frequency of usage), we usually have a case of LSA IV. We will also find a case of CSA IV. Usually this is because in addition to liking or wanting to use the product, we try to make a personal statement about ourselves or to individuate ourselves from others by picking a particular brand.

I include brand names, therefore, because they exist for the same reason that words in other LSA IV domains exist. Brand names are not an isolated phenomenon, nor are they simply the result of a rich capitalistic society.

But the distinctive behaviors that are associated with brand names are somewhat different from those associated with a set of concepts that completely differentiate a domain (i.e., where the domain is not a case of LSA IV). In the former case, the distinctive behavior reflects preference, considerations of status and prestige, or considerations of the social situation. In the latter case, e.g., the Eskimo words for snow, distinctive behavior depends upon concrete and pragmatic needs. An example of the domain of *automobiles* will illustrate this.

On the hierarchical level below that of *automobile* or *car* is a considerable degree of differentiation: *four-door, sedan, sports car, compact, convertible,* and others. There is an old saw that goes, "My car gets me where I want to go, and that's what a car is for." This is true. But he who utters the saw is using *car* on the same hierarchical level as *four-door* and *compact.* The primary function of the automobile is transportation, perhaps, but transportation is rarely as simple as the saw implies. A compact allows one to save on gas, park in small places, and get lower insurance rates. A four-door sedan allows one to transport up to six adults in relative comfort. A *car*, as used in the saw, allows at least one person to "get around," but with the additional specification that that one person doesn't have to worry about gas money, parking, transporting other people, speed, impressing other people, and so on. The varieties of automobiles mentioned have different functions, even though they are all transportation functions. The needs they fulfill are concrete and pragmatic. On this level, we do not have a case of LSA IV.

The state of affairs at the next lowest level (brand names) is entirely different. There are, for example, many brands of compact cars. Naturally, each manufacturer claims his is the best. Some of the claims appeal to the cars' transportation functions. And there are probably differences in this respect. But this is not all the manufacturer is appealing to, a necessity, as we shall see.

Americans have a love affair with the automobile. Let us take this meaningless generalization somewhat seriously for a moment. Usually when we speak of someone loving someone, the loved one must serve more than one function. More than sex is needed for us to say love is present in a relationship, no matter how wonderful the sex, although sex is one of love's criterial attributes. More than just a meeting of minds (between a man and a woman) is needed for the attribution of love. Some sex is needed. While only a little sex is needed to make a profound meeting of minds love, and while only a little meeting of minds is needed to make sex love, two functions must be present.

An automobile has many functions: status, sexual benefits, speed, fun, an outlet for hostility, luxury, and an opportunity to make a personal statement about yourself by owning the kind and brand of car you own (whether you like it or not).

Differentiation of transportation functions has allowed some of these needs to be fulfilled in a real sense. Sports cars can and do go fast and corner well. But many of these functions are not the kind that can in any real sense be fulfilled by an automobile.

Consider, for example, the personal statement one makes about oneself by owning the kind and brand of automobile one owns. Because one can't in any real or concrete sense make a statement about oneself or individuate oneself from others by owning a car, there will be restlessness. Proliferation of brand names is needed: One does not wish to be stuffed in with 10% of the population. Hence the proliferation of sizes of compacts. A few years ago, there were only compacts; now there are at least three sizes: intermediates, compacts, and sub-compacts. These cars differ somewhat in their transportation functions. But not that much. It may be that Americans will be happy only when there is a different brand for every person. But because one can't in any real sense differentiate oneself by owning a car, the restlessness will no doubt continue.

Wells, Goi, and Seader (1958) demonstrated that cars and the people who own them have images. But they investigated the images of Ford, Chevrolet, and Plymouth owners. Today nobody owns a Ford, Chevrolet, or Plymouth. The lower level names have taken over what reality exists in this area. One owns a Mustang. Even these sub-brand names are spawning. One owns a Mustang fastback. And so on. When will it stop?

It is hard to say, but the trend is unmistakable. And there are attempts to move in other directions. Some people are restoring "old" cars. I own an old (1967) Rambler convertible that is very beat up. Almost everything has fallen off it, and if my left window won't open so I can open the left door from outside (when I am inside), I have to crawl out the rear window. But it keeps running, and so I keep it. I don't care much about cars, but I can't deny the attention I get is pleasant. I am making, it seems, the kind of statement I would make if called upon to do so: I don't want to own anything I care about because I don't want to be unhappy if it is stolen or ruined or stops, and I do think it is silly to spend as much time with cars as Americans tend to. I didn't intentionally begin to make this statement, but now I am rather pleased with myself. Two friends of mine have independently done the same thing; I am sure they didn't intend to make a statement either. But they are, and they know it now. No doubt new directions will open in the future.

There are no clear criteria for determining whether an extra-transportational function has been fulfilled. Consider luxury. It makes sense that a car should be comfortable. But how should a car be luxurious? Luxury is more appropriate in a home, where one entertains and relaxes. In a car, it is not clear when to stop adding luxury features. In a home there are certain reasons for having certain features. Once you have all you need, you can stop buying. But because it is unclear what luxury is *for* in a car, one keeps adding features in the (magical) hope of attaining true luxury (just as one hopes one will keep hostility out of humor by introducing new words). Hence luxury cars become absurd. Some of the luxury devices now offered are not only rarely used, but are not really luxury devices. Some of them are (significantly) the antithesis of a luxury device. For example, if both front seats can be made into near beds, the car may be used to sleep in. But what kind of person would sleep in a car? A poor person who can't afford a motel. Here we can see the "pull" of the real name. Because (to a certain real extent) the essential function of a car is transportation, what is luxury in an appropriate place becomes absurd and antithetical to luxury in an automobile.

Unless a concrete, pragmatic function is being fulfilled, the only possible criteria are "being better" or "having more." Thus proliferation of kinds of automobiles and silly devices on automobiles can be expected.

Note that while there are more pen companies than American automobile manufacturers, brand names of pens are not commonly used, nor has there been a proliferation of brands or kinds of pens. For the majority of the population, for most occasions, pens are used to write with; there is no uncertainty. Pens do little else but write. So LSA IV is *not* descriptive of all brand name domains. In fact, it is descriptive of few of the many brand name domains. But whenever a product has an unclear, ambiguous, or a magical function, or whenever it has several very different functions, one can expect LSA IV.

But why not pens? They are small, relatively inconspicuous, and not very capable of doing much except writing. It seems likely that if pens could reasonably perform some magical function, someone would try to make them do so.

Let us consider a couple more examples. Why do we wash clothes? To keep them clean. But how clean? And how often should they be washed? And how should they be washed? And with what?

The last four questions are asked out of real uncertainty. In this culture, washing clothes well turns out to be, among other things, a sign that one is not a bad mother. Because of this association, one must be very good indeed. And just as it is hard to have a real luxury car, it is hard to be an artist at washing clothes. There are no clear criteria. In a more stable culture, washing clothes and being a mother would be done things, social practices. In ours, neither is a model *or* paradigm case of a social practice. In fact, they are becoming courses of action. But impossible ones; let's face it: clothes simply can't be whiter than white.

The decay of America can be seen in the decay of social practices into *impossible* courses of action.

Finally, let us again consider the American Negro. It was not clear to our Founding Fathers whether the Negro was a slave or a human being. At the present time, neither whites nor blacks are clear as to the status of blacks. Perhaps they are a separate race. Perhaps they are partially assimilated into the dominant culture. Perhaps they are still scapegoats. Perhaps they are spoiled trouble-makers.

Yet, as I have suggested, perhaps they are *really* human beings, in addition to their other possible statuses. That many white and black Americans, bigoted or not, believe this is partially attested to by the fact that we tend to show this uncertainty (LSA IV) about many other pseudo-classes of people, i.e., people who are sometimes people and sometimes not:

Consider the following terms: *creep, 258682, client, customer, undesirable, hunk of ass.* They cannot be considered multiple names because they purport to differentiate among men; but they cannot be considered instances of differentiating concepts, because they focus on incidental or vague attributes. These terms restrict the function of humans *(hunk of ass, customer, client)*; attempt to restrict the humanity of humans (258682); or attempt to restrict the domain of those who deserve to be called human *(creep, undesirable)*. In all cases, however, the user of one of these terms would feel strongly influenced by the real name and would probably agree to the statement, "But it's really a human being." Perhaps the user would have to calm down first, but usually he would eventually agree.

This state of affairs is probably necessary. While all human beings bear certain striking resemblances to ourselves, it is often desirable to attempt to dehumanize them. But there is bound to be some uncertainty about this process. And thus, store clerks sometimes feel guilty when they treat a customer badly; psychiatrists and psychologists sometimes wish they could cry with their patients (or tell them what fools, bores, or babies they are); and men in general sometimes feel bad after they have called someone a creep or an undesirable.

F: Some concepts permeate the language more than do other concepts. That is, some concepts can be expressed in several form classes; others cannot. Some concepts are often metaphorically extended; others are not. Some concepts belong to families that are used in many language games; others don't. These differences should be represented in the lexicon.

Brown has pointed out that the child who wishes to master his language must learn the words of the language. Bolinger has said, "The child who would rather not have to distinguish between 'jar' and 'bottle' is quickly driven into line" (1968, p. 257). The same would be true of the even more similar *drizzle* and *sprinkle.* Both pairs represent fine distinctions. The pair, *irritated-irritable,* represents as fine a distinction. The former term implies a fairly immediate cause; the latter does not. Clearly this distinction is more important in the culture than the first two distinctions given in this paragraph, at least from a pragmatic point of view.

Much more hinges on whether a hostile behavior has been caused in the recent past by a concrete event, is a mood of the day, or a more general personality trait. Degree of differentiation does not seem to be directly related to importance.

Consider the difference between the questions, "Is it raining or not?" and "Do you love me or not?" Again, the latter is more important and central in our culture. In almost all cases much more hinges on the answer to the latter question, although the former is probably much more frequent.

It would seem that it is not possible to distinguish the trivial distinctions from the important (but equally fine) ones on the basis of frequency. As illustrated, it is quite possible that trivial distinctions are more commonly made. It is not possible to differentiate them on the basis of fineness of discrimination or degree of differentiation within a domain, as illustrated. Analysis of number of names is also fruitless, since, for example, the two important concepts here vary greatly: there are several terms for love, but few instances of multiple naming in the domain of hostile behaviors. But the fact remains that the determination of love and the status of hostile behavior are extremely important in our culture.

On the other hand, the distinction between *jar* and *bottle* is one that would not be missed upon occasion. While the child does have to learn the words of his language, it seems that some of them are learned "because they are there," while others are learned because one would be lost without them. To put it crudely, some words are learned for linguistic reasons, while others are learned for "real life" reasons. Here we get at Brown's notion of central concern and importance. But it should be clear that neither degree of differentiation nor multiple names are enough to account for such differences.

It is for this reason that LSA VI was introduced. An explanation of why LSA VI is associated with the CSA of permeation, centrality and importance will now be given.

If a domain is of central concern or importance, the words *have* to be used as various form classes, and have to be extended somewhat metaphorically to other situations. And there has to be a family of meanings, because the domain has to be applied in so many situations. In other words, if a concept is of central concern or importance, it should extend into many language games. For example, the concept of rightness: In cases of criminal behavior, we use *legality* or *criminality*. It is not appropriate to use these words in unlegislated areas, so we use the similar concept of morality. In still other areas we use the concept of manners. It is very important in our culture to do the right thing, so the concept permeates our language, adapted to the various situations of the culture. Ethics are important for various professions, and it even seems sensible to add to this family various judgments of skill: There is a certain similarity between a man choosing the right fork and the surgeon choosing the appropriate forceps.

Put another way, if a cognitive domain permeates the culture, the linguistic domain *has* to permeate the language.

But what of the Hanunoo, with their ninety-two varieties of rice? It seems unlikely that the words would be used except as nouns; it is not necessary that any metaphorical extension should occur; rice should stick to language games related to eating and harvesting; with such fine distinctions multiple means would be a disaster. Are we then to say that rice is not important and central to the culture, and that it does not permeate the culture?

The schema already grants that rice is common in the day-to-day life of the Hanunoo, given that the total domain is used with high frequency. But food is usually taken for granted unless it is absent. If there was never a question in the mind of man whether he would have food, would he have gods of rice, or rain, or wheat? It is not possible to tell from Brown's description of the Hanunoo lexicon if rice is a central concern. If they have a god of rice, the schema would then grant rice a degree of centrality (metaphorical extension). Or if a great deal of slang is derived from food terms, as is the case with the American language (Wentworth and Flexner, 1960, p. xiii), the schema would grant centrality for the same reason.

The concept of importance or centrality must be distinguished from the concept of fascination. I will conclude this section with an additional example. The first state of affairs is a paradigm case of fascination with little or no centrality; the second state of affairs is a paradigm case of centrality with little or no fascination.

The lexical state of affairs for the domain of terms referring to the female breasts is a case of LSA III (somewhere between A and B). There are a large number of terms, and they function almost entirely as nouns. There is little metaphorical extension; there is but one reference, and therefore no family of terms. They fit an extremely modal sentence frame: "She's got a _____" (fill in descriptive term) of _____." In other words, usage is rather rigid.

American males are fascinated with female breasts. Otherwise, nudie magazines, which only recently began to show more than breasts, would not flourish as they do. But breasts do not play a central role in the culture. It would be considered pathological (or, worse, stupid) to choose a mate solely on the basis of breast size or quality. Even *Playboy* utilizes other criteria in the selection of its girls. That it does, while the cheaper variety do not, at least to any great extent, is significant: *Playboy* has (successfully) sought to become part of the general culture, while the others remain somewhat underground. In general, while many males feel it necessary to respond to breasts, most of them, caught in a sober moment, would probably admit that they are not terribly important, even in the selection of one's own mate. Or if they say they do think breasts are important, they would be vulnerable to attack. That is, they could be made to feel foolish. I have heard several females commenting on the complete lack of significance of breasts; however, paradoxically, it could be that breasts are of more centrality to females than to males. After all, breast size is a concrete unambiguous measurement. Capturing a man used to be and perhaps still is the central concern of many young women. Given that the other criteria for success in the male-female arena are not so concrete and unambiguous, it is possible that breasts are a central concern of women because men are a central concern of women. I think it is fair to say that men are much more concerned with penis size than women are. Therefore, perhaps I should restrict the analysis to the LSC of men.

Law, on the other hand, is a central concern of the culture. It permeates it in the sense that much that is pleasant is illegal, and much that is unpleasant is required by law. There are nouns, verbs, adjectives and adverbs. There are the associated concepts, discussed above. Yet there is no multiple naming (although recently there has been a proliferation of names for [what I shall call for convenience] the fuzz, but that is a whole other domain). And there does not appear to be fascination. "The law" is something people would prefer not to deal with. They do not approach it, but wait for it to approach them. This contrasts markedly with the situation regarding the female breasts.

Conclusions

The anecdotal, unsystematic, and cursory armchair analysis presented here suggests strongly that the present schema deals more adequately with the relationship between lexicon and culture than the previous superficial statement of the relationship.

It should be noted that while I have presented the schema as a schema, it has some resemblance to a theory. In the text I have offered explanations for why multiple naming is associated with fascination, why incomplete differentiation is associated with uncertainty, why several real names are associated with arguments, and why permeation of language is associated with permeation of culture. The explanations do make use of different constructs, reducing the legitimacy of the claim that this is a theory. But there is an assumption underlying all explanations: words are in the language for a reason. But this is no big surprise. What this chapter does show is that the reasons are varied and not very simple. That is, the typical assumption that words differentiate concepts so that we can communicate would seem to be an oversimplification. The assumption ignores the many other language games we play. I think the major contribution of this chapter has been the demonstration of the importance and commonness of word magical attempts.

Assessing the Schema

The analysis presented above may or may not strike the reader as true or reasonable. In some cases, it might be interesting to do some quantitative empirical investigation; this section discusses some possible approaches to measurement.

Frequency

Lists of frequency exist, but they are not compiled from the spoken language and they do not adequately sample the culture or the range of situations people find themselves in. Compiling a truly adequate list seems an insurmountable task. However, the list would be widely useful.

Movie, play, and television scripts, particularly commercials, would seem good sources for a record of the spoken language. Particularly since these sources are not only mirrors but disseminators of language. Slang is common, and swearing is common in movies and plays. Slang which is not known to the general public is not used as a matter of course, since the production must be intelligible. It is true that big words are not often used, but then they are not often used in society at large.

The major drawback, which is also a strength, of these sources, is that sub-cultures are excluded. Thus the focus is on the general American culture, which gives some guarantee of representativeness, but the fact that words exist which are used only by one sub-culture is often of significance. However, as I have said, this fact is much more significant when the word becomes generally known.

But the "sub-culture" of common man doing things which aren't particularly exciting *is* largely ignored. Thus we would probably find that *doctor* is more common than *flat tire, rain,* or *five o'clock.* Records of radio disk jockeys would increase the frequency of, for example, the latter two. One should probably add various popular magazines, the lyrics of popular songs, underground newspapers, and so on. The list seems endless, but for the most part these records are available in written form and could be transferred to computer cards easily, if only the money were available.

Degree of Differentiation

Subjects could be asked to differentiate two words. To the extent that subjects agree, can readily perform the task (short latency), and give the same differentiation on a second occasion, we would say that the two terms were differentiated. It may be noted that all three of these approaches to measurement were employed by Brown and Lenneberg (1954) in their initial study of color codability and color recognition (Chapter Three).

One would want to add measures of the general intelligibility of the differentiation attempt. It would be important not to attempt simplistic quantitative approaches. Subjects will be glad to assign numbers representing the size of the difference between concepts, but we are concerned here with differentiation that is clearly present and available to subjects.

Closure also suggests itself as an approach here. If, for example, we used an article written by an "expert on comedy," we could delete all names of varieties of comedy. To the extent that subjects filled in the blanks correctly, we would have differentiation. If subjects consistently got wrong answers, and if different subjects got different wrong answers, we would say that the domain was not differentiated. Degree of differentiation is similar to reality of names.

Multiple Names

Ask subjects to give as many names as they can think of for what is depicted. Then ask them to choose which words they would use, and which words they wouldn't use in a variety of situations. To the extent that individual subjects recognize situational constraints upon usage, and to the extent that different subjects give different lists of words, we have LSA III(B). It is wise also to look for clumps of words that always appear together.

I have asked classes a couple of times to give me some names for sexual intercourse. But I don't give them any names to start with. That is, I get the idea across without suggesting what names to start with. Getting the idea across this way necessitates some talk of the kind called lewd or suggestive. Even so, both classes started with the clinical terms and then slowed down. Then they took up the polite, denying terms, finished them off, and slowed down again. With pressure, one person would come forth with *fuck* and then, the barriers down, lots and lots of words would come forth, many of which I hadn't heard myself.

Both classes were in stitches throughout the whole proceedings. Afterwards, I asked them why they laughed (it is a sign they are repressed about sexuality—which is to say guilty—and are, given the scientific sanction of the classroom, releasing or relieving some of this repressed energy). I pointed out to them that they would feel very strange if the dean were to walk in, or their parents; and I suggested that the more repressed of them might dislike me the next day for tricking them into laughing at such things. Laughter can be a good indication of guilt.

Centrality and Importance

The concept of linguistic permeation of a language by a word or family of words is perhaps the vaguest in this chapter. I would suggest beginning with other techniques that approach the concept of the centrality of a concept from other theoretical positions. For example, there is a good deal of literature on the so-called central trait. In addition, one might use the semantic differential and consider concepts that load highly positively or negatively on the major factors (except for, perhaps, negative activity and negative potency). Then one could see if they had the features hypothesized to be associated with linguistic permeation.

The Schema and the Conduct of Social Science

Conceptual analysis is often a precursor of empirical research (although not often enough). Conceptual analysis may help investigators define what variables they are studying, and in what ways those variables differ from related variables. The use of conceptual analysis proceeds from the assumption that the social sciences should (or can profitably) study variables and phenomena which are represented by entries in the lexicon. Put another way, it proceeds from the assumption that ordinary language has or allows access to reality. (A very strong statement of this position was given in Chapter One.) While psychology in particular has often denied that it needed to make this assumption, in practice it has made it.

Conceptual analysis proceeds from the assumption that different words mean different concepts, and that therefore, for example, *prejudice* should be differentiated from *discrimination*. As this chapter has made clear, this assumption is not always valid. While what follows is often completely in disagreement with many of my strongest beliefs concerning language, it proceeds from the schema, and I shall therefore present it.

When the words in a domain are incompletely differentiated from each other and from the hierarchically higher name (LSA IV), conceptual analysis is not appropriate. If an investigator studied parody, finished his study of parody, and began to study satire, his operational definitions, the schema suggests, would be highly arbitrary. While there is nothing necessarily wrong with arbitrary operational definitions, in this case the investigator, no matter how well-intentioned, cannot be studying the two distinct phenomena suggested by the lexicon, because the lexicon is not codifying two distinct phenomena. He may, of course, be studying two distinct phenomena, but that is, of course, inappropriate in this domain. If there is chaos, one must study chaos, not attempt to impose order to study it. That is, one must not behave like the drunk who looked for his lost quarter near a street light because he could see better there.

Many of the most important areas of investigation have suffered from this misguided respect for ordinary language (although social scientists show little real respect for ordinary language). Consider, for example, the areas of intelligence, racial prejudice, and mental illness. In all of these areas, (rather unskilled) attempts have been made to define and sub-divide the subject matter. This has led to confusion and to a rather endless addition of concepts that need to be analyzed or defined.

However, the problems with conceptual work in these areas have been recognized, and an alternative approach, multivariate analysis, has been employed in a few areas. The usual technique has been factor analysis, which attempts, as I have discussed before (Chapter Three), to find underlying dimensions by putting variables that correlate together with each other and separate from other such clumps of variables.

However, what goes into a factor analytic study is largely determined by the experimenter's concept of what it is he is investigating; and what comes out of a factor analytic study is largely determined by this concept and by the investigator's philosophy of factor analysis. Furthermore, the large majority of those who use factor analysis and related techniques want to name the factors; many feel that a factor is "good" if a simple, ordinary language name can be used to name it. That is, it is felt to be indicative of the orderliness of human behavior if things are found that one has a reason (language) to suppose should be found.

An alternative is to refuse to name the factors. Ossorio, for example, in describing his factor analytic approach to information retrieval, speaks of "uniquely identifying a subject matter field even when, in the usual sense, no such field exists" (1971, p. 272). In reporting the factors, he makes no attempt to name them, since "in the present use, nothing hinges on whether the descriptive title for each factor is what that factor 'really' represents" (p. 286).

The reason that his approach is acceptable in this case is that something *does* hinge on the effectiveness of the information retrieval system. Users are able to get information they need, information they would be unable to obtain using the *Psychological Abstracts* approach to information retrieval, which assumes that the user knows what he wants to investigate, and can name it, and can find all the information he wants under that name (if the *Abstracts* has the name he needs). Ossorio's approach allows any relevant information to be retrieved, regardless of "name," and even if the user is quite vague about what he wants.

Unfortunately, when the aim of a factor analytic study is the discovery of truth (or of what is "really" out there), it is unlikely that anything will hinge on the effectiveness of the factors in representing what is there. If we can name a factor, it follows that we can do what we already can do with something that has that name, and nothing more. For example, suppose we find that a factor that looks like anxiety is a major component of mental illness. In the first place, that is no surprise. In the second place, that does not increase our ability to deal with anxiety in order to reduce mental illness one bit. If we can't name a factor, we show, by our inability to give it a name, that we don't know how to deal with it at all. Some psychologists (Cattell, for example) like to give factors strange names. This is word magic, of course. In short, the schema suggests that we often already know what is there; what we need to know is what to do about it.

However, the schema does allow for the identification of areas of investigation where ordinary language is a very poor guide. Where the domain of terms in the area may be described as a case of LSA IV, incomplete differentiation, neither conceptual nor factor analysis is appropriate. Where we find cases of LSA IV, it is probable that we will find areas that should be investigated, since the CSA that is hypothesized to be present is one of confusion and uncertainty. It is here that the social sciences, in their roles as inventors (rather than discoverers) of states of affairs or descriptions, are most urgently needed. In brief, here we need new ordinary language.

I have suggested in this discussion that language is not doing the fine job that ordinary language philosophers and linguists who reject the notion of "correctness" seem to feel it is. But this is not the fault of language nor of language users as individuals. Rather, where language is not doing a job it ordinarily does well, i.e., defining concepts and differentiating them from related concepts, the culture is not doing something very well.

In conclusion, the schema suggests that in areas where LSA IV obtains, investigators will have to avoid the existing language of the area. In other words, they must avoid being bound by the constructs that happen to be given us in language. The schema further suggests that it is these areas where the pursuit of new knowledge is important, precisely because it is these areas where the culture needs knowledge.

Another function of the social scientist, presumably, is social action. In some areas, social scientists have pursued understanding in the hopes that this understanding will eventually lead to viable approaches to solving social problems. The schema suggests that in some cases this approach is at best less than optimal, and often fruitless.

For example, consider the social problem of alcoholism. A good deal of work has been done on the etiology and epidemiology of alcoholism. This is all well and good. But consider what A.A. considers to be the major problem in this area: getting the alcoholic to face the "fact" that he is indeed an alcoholic. His resistance to this description of himself is usually described as a defense mechanism.

But consider some of the things "heavy drinkers" (by their own descriptions) say about charges they are in fact really alcoholics. "Look, Joe gets drunk all the time. Sure, he holds liquor better than I do, but is capacity a criterion for calling someone an alcoholic?" "So I get drunk occasionally, perhaps more often than most people. But how can you call me an alcoholic when I only do what others do, and only a little more often? Your cut-off point is arbitrary."

Clearly these are rationalizations. But there is some truth in them. Alcohol is a part of our culture, and a big part. Some people drink heavily all their lives and because they do not, for one reason or another, get into trouble, never get labeled alcoholics.

Our humor is saturated with jokes about drunks, leading the alcoholic-heavy drinker to have the right to say, "If you're going to joke about it there, what gives you the right to come on so serious now?" A meeting of people often does not become a social event until liquor is served. It is not necessarily the liquor that allows people to have fun. It is often the fact that liquor is being served that indicates to people that fun is now appropriate. And so the heavy drinker facing the charge of alcoholism faces also a rejection by society, and for reasons that he does not accept—or shouldn't.

We have here a case of LSA V, multiple real names, at least for many relatively heavy drinkers. Thus we should find, as we do, arguments of the sort presented above. The arguments have substance. P is at once a heavy drinker and an alcoholic. Which description will be applied, by the drinker (for the arguments can be intrapersonal too) or by another person, depends on the circumstances. If P gets drunk with O, an "alcoholic," P will be less likely to call O an alcoholic than if P has just seen O staggering around when he, P, was sober. If O, formerly a "heavy drinker," finds that he has ruined his family and broken some bodies, he is likely to be willing to accept the label of alcoholic. For both drinker and observer, both descriptions have reality. And therefore we have inter- and intra-personal argument. And it is my feeling that the arguments cause as much damage as the drinking, except in cases of drinkers who destroy property or cause harm to other people. According to humor and other observations, American men and women are in constant argument over the man's drinking. If the man were confident that he was not an alcoholic (or on the road to being one), i.e., if the man knew that all talk about alcoholism was garbage put forth by people who would like to drink but fear too much, he wouldn't take any protests from his wife (she can't tell him golf is hitting a little white ball around a cow pasture). And if the women didn't believe to some extent that the man really wasn't doing anyone (even himself) any harm by knocking back a few, she wouldn't put up with his drinking for more than a couple of weeks. But because both recognize the reality and legitimacy of the other's point of view, arguments persist, as, of course, does the drinking.

What are the implications of this for the conduct of research? We should resolve the argument. First, however, it is necessary to recognize that there is an argument, and this seems to be the major hurdle.

But there is no way to resolve the argument, precisely because it is a real argument, not a difference of opinion, not a misunderstanding, not a failure of communication (and none of the other things popularly put forward as the causes of our various problems as word magical attempts to dissolve them), but a real argument, a contest, where if one person gives in he loses. P loses his claim that O is causing trouble by his drinking if P admits that O is not an alcoholic, and thus O can continue to cause trouble. O will lose his freedom and his right to consider himself a human being with potential access to dignity if he admits to P that he might be an alcoholic. And, except in model cases, which label will be chosen is a matter of many factors. Most cases are borderline, at least initially. Often what makes an alcoholic an obvious and model case of an alcoholic is a readiness on his part to accept that label.

So what can we do as social scientists? In general, when we find cases of LSA V:CSA V associations, we must for theoretical reasons be pure applied social engineers, arbitrary but just. That is, we must recognize the validity of the claims of both parties, and attempt to discover a workable solution. In this case it seems simple. Drunken driving must be stopped, and there is evidence that extremely severe penalties would help. Bars should have free and compulsory taxi service. Wives should be able to charge their husbands with harmful drunkenness and get action. On the other hand, there should be no laws against walking down the street drunk (I am here referring to so-called victimless crimes).

It sounds too simple, of course. But all I am claiming is that this approach is the appropriate one. It will solve the social problem of alcoholism, and we don't need to know anything more about the *drinker* than that he drinks in order to plan social change.

In Japan (according to one anthropological article written in the 1950s), men are allowed to drink very heavily at more or less formal, ritualized, specialized times. It is a part of Japanese culture, a real part. The drinker is also at other times a human being, so there is no need to find out about *drinkers.*

But social science is too nice, and will object that the "real" problem, that people will still drink heavily, is ignored. (In Japan it is accepted; heavy drinking is a social practice.) Perhaps we can come back to the drunk later. But if someone wants to sit at home or in a bar and get drunk every night, he should be allowed to, as long as he injures nobody in the process.

We do not know enough about prejudice to effectively legislate against it; it seems to be the kind of phenomenon that cannot be legislated against. But we do know how to legislate against the problems caused by drinking (although America cannot, it appears, accept the fact that there are other ways of doing this besides making drinking itself illegal). And as social scientists, we should recognize the difference between the two kinds of social problems, and act accordingly. In cases of CSA IV, we should attempt to find out something new. In cases of CSA V, we would be better off doing what we already know how to do.

Other cases of CSA V abound. I won't analyze them, but here they are: Crime, drug addiction, poverty, suicide, divorce, and who gets the green sucker. In general, we know what we need to know about the poeple who "cause" these problems. What is needed is engineering.

The implications are more problematic when we find cases of LSA III:CSA III, i.e., where the culture is fascinated with something. These remarks have particular relevance to LSA III(B):CSA III(B) associations, where there is accompanying shame, guilt, or embarrassment.

It has yet to be determined if guilt, shame, and embarrassment are good or bad. Probably sometimes yes, sometimes no. On the whole, however, some guilt or shame seems preferable. We have the psychopath, for example, who is without guilt and without, perhaps therefore, joy. William Burroughs' fine description in

Naked Lunch of the perils of "over-liberation" is relevant. One peril is a total lack of humor, another lack of individuality, a third lack of joy.

Therefore, I would recommend that psychologists stop studying sex. Maybe we can stop sex from becoming like a good hamburger.

If anything does need to be done in such areas, it is guilt removal. That's all, and then you can leave people alone.

Finally, a brief comment on areas where LSA VI:CSA VI association are found, i.e., where the concepts are central and of importance to the culture. Here social science is not needed. For example, consider the "new morality." It is the new morality. It is a morality. There will always be a morality (not an immorality, not an amorality) in this culture. In general, where we find LSA VI:CSA VI associations, we will find that the culture is pretty well able to take care of itself.

In such conclusion, some suggestions as to when and how to do research have been offered. They are revolutionary and iconoclastic. I do not think many people will be upset to learn that ordinary language doesn't always do a businesslike job. But I imply that research on most of social science's favorite topics, from sex to crime to prejudice to deviance, is worthless from a practical point of view. I also suggest that the solution to these so-called problems is probably very simple. I can easily be accused of over-simplification; but then I can easily accuse people who research these problems of obfuscation.

chapter five

The Semantic Differential

In 1957 Charles E. Osgood, George J. Suci, and Percy H. Tannen-baum came out with a book entitled *The Measurement of Meaning.* MOM presented a theoretical approach to the problem of meaning and an approach to the measurement of meaning commonly referred to as the semantic differential (SD).

I will not discuss the theory here. As the authors admit, their theory and their measurement technique are not well related. The theory is a variety of stimulus-response theory, and has some nice moves of the sort one can make from the framework of a stimulus-response theory; but as a theory of meaning it is hope-lessly crude.

The technique was immediately adopted by social scientists despite the very tentative manner in which Osgood and his associates presented it and the results from some 50 studies that had already been done using the SD. The authors deserve great credit and praise for waiting as long as they did. They investigated their measurement approach with a rigor and ambition rare in the social sciences. MOM is rich in complexity of reasoned argument and sophisticated data analysis. And yet, the authors knew what the fate of their effort would be:

> Meaning is one of the most significant pivotal variables in human behavior, and even a crude and provisional measure of it, such as the semantic differential now is, readily finds uses. As a matter of fact, we are now more concerned that its applications—and claims for it—will outstrip the development and evaluation of the basic methodology, and this is one reason why our own staff has been concentrating more on these methodological matters (p. 329).

The SD is widely used, but the common level of precision, validity, and elegance of the methodology has declined since 1957. It appears that many of the many social scientists who have used Osgood's tool have used it so uncritically and carelessly that it is hard to believe they took the trouble to read the original book, which is, after all, some 346 pages long in the paperback edition. So it goes in the social sciences.

In this chapter we will explore the semantic differential. First I will discuss the methodology and its rationale. Then I will take up some of the major findings, some criticisms and qualifications of these, and their implications. The next section will take up selected topics of interest to our general concern that are contained in MOM itself. Finally, I shall review cross-cultural studies that use the semantic differential to explore linguistic and cultural differences between linguistic sub-communities.

Methodology

Osgood and his associates have attempted to discover the dimensions of connotative meaning of words by means of factor analysis. That is, they have attempted to find the dimensions of connotative meaning along which different words lie at different positions.

They use *connotation* differently than I did in Chapter Four. As is the case with humor terms, the connotation-denotation distinction is not clear. Therefore, various groups of experts have imposed order. Therefore, there are many correct distinctions and many proper concepts of connotative meaning. Osgood's is one. But let us examine the distinction to see where the problems lie.

Denotative meaning is at its best when we are dealing with discrete concrete objects such as pens. As they say, or used to, the referent and denotative meaning of *snow* is snow. The referent of *pen* is pens.

The referent of *USA* is the USA. But what is the USA? It is a certain piece of land and water. It is also an aggregate of people. It is also a nation, i.e., a governmental unit with various laws and rules and policies. It is a historical entity that has done this at this time and that at that time. And it is, among other things, also a concept that invokes various attitudes in people when they think of it. That is, the USA is that entity which, when you ask the question, "What is the USA?" will elicit long statements concerning the nature of the beast.

It is this latter aspect of the concept of the USA that Osgood considers connotative meaning—the cognitions and attitudes people have towards a concept.

It is clear that this aspect of USA has no clear-cut right to the term "connotation." For example, if we consider connotative meaning to be the cognitions people have about a concept, some of the referents of the concept USA that seem rather denotative can be included. For example, one way of getting at Osgood's theoretically rather vague concept of connotative meaning is to think of the question, "What does the USA mean to you?" We might expect many people to give answers that reflected love and respect of country, e.g., "The United States means freedom, honesty, activity, goodness." But we might find someone saying, with the same dreamy idealism, "The United States to me is the greasy spoon in Arizona on Route 66." In other words, a geographical, seemingly denotational response.

But there is no ambiguity when we get to the measurement technique. We shall later attempt to get at exactly what the SD does measure. We will now proceed with a discussion of the measurement approach with, I hope, an understanding of the fact that there is nothing whatsoever clear about meaning, so we should avoid premature criticism of the SD on the grounds that it doesn't measure meaning. It does measure something, and that's quite an accomplishment in these woods.

People must rate a number of concepts, such as (following MOM's practice of putting concepts in caps):

USA, RAIN, JUSTICE, FOREIGNER, MY MOTHER, ME, ADLAI STEVENSON, RICHARD NIXON, KNIFE, BOULDER, SNOW, ENGINE, MODERN ART, SIN, TIME, LEADERSHIP, DEBATE, BIRTH, DAWN, SYMPHONY, HOSPITAL, UNITED NATIONS, FAMILY LIFE.

Each concept must be assigned a position on a number of seven point rating scales, e.g.:

good_____:_____:_____:_____:_____:_____:_____bad

In other words, how *good-bad* is DAWN?

Some other rating scales used in Osgood's research are presented below, in italics, as all scales are in MOM:

large-small, beautiful-ugly, yellow-blue, sweet-sour, hard-soft, active-inactive, potent-impotent, strong-weak, pleasant-unpleasant, happy-sad, heavy-light, bright-dark, light-dark, fragrant-foul, honest-dishonest, near-far, healthy-sick, wide-narrow, thick-thin, deep-shallow, valuable-worthless, kind-cruel.

How yellow is justice? How dark is a symphony? How thick is the USA? How large is rain? How near is family life? How light is a hospital? How sad is modern art? How beautiful is the UN? How beautiful is a symphony?

These are rather different sorts of questions, and we shall look at some problems that might arise, given these concepts and these scales.

For one thing, different uses or meanings of words are required for different concepts. A good claim could be made that the United Nations, a symphony, rain, and the USA are beautiful in quite different ways, although the various uses of *beautiful* have a family resemblance.

For another thing, many of the possible questions don't make much sense. Where would you place justice on a continuum between yellow and blue? Where would you place a symphony on a continuum between dark and light? The first question seems totally nonsensical. The second makes more sense. There are light symphonies, which are simple, bright, with melodies you might want to hum or dance to. And there are symphonies that are profound, tempestuous, passionate. These we might rate as *dark,* although the lexicon of music critics' terms doesn't contain *dark* to any great extent (low LSA I). But *dark* makes some sense in the context.

Some of the questions are ambiguous. For example, is a hospital *light* because it has windows and the sun shines in, at least in soap operas? Or is it *light* because the atmosphere is bouncy, happy, and casual? Or because it doesn't weigh much?

A related problem lies in the presumed opposition of the terms defining the scales. Which of the three opposites to *light* implied by the above discussion of HOSPITAL is the real opposite? They are, respectively, dark, somber, and *heavy.* Although *somber* seems unlikely, the best answer is that it depends on the concept. For HOSPITAL the opposite of *light* is likely to be *dark.* For BOULDER, it is likely to be *heavy.*

Other questions are difficult to answer in any general way. How beautiful is a symphony? Which symphony? I like Beethovan's Fifth but I think his First is ugly. How heavy is rain? Well, yesterday a light rain fell.

A similar problem in generalization is illustrated by the question, "How good is dawn?" That too depends, but here the variance is within the person. Dawn can be very beautiful and good if one has had several hours of sound sleep but can be very bad and ugly if one has been up all night arguing about a trivial subject. Snow is nice if one can watch it all day but awful if one has to drive 30 icy miles to work. But some concepts have much more constant connotative meaning. I've always been partial to justice (although I may have disagreed with others as to whether what I received was justice). Who could be against leadership?

In other words, concepts differ in the stability of their connotative meaning. As discussed later, the connotative meaning of a concept, as determined by the SD, does not directly incorporate the extent to which people differ in their ratings of it on various dimensions; nor does it incorporate the extent to which people differ over time and circumstances within themselves in their ratings.

Some of the comments above have been leveled as criticisms of the SD.

Factor Analysis

Factor analysis is a technique designed to reduce many variables to few. Consider 50 scales similar to those listed above. Do we need all 50? Or do they form several clusters of similar scales so that we need fewer than fifty separate scales? The latter is the case. A cluster or factor is produced by correlations between variables. *Good-bad* is highly correlated with *pleasant-unpleasant.* That is, if a person rates a concept as being good, he is likely to rate it as being pleasant; conversely, if a person rates a concept as bad, he will probably rate it as being unpleasant.

That this is true is an empirical fact; however, the two scales are nearly synonymous in many or most language games, e.g., a good day is not much different from a pleasant day, although a good person is something more than a pleasant person (but most good people are pleasant also).

Consider two variables that are less synonymous: warmth and generosity. Being warm can be described as being generous with one's emotions and attentions. Generosity is a warm behavior. In this case the concepts are not synonymous but they are logically and conceptually related: If a person is warm, it is hard to imagine him being ungenerous.

It is synonymity, conceptual overlap, and other kinds of relatedness that lead to an assumption that our language has a good deal of redundancy. If this assumption is correct, and we will challenge it in a later section, there is a rationale for a reduction of this redundancy via factor analysis.

Factor analysis allows the user to determine how many scales he needs and what they are; once he has developed a model with a reduced number of scales, factor analysis tells him how good that model is. A particular solution to a matrix of correlations between scales accounts for a certain percentage of the total variance of the matrix. If we account for 75% of the total variance, what is left over? 25% of the total variance. But what is that?

Suppose one of our factors is called the evaluative factor. Think of it as sort of a super-scale. Say that *good-bad* correlates (or, technically, loads) highly (say .78) with this factor. That means that the evaluative factor is close to *good-bad* in just the same sense that *pleasant-unpleasant* is close. There are things called "factor scores," which represent a person's hypothetical rating on the evaluative factor. Thus a person who rated a concept as being good would have a high score on that factor for that concept.

If this correlation is high, a good deal of the variance of the *good-bad* scale is accounted for by the evaluative factor. What it doesn't account for is part of the 25% of the total variance that is left over.

If people judge SYMPHONY *good* and if it is high on the evaluative factor, that contributes to the loading or correlation between *good-bad* and the evaluative factor. If people judge HOSPITAL *bad,* say out of fear, but if HOSPITAL is high on the evaluative factor, say because on a number of other scales that correlate highly with the evaluative factor, people must admit hospitals are good, e.g., they are valuable, helpful, and kind, that will take away from the loading.

Let us consider an example of near independence (zero correlation) between variables. Consider *good-bad* and *strong-weak*. There are concepts that are good and strong (USA, MY FATHER) and there are concepts that are bad and weak (COCKROACH,

QUICKSAND); these contribute to a positive correlation between the variables. There are concepts that are good but weak (A BABY, NUN) and there are concepts that are bad but strong (THE DEVIL, DEATH, RED CHINA); these contribute to a negative correlation between the variables. The result should be a zero correlation.

(But it is unlikely that these two scales are generally uncorrelated. Notice that I said, "good but weak." Perhaps I should also have said, "bad but weak," since most bad things must be strong: Otherwise, they wouldn't be bad. And it doesn't seem quite appropriate to have said, "bad but strong." Similarly, "warm and ungenerous" or "cold and generous" do not sound right. "Warm and generous" comes easily off the tongue; it is almost a cliché. Thus correlations are implicit in our use of language.)

Factors are scales that *represent* many of the original scales. The higher the correlation between the factor and the scales it represents, the more variance accounted for and the better the solution.

So how does one decide how to "place" the factors? There are two ways of visualizing it.

Consider the scales as lines all originating from the same point. The angle between any two scales is small if the correlation between the two scales is high. One would place a factor so that it was a new super-scale that made as small angles as possible with the original scales. That is, it would be placed in that position where the sum of all the angles between it and the original scales would be smallest. (It is easy to see that mathematically this would not be easy.)

Or imagine a "meaning space," in which the concepts are represented by dots. The closer the dots, the more similarly the concepts have been rated. Suppose we use two scales, *good-bad* and *strong-weak.* Suppose USA, MY FATHER, and RED CHINA are all medium strong, but USA and MY FATHER are both equally very good, while RED CHINA is very bad. Thus MY FATHER and USA will be at the same point in the meaning space, a good distance away from RED CHINA.

A good factor analytic solution places the factors so that the distance between the concepts and the factors is minimized. Thus we would run the line of the factor through MY FATHER and USA and directly down to RED CHINA. It would make sense to call this an evaluative factor, since the concepts placed along it differ *only* in the extent to which they are liked. Thus a factor may bring order to chaos by aligning very different concepts on the same dimension. And thus we have codified and may talk about the differences in meaning. In this case, the only differences are evaluative.

Suppose we also have JET, which is neither good nor bad, but which is very strong, and SNAIL, which is also neither good nor bad, but which is very weak. We can represent this as follows:

                    USA–MY FATHER
    JET   SNAIL
                    RED CHINA

We *could* draw one line. This would be a diagonal, say the one from bottom left to upper right. It would be hard to name and we would not be able to talk easily about the concepts. For example, SNAIL and FATHER would be fairly close to and equidistant from the line. But, in terms of similarity of ratings, they are very different concepts. They differ on *good-bad* and also on *strong-weak*.

Or we could draw two lines, one between USA and RED CHINA, as before, and the other between JET and SNAIL. We could call this the strength dimension.

Here we have hit on a problem in factor analysis. We want to have as few factors as possible. But we want the factors to represent the concepts. That is, we would like to have each dot quite close to a factor line. We can't call a concept "highly evaluated" if it is far from the evaluative factor. In the one line solution none of the concepts is far from the line but none is right on it. So whatever we name the factor, none of our concepts will be paradigm cases of it. Furthermore, whatever we name it, the difference between two concepts will not be as easily expressed *(codable)* as the difference between USA and RED CHINA on the evaluative dimension, which are the same except for a difference on one dimension.

Suppose in describing the United States we have two lines, one running from Chicago to New Orleans, the other from San Francisco to New York. We can say that New York is an Eastern city. We can say that Denver is quite far West. We can say that Memphis is half-way South. But what of Miami? In this case, we are not uncomfortable saying it is a South-Eastern city.

But what of a concept that is, for example, very strong and very good, i.e., as good or better than USA and as strong or stronger than JET? We would have to place it above JET and on a level with or above USA. It would be far from any factor line. Furthermore, we could not name it easily in terms of our reduced set of scales. In terms of codability, we would have to give it a two name description instead of a one name description, i.e., very strong and very good. The other concepts in our diagram can be encoded with a one name description. JET is very strong. USA is very good. So our new concept is awkwardly named. So if we are trying to represent the lexicon of the language without ruining it, the solution above would not be very good. As much as possible, we want to preserve the real name of the concept.

Suppose this concept is GOD. GOD is not something we want to represent in bits and pieces. GOD doesn't seem to be made of the same materials as jets and countries. GOD is more than "the strength of a jet combined with the goodness of the United States." So we would perhaps be tempted to run another factor through GOD and call it superhumanness.

Osgood uses orthogonal factors, i.e., factors at right angles to each other, making it easier to talk about and represent concepts. The approach used by Osgood finds factors that account for as much variance as possible. That is, his first factor will be the line that minimizes the distance of all dots to it. A good deal of distance will be "left over," and the second factor will take away as much as possible of that. So the first factor will always account for more variance than the second, and so on.

This is an extremely oversimplified explanation of a technique that many books would have been written about if enough people understood it sufficiently. I have made it sound too effective and too easy to apply. My brief comments in Chapters Three, Four, and Seven could serve as something of an antidote to this discussion. I have left out countless complexities and have sometimes been slightly inaccurate in the interests of a simple clarity. But the basic purpose may be briefly recapitulated:

Factor analysis attempts to reduce many variables to a few super-variables called factors that adequately represent the original variables. To the extent that concepts, represented by dots in a multi-dimensional meaning space, cluster together or arrange themselves along lines, a solution can be found that will allow us to talk about the concepts with a less complex and redundant vocabulary. If the dots are scattered, we *can* use a factor analysis, but our talk about the concepts will be awkward and clumsy. We want solutions that retain normal codability and we do not want concepts represented by bits and pieces of diverse factors. Some sets of concepts and scales simply won't yield a satisfactory solution. So factor analysis is often ineffective.

Factor analysis is often called arbitrary, and it is true that there are many points of choice along the way where one can go one of several ways, each of which is equally valid mathematically. For example, one can choose a form of cluster analysis rather than factor analysis. One can choose oblique (correlated) rather than orthogonal factors. One can "rotate" as many factors as one wants. In addition, there are no clear-cut standard procedures for interpreting a solution or even for deciding how good a solution it is.

These criticisms are often leveled at factor analysis. However, as we have seen, behavior can be variously described and negotiation, involving the use of human judgment, is the process by which we resolve difficulties and disagreements. There is no single way to do a factor analysis; nor is there a single way to describe human behavior or to behave. But that doesn't stop us from exercising our judgment. In fact, it is because there is no one right way that we have to use our judgment.

General Results and General Considerations

Repeatedly, in study after study, with different sets of concepts and different sets of scales, with paintings and sonar sounds and other esoteric stimuli, in culture after culture, year after year, three factors emerge and account for a large proportion of the variance. These factors are called *evaluation, potency,* and *activity.* In some studies only two important factors emerge, the second being a combination of potency and activity called *dynamism.* Other factors have been found, but these two or three consistently emerge and consistently account for a lion's share of the variance.

Evaluation always accounts for the most variance. Potency and activity differ somewhat in relative strength from culture to culture, and sometimes they are fused.

Some examples of scales that define the various factors (I will give more than a few so that the reader can judge for himself):

Evaluation: *good-bad, kind-cruel, grateful-ungrateful, harmonious-dissonant, beautiful-ugly, successful-unsuccessful, true-false, positive-negative, reputable-disreputable, wise-foolish, optimistic-pessimistic, complete-incomplete, timely-untimely.*

Potency: *hard-soft, masculine-feminine, severe-lenient, strong-weak, tenacious-yielding, heavy-light, mature-youthful, constrained-free, constricted-spacious, serious-humorous, opaque-transparent, large-small.*

Activity: *fast-slow, active-passive, excitable-calm, rash-cautious, heretical-orthodox, intentional-unintentional, complex-simple, meaningful-meaningless, important-unimportant, progressive-regressive.*

The cross-cultural generality tends to indicate that human beings, regardless of what language they speak, differentiate among concepts primarily in terms of their differential goodness, potency, and activity. Carroll (1959) has pointed out that the concepts are usually nouns. I don't feel that *this* lessens the generality of the findings. In the first place, this is not as true as it once was. Cliff (1959), for example, has investigated the effects of quantitative modifiers *(slightly, many)* on the ratings of concepts. They have a predictable effect. Osgood and his associates report some interesting work on the connotative meaning of adjective-noun combinations as a function of the connotative meaning of the adjectives and nouns alone in MOM itself, and they inform us of the interesting tidbit that GOOD is evaluatively better than BETTER, a finding I don't believe advertising has seen. And, as we have seen in Chapter Three, several studies have used verbs and even nonsense syllables. The very fact that many nouns have verb, adjective, and adverb forms suggests that the generality is true. And if trained Navy men judging the meaning of sonar signals produce a matrix of correlations that yields the usual three factors, I for one am convinced. The regularity is incredible, especially when viewed in relation to other findings in the social sciences.

But writers in this area are not clear as to what these findings are about, although they are usually considered to be findings about language. They are more appropriately considered to be findings about people. The semantic differential indicates how people deal with concepts and what they do with them. *People* judge concepts as to their goodness, potency, and activity. The factors represent modes of human behavior rather than modes of meaning.

In an important sense, goodness, potency, and activity are not part of the meaning of words. If they were, since people differ in their evaluation of concepts, we would be forced to give credence to the old excuse for poor use of language, "Words mean different things to different people; this word means what I want it to mean."

While people know what USA means (otherwise you wouldn't know what I was talking about now, i.e., you wouldn't know what concept's meaning we are debating), they differ in their evaluation of it. And people *can* say of the United States that they can feel about it as they want to. After all, one can judge or rate a concept only after one knows which concept it is. Nevertheless, there is little or no point in quibbling over whether the SD does or doesn't measure a valid aspect of meaning. We shall try to specify further what it does measure, and assert that it's something like meaning.

Given cross-cultural generality, it appears that humans have similar sorts of reactions to concepts. Therefore, the claim can be made that the major or common reactions to concepts are universal and have been specified.

Different cultures assign various concepts quite different positions in semantic space, i.e., concepts differ across cultures in the factors they are strongly related to. This does not reflect on the universality claimed above. For example, it is not indicative of any qualitative difference in behavior with respect to concepts between Russians and Americans that Russians rate COMMUNISM as *good* (if they do) while Americans rate it as *bad* (if they do).

Scales differ in the extent to which they load on different factors. These cross-cultural differences reflect cultural differences. For example, *clean-dirty* is primarily an evaluative scale for the Japanese; this is not the case for Americans. This means no more than that the Japanese value cleanliness more than do Americans. The Japanese and American evaluation factors are similar enough in other ways that they both can appropriately be called evaluation.

Thus these two types of differences between cultures leave us with the same conclusions: The major dimensions of reaction to concepts are universal. But this conclusion is not particularly sweeping, and it is over-simple. Let us consider some other things the SD does not measure.

Connotative meaning as measured by the SD has little to do with meaning which is operative in usage *in ordinary discourse under ordinary circumstances.*

Consider the concept, USA. Americans, generally, evaluate this concept positively, and consider it potent and active. Suppose a history teacher says, during a lecture, "The USA joined World War II in 1944." The teacher is *not* saying, "The good, powerful, active USA joined the bad, powerful, active World War II in 1944." In this sense, connotative meaning as measured by the SD is not an important part of meaning in ordinary discourse.

However, connotative meaning has an effect in many circumstances. Consider the connotations of *nigger*. The English used this word for many years in a purely referential manner, with no pejorative intent. A slightly different situation is presented by the whites in our society who have absolutely no idea that any other white would find the word objectionable (if such people still exist). The English and these Americans give *nigger* a different connotation than most Americans. As we shall see, this may have effects.

In some situations the connotative meaning of words is *used.* For example, at a political rally, the word *Democrat* may be enough to elicit cheers all by itself, while a mention of *Republican* may elicit boos. And I mean the word all by itself, not as part of an implied utterance (as discussed in Chapter Two).

This example illustrates some restrictions on the use of connotative meaning. One, the connotation must be shared if it is to be effective. Two, connotative meaning would seem to be valuable only in what might be termed S-R situations, i.e., where a concept is being used as a stimulus in order to evoke a response.

In some cases, connotative meaning is operative without the intention of the speaker. A concept the speaker did not intend as a stimulus, i.e., that he did not intend to have taken out of context to serve as a stimulus separate from that which his entire statement constitutes, is responded to separately, usually to the loss of the whole statement, thus effectively disrupting the smooth flow of discourse. For example, many whites object when another white uses the word *nigger.* Some interruptions can be less laudable. For example, the kind of playing around with pronouns and the decision whether to say *woman* or *lady* or *female* so that the woman will not take the word out of context and object to it is disruptive of the flow of discourse and also of thought, and is one of the most obnoxious aspects of any liberation group's appeal. Which is not to say it is ineffective or unnecessary. In some cases, however, it is more a verbal tic on the man's part, and it is not as necessary to respond to.

Let us conclude by taking the position that connotative meaning as measured by the SD is *activated* when someone (speaker, addressee, or hearer) wants to or has to take the concept out of the context of the sentence in which it is embedded and attend to it separately.

Most discussion of the semantic differential takes it for granted that a word has one connotative meaning. In point of fact, the connotative meaning is the average rating of a goodly number of people on a goodly number of scales. Different people give words different connotative meanings, just as different cultures do. And no attention is paid to different distributions of judgments. For example, consider the evaluation, on a seven point scale, of two different Presidents of the United States. Let us say that President A has a mean evaluation score of 4.0 which is produced by half of the population giving him a 1.0 and the other half giving him a 7.0. He is loved and hated. President B also has a mean score of 4.0, but everyone in the country has given him exactly that score. He is nothing special to everyone. Yet the SD doesn't discriminate the two situations.

Furthermore, the connotative meaning of a concept varies for specific individuals according to the situation, as I have indicated. To give another example, if a person evaluates *love* highly, that person will not swoon when just anyone says he/she/it loves that person. Given that the connotative meaning of a word can be buffeted around as easily as it can (e.g., if you hate someone or find someone disgusting, their "love" will be evaluated very negatively), it sometimes seems somewhat pointless to have it *in vacuo.* As I commented on Wilson's approach to conceptual analysis, it is a somewhat academic language game.

To conclude this section I must once again return to the contrast between denotative and connotative meaning.

While the clear implication of studies using the semantic differential is that people evaluate concepts and decide how powerful and active they are, it is also clear that people make many other judgments. For example, it is possible to judge whether a person is clean or dirty. As I have mentioned, the Japanese use the scale much more evaluatively than Americans do. Americans can, however, make the judgment of "dirty" just as evaluatively bad as the Japanese can, by intonation and context, which again illustrates the somewhat academic redundant aspect of the semantic differential.

In fact, almost any concept, no matter how neutral it may be on the evaluative dimension, can serve as a pejorative. For example, an old Quaker joke involves an old-style Quaker lady, mad at her son, saying to him, "Oh thee little you, you." *You* was, in that language, the formal distant form, and the lady's son would feel much less favorably evaluated than would an adult male greeted by, "How're you, you old son-of-a-bitch." Thus connotative meaning is also a function of intonation, interpersonal context, and the extent to which connotative meaning is intended. There are many "fighting" words that we all know how to say without starting a fight; we also know how to start a fight with them.

More important, the Japanese can no doubt decide if a person is clean or dirty without evaluating the person on any other dimension. If Japanese parents are about to take their son somewhere, they may need to decide if he needs a bath. If they decide he does, they are not deciding he is bad.

The judgment of *clean-dirty* is not necessarily a judgment of anything else. The Japanese may have many more situations where cleanliness is valued, and consequently they use the scale more evaluatively. But the judgment may not be different in terms of the criteria involved. The semantic differential cannot establish what criteria are involved, nor where on the clean-dirty scale a person must be to be judged adequately clean (perhaps an American might accept 5 points of cleanliness, while a Japanese might require 6 points). But the fact that the Japanese use the scale more evaluatively does not imply that their criteria are more stringent.

Despite all these (relatively minor) problems, the research is overwhelming in its consistency. Carroll (1959) has offered an interesting rationale for the consistent emergence of the three factors. Evaluation is the approach-avoidance aspect of response to a stimulus; activity is the rapidity of adjustment necessitated by the presentation of the stimulus; and potency is the amount of adjustment required.

I have emphasized that the semantic differential measures dimensions of reactions to *concepts,* while Carroll suggests that it measures dimensions of reactions to stimuli. While *stimuli* is broad enough to include anything, it is clear that if Carroll, as seems to be the case, means real live stimuli rather than mere words, he is wrong. An ant is active, but we don't have to actively avoid ants; when we rate an ant as active, we are rating the *ant.* The USA is good, but it is hard to see how those of us who live here can approach it.

This section has been quite general. In the next two sections we shall get down to cases.

Fine Points and Issues in The Measurement of Meaning

In this section I will take up two subjects from MOM that are relevant to the general purpose of this book. The book has many other interesting complexities.

More on Evaluation

In Chapter Four I described the domain of evaluative terms as a case of LSA IV, associated with confusion and uncertainty in the culture. Perhaps, that analysis implied, we don't really know what we are doing when we evaluate; perhaps we are attempting to force order on chaos. MOM sheds some light on this issue.

Osgood reports that if subjects are asked to give the first descriptive adjective that comes to mind when presented with a stimulus object word (a modified word association game), half of the 50 most frequent adjectives are "clearly evaluative in nature" (p. 33). This corroborates the consistent emergence and strength of evaluation and Carroll's notion that evaluation is a ubiquitous and omnipresent "real behavior" of most organisms, the approach-avoidance aspect of their behavior. The first thing we do is to evaluate, i.e., decide whether to approach or avoid.

Osgood also reports "a tendency to collapse semantic dimensions toward a single evaluative factor when judging highly evaluative concepts" (p. 179). In other words, it is suggested, highly charged concepts (people and policies versus objects, to use Osgood's distinction) are evaluated, nothing more. The evaluative dimension accounts for most of the variance. We do not make fine discriminations.

This is not very encouraging if we are in the business of rating man on the *good-bad* dimension. It suggests that man, for all the talk about his incredible cognitive capacity and ability, does nothing more than animals do when faced with a salient object. America, for instance: we *do* "love it or leave it."

In fact, the above paragraph illustrates the kind of simple-minded thinking this evidence from the semantic differential suggests. Why would any full-fledged, intelligent, cognitively able human being be so simple-minded as to "examine man on the *good-bad* dimension"?

In addition, there is evidence (p. 157) that we react more quickly (operationally, by rating a concept on a scale) to concepts that are on the extremes of the evaluative dimension. This may be interpreted to mean that we of necessity must have practice in reacting to stimuli to which it is highly important to react. But it may mean that we react in a more stereotyped manner to extremely important stimuli.

There is in psychology an old and well proven inverted U shaped curve describing the relationship between arousal and performance. With low arousal we don't do so well. At medium arousal we do best. At high arousal we do very poorly.

Thus, it is suggested, stimuli at the extremes of the evaluative continuum provoke high arousal, which in turn causes us to behave very quickly in very undiscriminating ways. That is, when we should be thinking clearly and deliberately about the complexity of a situation, we are jabbing away at the old button in rigid, stereotyped, habitual movements like a pigeon in a Skinner box.

Part of the problem with evaluating, which goes along with the description of evaluating in terms of LSA IV:CSA IV, is that the evaluative dimension is almost completely free from denotative meaning. Potency and activity are highly connotative, but are tied to some extent to the denotative world. A thunderstorm *is* more powerful than a breeze and a shrew *is* more active than a slug, but a mother is *not* necessarily good.

As some proof of this contention, I offer Osgood's comment that "evaluative scales are less stable, more susceptible to variation across concepts, than non-evaluative scales" (p. 179). For example, *soft* and *good* go together with MOTHER, but *hard* and *good* go together with FATHER. The implication is that every time we have to evaluate a new object we have to bring to bear a new set of criteria (no wonder we get confused sometimes). *Softness* is a criterial attribute for the concept GOOD MOTHER. *Hardness* is a criterial attribute for GOOD FATHER. And these concepts are easy. What will go with *good* for ENGINE? That is, take a person who rates ENGINE as *good*. On what other scales does he give ENGINE a high rating? It's not very clear.

There are other problems. The authors have had difficulty finding scales that are "pure" representatives of the factors. That is, they can't find an evaluative scale that is neither potent nor impotent, neither active nor inactive. Nor can they find a potency scale that is neither good nor bad, neither active nor inactive. This is partially because the scale words are concepts too, and evaluation is therefore very much a part of *their* meaning. GOOD is not only *good*, but also *powerful* and *active*. Potency and activity are, in this culture, very good. Potency, activity, and evaluation are orthogonal, independent factors, but that does not mean that we judge an object's goodness, potency, and activity separately *or* independently.

Therefore, it is not surprising that the scales that load (correlate) high on potency and activity often also load high on evaluation. Therefore, I find slightly unjustified the authors' comment that, "We can say that there appear to be independent *factors* operating, even though it is difficult to find many specific *scales* which are orthogonal with respect to evaluation" (p. 38). It is not very sensible to intrude factors where ordinary language words don't go; the arguments to this point in Chapter One hold here also. The scales are the ultimate reality and the factor solution should attempt to deal with that reality.

But I do not consider my criticism too damning here. In an area so clouded by confusion and uncertainty the authors have done much to attempt to clear things up. One of their major efforts in this direction, which seems to be widely ignored, is a factor analysis of the evaluative dimension (p. 62). This was an attempt to discover varieties of goodness. There was a good factor analytic solution which yielded the following varieties of goodness (defining scales in parentheses): Meek goodness (altruistic, sociable, kind, grateful, clean, light-dark, graceful, pleasurable, beautiful); dynamic goodness (successful, high, meaningful, important, progressive); dependable goodness (true, reputable, believing, wise, healthy, clean); and hedonistic goodness (pleasurable, beautiful, sociable, meaningful).

Thus some things are good in that they are meek, others in that they are dependable, others in that they are dynamic, and others in that they are pleasing to the senses or to the needs. Note that these subfactors are much more closely tied to denotation.

This same study yields some additional factors besides the usual three, and I will report them here, as the picture of the semantic differential usually given is that the triumvirate always and only emerges. It should be noted that these factors do not account for much variance compared to the big three, and they should be considered to be rather specific factors, i.e., they are the result of the specific concepts and scales used in this particular study. Osgood and his associates were quite aware that the three factors did not come close to exhausting the total variance of the meaning space and that a good deal of further work was necessary to find out what else was going on. Not much of this work has been done, so the factors reported here do not have the monumental stability of the big three.

They were as follows, with defining scales in parentheses:

Stability *(sober-drunk, stable-changeable, rational-intuitive, sane-insane, cautious-rash, orthodox-heretical)*; Tautness *(sharp-blunt, masculine-feminine)*; Novelty *(new-old, unusual-usual)*; Receptivity *(savory-tasteless, colorful-colorless, sensitive-insensitive, interesting-boring, refreshed-weary, pungent-bland)*; and Aggressiveness *(aggressive-defensive)*.

Thus things are not as simple as they are often represented. In the next part of this section, I take up another major aspect of MOM that is ignored in accounts of the SD.

Dominant Characteristic Attributes

While factor analyses of many different samples of concepts have yielded the same two or three factors, the two or three factor solution is not always the best description of the data. It often is best to find a dimension that makes a line through the concepts, enabling us to accurately and with maximal simplicity represent the differences between the concepts. That is, we want the concepts to differ on only one dimension so that we can talk about their difference with ease. As Osgood puts it, "A *dominant characteristic attribute* (DCA) is defined as that line through the origin which is as close as possible in the least-square sense to all the concepts in the scatter. The dominant characteristic attributes of a structure are analogous to the factors in a simple structure" (p. 119).

The usual two or three factor solution is adequate, but fitting one or more DCAs to the data allows a better psychological interpretation. Thus Osgood explains the emergence of dynamism when the concepts are people or policies as follows: "It is as if things in this frame of reference that are 'strong' are also necessarily 'active' while things that are 'weak' are also necessarily 'passive.' " In order to be powerful, a person must do something, i.e., he must exercise his power; but we do have the image of the powerful individual sitting in state commanding his domain without demeaning himself with frenzied activity. We have the general belief in this culture that activity (hard work) leads to power or potency; but we do have the image of the impotent little man, the bureaucrat or underling, working hysterically but getting nothing of any significance done. So I think Osgood's interpretation in terms of an inability to make fine discriminations when dealing with salient objects fits well in this case.

The concept of the DCA gives the SD a flexibility not usually encountered in semantic differential research. The DCA solution can be tailored for the domain. Osgood says concerning the concept ATHLETE that all scales will tend to "shift in meaning toward parallelism with the dominant attribute of the concept being judged." He assumes the DCA to be active-potent dynamism, i.e., that is the major dimension along which athletes are seen as varying. We rarely evaluate athletes positively unless they are dynamic, so even the evaluative dimension should shift towards the DCA. Osgood asserts that such terms as *clean, successful, timely,* and *colorful* will become more potent and active in meaning in the context of the concept of ATHLETE. Thus a timely athlete is not one who is on time but one who is at the right place at the right time. The clean athlete has a "good clean stroke." I have commented on such shifts in meaning in the section on methodology, but in this context it seems less like an error.

In a study of politicians, policies, and programs (p. 120), three DCAs were found: benevolent dynamism vs. malevolent insipidness, malevolent dynamism vs. benevolent effectiveness, and weak-active vs. strong-passive.

Note that this last DCA codifies the two "images" I discussed earlier of the quiet powerful person and the frenzied little man.

Note also that the factors (DCAs) are made up of various combinations of evaluation, activity, and potency. The same dimensions of judgment are operating; however, people, policies, and programs tend to align themselves along the dimensions implied by the DCAs, so no new information is added. In general, this is the case with usage of DCAs in MOM. However, the potential for describing the structure of the lexicon in a more specific and denotative manner than the semantic differential usually does, especially when the technique is applied to one lexical domain instead of to the rather sparse sampling of concepts typical of the SD, is enhanced considerably by this technique.

Cross-Cultural Studies Using the Semantic Differential

In this section I will examine some of the cross-cultural studies that employ the semantic differential.

The most ambitious and the best of these is Osgood's (1964) study. Osgood points out that earlier studies used scales that were direct translations from the English scales used in the studies. Therefore, it is questionable whether the adjectives were common in or important for the other cultures. For each of his six language groups (e.g., Indo-European, Sino-Tibetan), Osgood asked speakers from the group to select a large number of important adjectives by qualifying nouns that had been translated from English.

The nouns were not selected by speakers of the different language groups, which introduces a possible similar bias. However, the nouns were largely names of common objects or events. Only about 20 had no obvious referent in physical reality. While this mitigates against the possible bias in the sample, it is a flaw in its own right, common to all cross-cultural studies using the SD. The denotative meaning of *rain* is easily separated from the connotative meaning. The connotative meaning can easily be thought of as an attitude. In the case of *justice,* connotative meaning and denotative meaning cannot be so easily separated. It is probably generally the case that where there is no clear denotative meaning, there is no clear connotative meaning, i.e., the distinctions merge. In Chapter Seven we see that this is the case with the distinction between style and content. Put another way, one might request a conceptual analysis of *justice* but not of *rain.* When the boundaries of a concept are unclear, it may be harder to have anything as distinct as an attitude towards the thing (which is less of a thing if it has fuzzy outlines). For concepts such as *inference* and *importance,* it is hard to imagine that anyone could have anything that resembled an attitude towards them. Osgood's sample does contain a few abstract nouns, but they are all, like *justice,* the kind of thing one can imagine people having an attitude towards.

So we will have to restrict the generality of such studies as follows: They study dimensions of meaning of rather common, concrete physical objects. With this qualification in mind, let us return to the study.

One hundred subjects from each language group gave the one qualifier they thought most people in their culture would give, for each of the translated nouns. An index, *H,* was formulated, which was a measure of diversity and frequency of qualifiers. Qualifiers (adjectives) were then ranked according to their H value. Rank order correlations between language groups of the 40 highest ranking qualifiers (translated into English) were all positive and quite high. Osgood suggests that this means that "the relative importance (frequency and diversity) of various modes of quali-fying experience appear to be shared despite differences in both language and culture." This is not very surprising, given the com-monness and concreteness of the nouns. Physical objects and natural events are not that susceptible to culturally biased percep-tion.

Opposites of the qualifiers were found in the original lan-guage. It is not reported if the opposites of the qualifiers were similar to the English opposites (there are indications that they weren't in all cases).

The usual three factors emerged for all language groups. Evaluation was always first, while activity and potency had varia-ble rank.

There is considerable variation in the amount of variance accounted for by evaluation. For the American sample the figure was 45% (which is lower than the figure usually reported for studies of American culture alone); for the Dutch sample it was 28%. Osgood doesn't explain this. It could be that cultures differ in the extent to which they evaluate objects and events; but it is also possible that the sample of concepts, because of cultural differences, differentially elicited evaluative tendencies. For ex-ample, one would not expect a person who had never seen a cow to have much reaction to it. I consider 29 of the 100 nouns to be concepts that *could* be unfamiliar in other cultures. Therefore, we cannot conclude that cultures differ in the more general tendency to evaluate.

There were numerous differences between languages as to the scales which defined the particular factors, although in most cases the naming seems valid, due to the presence of content-free scales such as *good-bad.*

Osgood found that all language groups tended to make unequal use of semantic space. More concepts appeared in the positively evaluated part of semantic space, more appeared in the more potent half, and more appeared in the less active half.

As Osgood points out, this could be a function of the concepts he used. He also suggests that it could be "characteristic of the human species." And there is much research which suggests that this is true with respect to the evaluative dimension. Perhaps we don't allow things we don't like to stay around. Or perhaps we can say that humans are pragmatic. If something is here to stay, we might as well like it. It doesn't seem possible to settle this kind of question empirically.

Triandis and Osgood (1958) report a similar study with Greek and American college students. They used only scale words that could survive a rather rigorous test. The words were translated into Greek by three individuals, and back into English by three others. The scale word was not used unless there was unanimous agreement. This introduces bias. Only a certain sort of qualifier is used, namely one that can be easily translated from English to Greek and back again without ambiguity, i.e., one which would not be expected to show cultural differences. It is in the areas of experience where the languages differ that we expect to find differences between the speakers of the language on various tasks, as the evidence in Chapter Three indicates.

In this study only two easily interpretable factors emerged, evaluation and dynamism. This was true for both Americans and Greeks. The factors were similar across cultures. The Greeks, comment the authors, tend, "to use all scales of judgment somewhat more evaluatively." While the percentage difference in proportion of variance accounted for by evaluation is small, the authors offer

an explanation: Greeks have a more "militant" "frame of reference." They seem to mean that the Greeks are more conformist,
and evaluate according to how well an individual conforms. The
authors find some specific differences to support their contention,
e.g., the Greeks positively evaluate "straightness."

More interesting and more valid is the finding that Americans
judge what the authors call "abstractions" (justice, soldier, police,
labor) to be colder and less sociable than do Greeks. Americans
also judge everyday objects as being more exciting and warm than
do Greeks. These authors interpret this to mean that Americans
romanticize. I don't understand the rationale for this interpretation and I would submit that the "well-known" materialism of
Americans would explain particularly the latter finding. At any
rate, these examples illustrate that the semantic differential can
potentially be used for broader assessments of culture than are
usually attempted in studies of this nature. However, the results
are bound to be problematical and the kind of interpretation offered in this study is too vague and offhand to be of much value;
similarly, the broad comments of anthropologists are often insufficiently related to concrete data. Psychologists perhaps feel
that if they have the kind of sophisticated tools that they have
they needn't worry about interpretation.

Suci (1960) reports another study of this sort, with Spanish,
Zuni, and Navaho speakers. It has a good many methodological
flaws. Due to translation difficulties and sensitive areas, the
groups used different concepts. There were varying degrees of
bilingualism, an important factor that was not controlled for.
Instructions were given in the native language only to the Navaho, who were the most distinctive group and the most different
from the sample of American college students who rated all the
concepts rated by any of the experimental groups. The Indians did
not use the usual paper and pencil format, which may or may not
cause trouble.

Only two factors that were interpretable emerged. The first
three factors accounted for only 39% of the reliable variance for
the Navaho, and for only 52% of the Zuni variance. As the au-

thors point out, for these two groups a great deal of attribute space remains undefined. This could result from the methodological problems.

Somewhat paradoxically, because none of the studies in this area are free of methodological difficulties, I tend to consider the findings reliable (the other studies, such as those of Kumata and Schramm, 1956; Maclay and Ware, 1961; offer no new methodological problems). If you get the same results from studies that have different flaws, you can have more confidence in the results, although this is a rather shoddy approach to empirical research. On the other hand, there is a tendency to say of the kind of criticisms I have given here, "So what? The basic findings are the same." But when one needs various controls, one is not so casual. For example, I could have deduced from the arguments of Chapter Four that cultures with many evaluative words would have strong evaluative dimensions. I cannot use the literature to test this proposition due to its flaws.

Conclusion

The semantic differential has had a history and it should have a future. I would like to see more of the methodological work that distinguished *The Measurement of Meaning* and the application of the technique to various more specific domains. Perhaps dimensions would emerge that would be more closely tied to the denotative world. But as I have said repeatedly, the monolithic consistency of the research is remarkable. Every social scientist should know about the semantic differential, for the emergence of the three factors is one of the few things that social science has found out by itself, of which nobody can say, "Oh, of course, I could have told you that." Unfortunately, most of the findings that are not obvious tend to arouse a feeling of sleepiness in the non-social scientist. I don't know where the semantic differential stands on this dimension.

chapter six

Naming Behavior

This chapter deals with what we call various kinds of people under various circumstances. The accounts of the empirical literature in this area indicate that there is a paucity of evidence, although all of us have a good deal of evidence of our own. I will first briefly discuss the excellent work that has been done in this area (Brown, 1965; Brown and Ford, 1961; Brown and Gilman, 1960). With that research as a framework I will delve into my own experience, which will provide a valid piece of hard empirical data. I am pulling participant observation in this chapter, as I said I would in Chapter One. So I will also feel free to comment on the behavior of others.

The review of the research by Brown and his associates will be brief because I introduce many of their findings in the account of my experience.

They have used modern American plays, history books, usage in a business firm as reported by an employee of the firm, self-reported usage of business executives, recorded usage in the Midwest, foreign informants, and other sources. Their research is methodologically sound, and I will not discuss that aspect of it further.

Two variables, status and solidarity, govern naming behavior. Status is a vertical dimension on which people differ in rank; solidarity is a horizontal dimension on which people differ in personal distance (Brown, 1965, p. 57). A slight problem with Brown's model is that status is a single dimension if treated in the abstract, but in the real world there are many status ladders. The position of P relative to O depends on whether he is X rungs higher on the same ladder or X rungs higher on a different ladder.

Some languages, such as German, Russian, and French, have (at least) two forms (where we have but one) for *you*. (Is the domain of "youness" more highly differentiated for Germans than it is for us?) Brown and his associates call these two forms T and V. V is usually the plural form and may also be used to indicate that the speaker is addressing more than one you. German has three forms for you, singular, plural, and polite.

T indicates intimacy if two people say it to each other, but condescension when a person gives T but receives V from the other. V indicates distance or remoteness if two people give it to each other, but deference when a person gives V but receives T. (These terms are Brown's; 1965, p. 59.)

Brown reports that "the principal historical change in the semantic of T and V has been the suppression of the status norm in favor of the solidarity norm" (1965, p. 64). That is, non-reciprocal usage patterns, where the superior gives T and receives V, are much less common than in feudal times. And while there is still reciprocal V, between strangers and people newly acquainted, there is a tendency for people to move more quickly to reciprocal T.

But, Brown notes, the expression of status continues via naming behavior. Dagwood calls his boss *Mr. Dithers,* but Mr. Dithers calls Dagwood *Dagwood* (or *Bumstead*). Brown suggests that Western civilization has retained this mode of expressing status because it is possible, as it isn't with pronouns, to avoid expressing it in all conversations. In the terms of Chapter Two, it is no longer obligatory to express status differentials.

Status is a very strong and important dimension in this society, although we are, I think, attempting to suppress it with word magic. I further believe that this is one of the cases where the word magical solution actually makes the problem worse.

Why does intimacy go with condescension and personal distance with deference? It could have been the other way around. Brown and his associates have an answer. Status ordering is painful, particularly for the inferior. Furthermore, Brown assumes, inferiors should desire and would profit from contact with their superiors more than vice versa. So they might be expected to attempt to initiate such contact more often. If this were allowed, inferiors would always be being rejected. They would then be unhappy and feel left out. Eventually they would rebel. The superiors might feel guilty because of all the constant rejection they would have to do.

So, Brown and his associates argue, society has ruled that it is the superior who will initiate intimacy and contact (if intimacy and contact *are* initiated). When he does, inferiors will be happy.

Therefore, the superior must hold the verbal keys to intimacy. "His" form, T, must be the one that he offers, since such relationships move from a status-differential codified to a status-differential uncodified position. Since the superior must initiate change from his giving T and receiving V, naturally "his" mode of address would be adopted. It would give the inferior little satisfaction to find his own mode of address adopted. That would be like a boss asking his employee to dinner at the employee's house (Mr. Dithers has done this).

I prefer to make the connection with a more conceptual approach, although Brown's is just as valid. Personal distance and deference have a distinct family resemblance. In Brown's terms, personal distance is a large difference of position along the horizontal axis, while deference is a large difference on the vertical dimension. The two concepts may have a semi-generic term: *dis-*

tance. Similarly, intimacy and condescension have a distinct family resemblance. If P can afford to be condescending (or more neutrally, to pull rank, however gently) with O, then O is in P's sphere of influence. That is, P is higher than O in both status and power. In terms introduced earlier, O is one or more rungs below P on the same ladder. A corporation president can get away with condescension with one of his $80,000 a year vice-presidents much more easily than he can with a taxi-driver. The status differential between corporation president and taxi-driver is abstract; they are also distant on the horizontal dimension, which detracts from the felt reality of the difference on the vertical dimension, and which, in a geometric sense, increases the absolute distance between them. The president and his vice-presidents are in the same family (I use *family* deliberately to bring paradigmatic families to mind). Their distance is purely on the vertical dimension. Thus both intimacy and condescension can occur only in the context of a family.

In English, of course, we don't use T and V. We only have various forms of address. Brown and Ford suggest the following ordering, from most distant and/or deferential to most intimate and/or condescending: Title (T); Title Plus Last Name (TLN); Last Name (LN); First Name (FN); and Multiple Names (MN), which we have met before in Chapter Four.

Brown and his associates are also aware of the practice of using no form of address, which is done when the status of a relationship is unclear or in transition. We shall abbreviate this NN, for No Name.

But the same patterns of relationship obtain in America. Strangers begin with mutual TLN (V). The superior, if there is one, will switch to giving FN (T) but receiving TLN. He may later offer the inferior the privilege of calling him FN. In relationships where there is no difference on the status dimension, the progression is from mutual TLN to mutual FN.

The five forms of address progression presented above is like a Guttman scale. That is, one moves from left to right but not from right to left. But while a relationship may move from T straight down to MN, it is common to start late (e.g., begin the relationship at TLN), end early (e.g., never get beyond FN), or skip steps (e.g., move from TLN to FN).

It should be clear that a good deal may be discovered about relationships and society, as well as about people, by examination of their naming behavior.

I have covered the main points and arguments given by Brown and his associates. They have fleshed out their theories and arguments with many interesting anecdotes from literature, history, and their informants. I will now present my account, which gives some recent history and some new anecdotes, explores some differences between my data and Brown's, applies some of the concepts we have been using in this book, and, I believe, offers a couple of new insights into the dynamics of naming behavior.

My Account

"A substantial difference of age seems to call for non-reciprocal FN and TLN; children say TLN to adults and receive FN" (Brown, 1965, p. 68).

When I was a child living in California in the early and middle 1950s, I called my parents' friends FN. My father is a professor in the humanities. Consequently, he and his friends could have received Dr. LN (DLN) from me. I know this is done in at least two circles of friends; and according to Brown it is common for children to give TLN and receive FN. (I doubt if it is common for children to give DLN to academics; the people in the circles in which this is done are extremely insecure and pompous.)

How can we explain my apparently deviant experience? California was not then a particularly informal place. My parents and their friends had good times and seemed to like each other, and they were intelligent and erudite and all that, but otherwise they were nothing special.

I have suggested that pomposity and insecurity are associated with formal naming behavior. And the relationship makes sense. If people are unsure of themselves, they logically should make the most of what they have, even if all they can do is play word magical games. So perhaps my parents' friends weren't pompous. And they weren't. And perhaps they had enough real status and prestige to be able to afford to forego the mere verbal trappings of status and prestige.

But although confident enough, my parents' friends were young and, though promising, hadn't yet arrived, and they were in a very competitive department. Nor were they models of total stability and certainty about right and wrong and up and down. So that isn't a sufficient explanation, although, slightly paradoxically, it is the unstable and undercontrolled who, in my experience, do not insist on formality in address or in other areas of life. Lack of stability and controls can be equated with lack of socialization. People who are not well socialized are likely to know that the status hierarchy is a convenience at best and a breeding ground for exploitation at worst and therefore people should avoid emphasizing it.

Most of the children in our circle were between 7 and 13. In those days, children that age showed and felt respect for their elders. We knew our places, to put it bluntly. Given this respect (but not obsequiousness, cringing deference, or servility), there was no need for the verbal trappings of respect.

But that is not all. We all had fun together. Intimacy is associated with intimate forms of address.

But this intimacy was based on a substrate of awareness of inequality. It seems to me that this substrate is less firm today. Consequently there is perhaps more formality (real and word magical) between adults and children. I believe that status, distance, and non-reciprocity are having a resurgence today, perhaps as a reaction against the excesses of equality. The gradual evolution of the solidarity norm, as traced by Brown and Gilman and by Brown, suggests a similar reaction to the excesses of the status norm, e.g., treating inferiors too poorly.

Perhaps for people of different status, age-graded or otherwise, a certain distance is needed for intimacy and friendship (which is paradoxical only on the face of it). When we went places the children played together and away from the adults a good part of the time. And there were times when it was appropriate for adults and children to have free interaction. This segregation was accepted and maintained. Therefore the adults did not have to fear the unpleasant task of pulling rank. So when they did play with us, it was because they wanted to, and we knew it. I believe that today children are less content to leave adults alone; and vice versa, for we are as youth-oriented as we can be. And this makes the relationship between the generations strained.

In summary, we could enjoy the friendship of adults because they did not feel *generally* threatened. Free adult-child interaction was the rule part of the time. The rest of the time the adults could relax, because segregation was the rule.

A slight digression in this connection: I always called my father's brother Uncle X and his wife Aunt Y, but I was and always have been on a strictly FN basis with all my aunts and uncles on my mother's side. I saw my mother's side more often and my mother is closer and more intimate with her sisters than my father is with his brother.

Putting this in the familiar framework of real names, because my aunt Jean functioned as *Jean* rather than as my *aunt* (an *aunt* is a formal role with prescribed and proscribed behaviors and with the distance and difference that is proper in the aunt-nephew relationship), I called her Jean. That was her real name. Aunt Y was usually my aunt. If she had been very little more than an aunt, I might have called her just plain Aunt (recall that Title is more formal than Title Last Name). So it may be that in such relationships as this (which I will call RFN for Role First Name) the given name is used less as the person acts less as a person and more rigidly as the role dictates. If Brown's analysis of titles holds for role relationships, the answer should be yes. But there are differences between role relationships in the family and title relationships in the outside world, as we shall see. Suffice it for the moment that I think I felt more intimate with my grandparents when I called them R than when I called them RLN. Note also that grandparents often have pet names.

Returning to the main thread, we moved from California and didn't return for five years, at which time I was about to begin my senior year in high school. Nothing particularly atypical occurred in the life of any of the cast of characters; I hadn't thought once about naming behavior; and I was not alienated or rebelling against society.

I didn't feel comfortable calling my parents' friends FN; but given the past it would have been strange to call them TLN. It would have seemed insulting and it would have codified a change in our relationships that I didn't feel. Perhaps if I had continued to live in California there would have been no conflict, but I doubt it, for I called some of my parents' friends in Indiana FN and by the time I was 15 I was experiencing the same conflict (I should point out that I was going to high school away from home nine months of the year). Perhaps then it was simply the loss of intimacy. With my parents' friends in California it was just a visit; with my parents' friends in Indiana I was hardly ever home. I don't think so. At any rate, I resolved the issue by calling them NN. Note that here we have an exception to the usual progression from formality to informality.

Perhaps the change came because I was closer to my parents' friends in status. But I was only 16, and by now my parents' friends had attained a good deal of status and prestige. So there was no status conflict.

Perhaps it was because I didn't trust adults. For me, to give FN is to manifest and sometimes to intentionally display liking. I rarely use FN with people I don't like. There are many people whom I don't dislike but who are not my friends. I use FN with them rather sparingly. But with my friends, I use FN often, perhaps more often than necessary. If we use multiple names with our best friends, we may also use these various names frequently. Not that we use them inappropriately. "Don't you see that X is the case?" is appropriate, but so is, "But Fred, don't you see that X is the case?" The latter locution adds a personal touch and may indicate that your opposition is less important than your relationship, while the former indicates the argument is more important.

But I still liked my parents' friends. So that explanation will not suffice, although like the others I have rejected, it would be a good explanation in some circumstances. The next explanation is satisfactory.

As has often been said, adolescents have no place in society. It is not clear *what* relationship an adolescent has to the rest of society. If naming behavior codifies the nature and quality of interpersonal relationships, then if you have no relationship with the mainstream of society, how appropriate it is to use No Name, as I did, caught as I was between FN and TLN.

Looked at in another way, in a sense the mainstream of society sends adolescents an incongruent message: You are a child, yet you are an adult. Sometimes you will be treated as a child—generally, those will be the times when you are trying to act as an adult. Sometimes you will be treated as an adult—generally, when you are acting as a child. No wonder adolescents move away from the mainstream for a time.

We have no distinctive social practices for dealing with adolescents. Instead, we borrow from either childhood or adult games. No wonder adolescents use NN, which attempts, symbolically at least, to deny relationships.

One is still a part of one's family (even if relationships in adolescence get rather stormy). At least my parents didn't throw me out, although they had good reason to. Families, many of them, exist and have reality (in the sense of real names) despite the most incredible incidents. So it is not surprising that I had no trouble with my aunts and uncles on either side of the family. I called them what I had always called them and what I will always call them.

One further possible explanation: It may be that it is very difficult for adolescents and adults to be intimate. Adults either have almost uniformly not succeeded sufficiently, or have been unhappy, without the hope (that all adolescents have) that the unhappiness and its cause will go away. Adolescents don't know what life in the world is like, but they know of its existence and are about to go out into it (unlike children). Therefore, they pose a threat to adults. Adults pose a similar threat to adolescents, who would rather not see (especially in adults they hold or held dear) the various weaknesses that come with adulthood.

Let us return to childhood. Tom Sawyer grows up with his aunt. So does Nancy, the comic strip character. Donald Duck is raising his three nephews. Snuffy Smith has a nephew (he and his wife have had a baby, and I'll bet he remains a baby). There are other fictional examples of this. In two comic strips (*Peanuts* and *Tiger*) adults are never to be seen and rarely heard.

Why? Humor depends on the reader's ability to keep his distance from the situation. We can't laugh when things get "too close to home." The kind of semi-hostile interchange between uncles and aunts and their nephews and nieces found in these comic strips would be hard to dissociate oneself from if it involved parents and their children. If the relationship is aunt-nephew, however, it is less close and significant; therefore, the hostility is not so dangerous or threatening; nor does it seem as real, important, or significant.

Notice in *Dennis the Menace* that Dennis has trouble with Mr. Wilson his next-door neighbor, but not with his parents. They—or we—may find out what he has done to Mr. Wilson *or* themselves, but always *post facto*. We see Dennis in the corner; but we don't see hostility towards the parents directly represented in the strip. In *Peanuts* and *Tiger* there are no adults and therefore no hostility.

I suggest, then, contrary to the tone of the preceding, that there is much value in relatively formalized relationships that aren't as close as parent-child relationships. In a family open displays of hostility are significant. That is, they cannot be (or are not, in this culture) taken to be merely outbursts of ill-temper. If the son is throwing temper tantrums, the son is having problems, although an uncle might put it differently, e.g., "He's just in a stage, and a good spanking will bring him out of it quickly." Furthermore, if the son is throwing temper tantrums, the parents feel at least partially to blame. Thus hostility threatens the family itself and its worth. The same holds true for friendship, love, and most marriage relationships—either the relationship must change, or the hostility must be dealt with. But where there is a relationship that is not as close to the center of the person, hostility may be released without danger. We know that Dennis and Mr. Wilson will always be together and will always be in conflict, but we can laugh because the conflict won't hurt anybody any more than various animals are hurt in movie cartoons when they are run over by trucks.

I have had some hostile interchanges with my aunts and uncles—hostile enough to destroy a different sort of relationship. But I have more or less forgotten about them, and I think they probably have too. I would feel free to drop in and sponge a couple of days' rest if I was in any of their areas. After all, I'm Dora's son, and any son of Dora's can't be all bad—nor can any sister or brother of Dora's be all bad either.

Similarly, Aunt Polly will always take care of Tom Sawyer. But he can go on long trips that would nearly kill a mother with worry. And while Aunt Polly says she has been nearly killed with worry, we don't believe her completely. Her suffering seems less real to us because Tom is not her own. But she will always care for Tom, as he will for her, for a reason that is extraneous to and, most important, *independent of* the relationship itself: Polly happened to be Tom's mother's sister. In addition, because the hostility isn't of as great personal significance, the child may without great trauma receive what psychologists like to call negative feedback, as well as just plain nastiness or grouchiness. This is certainly good training.

Social scientists sometimes bemoan the demise of the extended family because, they feel, it was good for children to have many adults to go to, adults who could, for example, comfort a child who had been in a ruckus with his parents without saying anything bad about the parents or the child. The extended family may be good because a child can learn not only that he is a confounded nuisance at times, but that he can count on being picked on for no other reason than that he was available. Spare the scapegoating and spoil the child. Once when I was an adolescent and threatening to do something rather foolhardy, my father's father said, "What that boy needs is a good kick in the ass." Simple-minded of course, but when my father related it to me we both laughed. One can accept being criticized by someone who one, is part of the family, and two, has enough distance to laugh at the situation.

But now we must deal with parent-child naming behavior and its significance, and I will not rely much on my personal experience. This may simply indicate that my experience was not at all out of the ordinary with respect to naming behavior, but it may also indicate I don't want to talk about it.

Let me present the paradox immediately: We call our parents the most formal term possible—*Mother,* or some variant, and *Father,* or some variant. This is equivalent to Title. Yet there is no relationship as intense, close, and personal.

Mother and *father* are generic terms. The lower level terms are the names of all the mothers and fathers who have ever lived. Thus children call their parents a very general term, just as taxi-drivers (are supposed to) call everyone *Mac.* Perhaps mothers and fathers function almost entirely as mothers and fathers rather than as individual human beings, i.e., perhaps *mother* and *father* are the real names. This is no doubt the case. But still, parents see their children and children see their parents in as bright and close a light as exists in human relationships, so that while John Doe may be *daddy,* he is also very definitely . . . who? Not John Doe, because the face we put on for the world is not the face we put on for our parents and children. *John Doe* fits our friends and our mates but not our parents. When we are children, our parents are much more to us than their regular given name.

Thus we may examine two possibilities: Parents are so important to and personal with their children that children, in order to (word magically) avert their faces from so bright a glare, call the parents by a name that codifies the formal nature of the relationship. (Similarly, parents like this name. It allows them to word magically forget the remarkable personal power they have over their children.) Or: Parents aren't people nearly so much as they are parents.

Both are appropriate descriptions, and they are not mutually exclusive. There can be little doubt about the reality of *daddy* and *mommy,* at least for children. The question, "Who is that?" would elicit those words and no others. Children often have difficulty thinking of their parents in any other way. Brown's example is that his nephews could not grasp the fact that their father was Brown's brother. They did not understand that their daddy stood in relationship to anyone else. In other words, if you take the view that words tame the world and categorize experience so that it doesn't overwhelm us, mothers and fathers can only be captured by a totally generic term, broad enough to cover most experience.

In terms of Chapter Four, I am speculating that children are fascinated by their parents, with some embarrassment or related feeling. *Mommy* and *daddy* are euphemisms of one sort, but we can't think up a word for the "too real" aspect of our parents. Note in addition that there are other terms: As an adult, one *can* regress and say *mommy,* but one usually denies one is saying it (i.e., makes the message incongruent) by putting a jesting or other tone on it. There is the somewhat assertive *the old man,* although this phrase also functions as an attempt to show an indifference that is, of course, not really felt. Thus, as was the case with words referring to Blacks or blacks, we find that the usual connotations found with LSA III(B) are present but not quite themselves. That is, if we had a true case of LSA III(B), we would not have to say *mommy* with a denying tone. Thus there is a suggestion that we are uncertain what to do and feel about our parents (i.e., in Freudian terms, that we are ambivalent, but it is more complicated than that). There does seem to be some attempt to impose a naming system on an uncertain situation. And the uncertainty is clearly present: neither we nor they can ever be sure if our parents "love" us because they really love us or because they are our parents. Nor can we be sure if we love them because we love them or because they are our parents. (In some cases, we can be, e.g., if we love our father even though he shows up once a month drunk and beats us up. Then we know we love him because he's our father.) And this uncertainty is mirrored in the overwhelming strength and reality of *mother* and *father* juxtaposed against the incredible impersonality of such a form of address.

Leaving childhood behind, let us return to academic life many years later.

Although I grew up with academics I did not hear DLN used except in addressing medical doctors until I got to graduate school. While I think DLN use by undergraduates is on the upswing, it is still the general practice at the "better" schools to call the teachers MLN (or Professor LN, PLN), and when I was an undergraduate in the early 1960s at Ivy U and at Rocky Mountain U, which was not one of the better schools for undergraduates, I never heard nor used DLN. However, I was an English major, and it could be that English teachers prefer to dissociate themselves from science and scientists. It seems to be the case at Seven Sisters College that DLN is more commonly given to scientists than to humanists.

When I began graduate school I met with the director of my program and naturally called him MLN. Shortly after meeting him I was in an outer office and heard DLN for the first time. I was shocked and horrified at the pretension of it all. I was equally shocked and horrified that I had called DLN MLN. I guess he forgave me, but I am sure he noticed it.

Once you get used to something, you are used to it, and I got used to DLN rather quickly. In fact, while I call many of my former teachers by their first name, while calling them DLN seemed very natural when I was a student, and while hearing others saying DLN to them seems natural to me now, I would find MLN applied to them by anyone very queer.

Sometimes I have heard them addressed this way by undergraduates and it does sound funny. MLN is not their real name. They function as DLN with graduate students. That is, they have power, expertise, and no need to please you; while for undergraduates they are not great scholars, but only teachers, subject to snide comments, course droppings, and face-to-face complaining (someting a graduate student would never do at Rocky Mountain U). Thus MLN is all they can expect.

However, I had soon to face another rude shock, in my second year of graduate school. I heard graduate students addressing DLNs by FN. Later in my second year the first attempt was made by a professor to seduce me into calling him FN. Why this term is appropriate will be made clear.

In graduate school the faculty has a good deal of control over the graduate students (as much as a boss has over his employees, or perhaps more: If you've been thrown out of one graduate school, it is unlikely you'll get another chance). It is hard to get jobs unless you get good recommendations; in some fields you may need the sponsorship of a big name. In your first year or two you may be dropped from the program, and if you make enemies, even one strong enemy, you are done for. And there is some professional jealousy. The faculty don't enjoy having their years of research sneered at by young punks, and who can blame them? Sometimes if you do research with one person and decide to change to another, you make an enemy. It is a characteristic of the structure of graduate school that the graduate student is in a definitely subordinate position, to a far greater extent than an undergraduate, who can only be punished or rewarded by grades, and with whom the faculty is generally less professionally involved.

Thus FN would seem highly inappropriate and highly unlikely. Why did I find it in use at Rocky Mountain U? It may be that it was an attempt by the faculty to make the graduate students feel they weren't really as lowly and dependent as they actually were, as Brown would suggest, although Brown would impute to the faculty much more generous motives than I would. But let me describe the situation more fully.

Some of the teachers, the young ones for the most part, were more "the FN type." They were just out of graduate school, young, and not yet secure. Therefore, they found it difficult to act as if there was a large status differential between themselves and the graduate students. Others were simply not very formal types.

Students were another variable factor. Some students took rather quickly to calling faculty FN. Brown has suggested that it is almost universal that the superior initiate more intimate forms of address. But there are exceptions. One time I heard a "brash young punk" calling one of the stern and powerful professors FN. I was in a state of fear and anticipation. Fear for the graduate student, for I thought he would be asked to turn in his computer project number on the spot. Anticipation because he was in his first year and I was in my third; I had worked for this DLN for a couple of years, had done good work, and had never used FN. The brash young punk hadn't even worked with the DLN. I was jealous, in a sense.

The student wasn't struck down by lightning, the DLN was cordial, and I believe the student accomplished something.

What happens to brash young punks? Here perhaps research is needed. It may be that the superiors are flattered to be considered human (rather than the enemy); or perhaps they are threatened and feel somewhat in the power of the subordinate. After all, they have passively accepted FN even when inappropriate.

But what should they have done? It is a bit silly and beneath one's station as a seeker after truth to make a fuss about forms of address. As scientists in hot pursuit of knowledge, we are more or less indifferent to such matters. Similarly in the business world: "He may be a brash young punk but what matters is that he gets the job done."

But I wouldn't be surprised if the superiors felt taken. An inferior uses FN. The superior has not offered it, but accepts it without protest. An outside observer could not tell from the naming behavior that there was a superior and an inferior. It looks as if there are two equals. Furthermore, Bem (1967) has presented a theory with supporting evidence that in many cases we find out the truth about ourselves not by looking inward but by looking at our behavior as if we were outside observers of ourselves. From the point of view of this theory, the superior should have a tendency to believe that the inferior is not really an inferior.

So perhaps the brash young punk makes off with a gain in status. But what of his ultimate fate? In the last few years I have noticed an increasing tendency for bank tellers and others who can easily discover my first name to address me by FN on first meeting. They even do this to my mother, who is in her fifties. This irritates me even more than it irritates my mother. But I can't express this anger even to myself without feeling foolish. After all, my FN is not my virtue, although I should have the right to reserve it for use by my superiors and friends.

I subvocally vow to get revenge, and yet I feel ashamed. As yet I have not hurt anyone who has abused my name. But then I am not a very powerful person and I don't like holding the power I do hold. Perhaps power does corrupt. And so perhaps many brash young punks do come to grief by being brash with a superior who is just as annoyed as I am and just as ashamed of his annoyance, but willing to seek secret revenge.

I do have a standard tactic for dealing with such unauthorized traffic with my FN. I studiously refuse to return FN. In fact, I often use TLN (although casually, not with the "watch who you're talking to" tone of Brown's example of a boss whose employee has given him FN after a party. To be that heavy handed would be to appear more pompous than I want to appear, because that's precisely what this new generation of FN users would call me).

I don't think more severe punishment is called for. Probably most people who use FN in a manner I consider inappropriate don't know any better. Which is to say they don't see things the way I do. They didn't have the proper training. Which is to say they weren't brought up the way I was. They don't find using FN particularly significant. It is natural to them and signifies nothing special about themselves or the persons they are addressing. It is only from my point of view that the use of FN is significant, so I retaliate with a weapon that will probably give only me satisfaction.

While in the past the higher status individual gave T and received V, it is just possible that the trend will be reversed. One will signal that he is conservative and is maintaining his distance (and perhaps that he is or considers himself of higher status) by using formal address while accepting familiar, intimate forms. In the past one asserted oneself by the intimate form. Soon one may do so by the formal form.

I have said that students were one variable factor. Another was number of years in graduate school. In my first year I never considered using FN, nor did any of my friends. By my second year I knew of the practice, and by my third year I had called a teacher or two FN. By the time students get close to the Ph.D., most of them are calling most professors FN.

However, let us consider again Brown's contention that the superior initiates intimacy. His theory rests on the assumption that subordinates desire contact with their superiors. I do not think this is a complete description of the state of affairs. Brown as usual has the answer, but in another part of his great book, *Social Psychology,* in his section on "The dark side of high status."

Overt overtures are the exception to the rule today in America. In Germany they have a ceremony, but here a direct request for FN is unusual.

I was the recipient of two fairly direct overtures. I haven't heard of anyone alse having their virtue assaulted in that manner, probably because most people slip into use of FN when the time comes. One mumbles FN to see if anything will happen and pretty soon one is open about it. But I was recalcitrant.

When Brown wrote about this very same transition, he implied that it occurred after one got the Ph.D. and in fact became the equal of the teachers, at least with respect to degrees. Things have changed, at least at Rocky Mountain U. The time for using FN is more like two years.

As I have said, there is plenty of inequality, but the rule is to make sure it isn't codified and made perfectly clear. So one uses FN in a word magical attempt to make believe that there are no status differences, and, as my examples will illustrate, the anxiety that this be so is just as strong or stronger on the superior's part. The move towards equality Brown described in his 1965 book has continued, but in 1974 it is getting somewhat pathological. It made at least one of my teachers much more uncomfortable than it made me that I called him DLN.

"Nobody wants to play God anymore," is one way of talking about the change; but people continue to play God, and perhaps it is easier to do away with someone who is equal in address. Perhaps superiors fear they will feel guilty if they destroy an inferior, who is by definition less powerful. Picking on someone smaller than you makes you a bully. So the superior word magically creates an equal. He allows the inferior to call him FN. Then the inferior is no longer an inferior, and he can be destroyed. I am reminded of Orwell's *1984.* Winston, the "hero," is not killed until he truly believes in Big Brother.

When you get down to cases, however, it is hard to imagine such evil but basically devious motives. In my second year, Dr. Fred Farquist said to me with something of an embarrassed smile that I was the only "person around here" who called him Dr. Farquist. I was sorry for him, because he was a nice guy, and he knew my story about my shyness was something of a lie. It is fortunate that he wasn't a powerful person. I said I'd try, but for two more years all I could do was to give him NN.

More interesting was my run-in with Dr. John West, for whom I had done some good work. He hinted relatively directly that I should call him FN. I demurred and laid it on thick about my FN neurosis. He wasn't fooled and made several references to it over the course of a couple months.

One night at a party at his house I got drunk and informed him that while I couldn't call him *John,* I would call him *Old Shit.* He forgave me the next day, so the story doesn't have an unhappy ending. But here I was calling a man I respected and feared *Old Shit.* And feeling much more comfortable about it than calling him *John.* I suspect I got drunk that night so that I could call him *John,* but the truth will out, and the power structure made him Dr. West.

We have here a clear case of multiple naming with no real name (in my lexicon). His real name was and subsequently became for me *John,* but at that time it wasn't real to me, or, as I suggested with reference to *mother* and *father,* it was too real to face. *Old Shit* is obviously the rude and assertive term, *Dr. West* the polite euphemism. I also used a term (not around him) which can only be described as regressive: *Uncle Johnny.* This had the (word magical) function of showing that he was really a nice guy. And note that I chose *Uncle.* But as was the case with *mother* and *father,* the assertiveness isn't really assertive, nor is the regressive term really regressive, and it seems as if we may again have LSA IV.

Eventually I settled down and called him John, and now I feel comfortable with it. Perhaps psychology should attempt to find out how to get out of cases of LSA IV.

Both of these teachers were, I think, attempting to accomplish something by getting me to call them FN. Dr. Farquist didn't feel like a very powerful man and didn't like to be treated as one. He was mild-mannered, pleasant, and not very competitive. He was fired of course—that kind of mentality doesn't belong in an area where truth is being actively sought.

Dr. West was somewhat lonely professionally, due to his honesty and his lack of interest in playing academic politics, and perhaps wished to think of me as a friend of sorts. After all, I was one of the few people in the department who read any of his work. I have seen this kind of loneliness in other non-political and honest academics. It is understandable, but the victim refuses to accept the power structure and all that it implies. This is the dark side of high status.

However, with one teacher I found myself using FN rather quickly with no direct or indirect overtures and without a great deal of friendly or personal talk between us. In fact, the relationship was strictly business and still is. I like the man a great deal but I don't know him or care to know him except as a psychologist. In general, this is the way I feel about the psychologists I respect most as psychologists. There is no reason why all relationships should be the same. Friendship is inappropriate and impossible between non-equals who are as separated as graduate students and their mentors, and one can't have a good professional relationship if friendship is present or in the offing. And it was precisely for this reason that I felt most free to call him FN. It had no significance to call him FN. DLN would have reflected a personal distance that did not exist, simply because there was no personal relationship. The FN was for convenience's sake.

Thus, somewhat paradoxically, it was only in a relationship that was of the sort one would expect between teacher and student that I could use FN. There was really no paradox: since the relationship was strictly teacher-student, I was no more threatened by FN than my parents' friends were. And since I was willing to be a student, perhaps, this teacher didn't feel that I was trying to get inappropriately personal.

If it sounds as if graduate students are under the thumbs of powerful and devious professors, that is sometimes true. But the professors have their troubles too. As is the case in all walks of life, the academic world has some back-stabbing; furthermore, almost everyone is scrambling hard to make a reputation and keep it, so there isn't much time for a shared life of the mind. The notion of a community of scholars is usually no more than a notion. So it is not surprising that professors attempt to have intellectual relationships involving cooperative endeavors without constant competition and one-upmanship.

But recall that we haven't any social practices for dealing with adolescents—we have to borrow them from those we have for dealing with children and adults. Similarly, the so-called intellectual relationship is not easily attained; most of us do not have the appropriate behaviors at our disposal. We do not *know how*, for example, to disagree strongly with someone without either hurting their feelings or fearing we have hurt them. And most of us don't know how to take criticism that is not to be taken personally. This inability may stem in part from the fact that most criticism doesn't come off right, and that is because the critic doesn't know how to do it without implicating the person as well as his works.

As Ossorio has said, if the situation calls for something we don't know how to do, we will do something we do know how to do. In this case, people may try for an impersonal intellectual criticism, but it "comes out" as coldness and unfriendliness. Or it affects the person being criticized as if it were (merely) coldness and unfriendliness. And it is impossible to determine who is at fault, the critic or the criticized, although a person who has been a successful critic for many years (i.e., one who can criticize without hurting) may legitimately believe that the one person in a hundred who breaks down in tears is in fact unusually sensitive.

On a more general level, if a person doesn't know how to offer an intellectual relationship, he will offer the kind of relationship he does know how to offer, in this case friendship. Because friendship is inappropriate in this and other similar situations, where there is not only a status differential but a power relationship, it is no wonder that the inferior, contrary to Brown's law, sometimes attempts to back off.

This is all I have to say about name calling in the academic life. I could detail my experiences as a teacher, but no new principles would be brought forth. For example, for a year I taught at a college that was going downhill in many respects (as many small colleges are) and which had a huge inferiority complex. There the status gradations were rigidly held through naming behavior. There were DLNs, who had the Ph.D., there were PLNs, who didn't but were close, and there were MLNs, who were Instructors and not close. This is another example of using word magic. Teaching at Seven Sisters College is an entirely different experience. Students, unlike the students at the other two institutions where I have taught, do not want to get on a FN basis with you. They have ambition, and they know they are bright and very hard-working, and they don't want to be taught by a FN or even by a MLN. They want the best, and in the best verbal clothing. That is yet another example of belief in word magic. I think the various principles I have suggested would hold for other situations besides the academic one.

Let us now consider briefly romantic-sexual relationships. Brown and others have commented upon the use of *mother* or *father* by husbands and wives who have lost (temporarily or permanently) their status as husbands and wives. Here I will focus on less dead relationships.

It is a big step in a relationship to say, "I love you." Equally big is the first use of terms of endearment (*sweetheart, darling,* the blander *dear,* the secretly financial *precious,* the clearly regressive *baby,* the orally regressive *honey*). In the beginning the more neutral *sweetheart* or *darling* appears to be used, being most unambiguously terms of endearment and being (perhaps therefore) the most tender of those listed above.

Why are such names used? As I mentioned, multiple names are often applied to our best friends (Brown and Ford, 1961). Several explanations of that phenomenon were offered in Chapter Four, and it could be that they apply here. That is, these words could indicate fascination or word magical exploration. I also suggested, however, that sometimes, especially with couples who have been together for some time, it seems as if they are denial of function euphemisms or avoidances of the real name.

We are now in a position to put that interpretation alongside a more favorable one for comparison. As we have seen, using a more generic term for a human being than his or her name may indicate that the interest in that human is so intense that the generic term must be used to depersonalize the situation sufficiently so that it can be handled. This could be the case here.

However, that interpretation would imply that people in love eventually attempt to reduce the intensity of the love. It could be that it is more appropriate to look at love as something that needs to be expressed, and that terms of endearment provide a means for expressing love. That interpretation is more consonant with our experience of love, which indicates that at first at least such terms are used with much tenderness. That they may later be overused and used to avoid the real name is not denied by the above argument. In fact, they have several possible uses:

The wife who says to her husband, "But *dear,* you were stumbling around so, of course you were drunk," may be described as word magically attempting to show she really isn't mad, which puts the husband in a bind. She clearly is mad, but the use of a term of endearment makes it difficult for him to react directly to her anger.

Or they may be used as *mother* and *father:* When they have a relationship that operates so automatically that they have ceased to respond to each other as human beings, the use of the given name would be a shock. (It would be almost like addressing oneself with one's FN.) And I have observed in older married couples that they use the FN only when they are mad (and also perhaps when they feel some of the old tenderness, but I haven't been around for that). In other words, the real name of the person is used only when one has to deal with the person in a new way, and not when one is dealing with one's partner is a programmed relationship.

Finally, such terms can be used when it looks like the relationship is very bad. To say *sweetheart* pleadingly is a word magical plea for the relationship to return to its former state when the term was entirely appropriate.

It would be wise not to lose sight of the fact that most of the time names are used in a habitual manner and that most of the time the people using them are not attempting to express or even mirror the power structure, the nature of a relationship, or anything else. In this chapter I have chosen to lose sight of that fact in the interests of investigating some of the possible factors operating in naming behavior. But I did suggest that examination of an individual's naming behavior would allow us to make some statements about him. We have seen some examples of this process. For example, I have described a student who addressed a professor by FN as a brash young punk. In general, the attributions we make on the basis of a person's naming behavior are similar to, and are made on the same bases as the attributions we make on the basis of a person's other behavior. To make it clear that we are not always making metaphysical statements when we say, "Hi, Fred. How's the boy?" (any more than we are expressing our view that nouns and verbs bifurcate reality when we use nouns and verbs), let me conclude this chapter with another personal note.

The kind of person who would pay as much attention to naming behavior as I have and who would be as fascinated by the few pieces of evidence gathered to date (not every psychologist I know considers this work by Brown and his associates to be of major importance and elegance) is clearly the kind of person who would make too much of things in this area. A person who is probably rather suspicious about human relationships. Fortunately, I can play more than one language game. We all have heard the story about the psychiatrist who receives a friendly good morning and says to himself, "I wonder what he meant by that." In real life psychiatrists don't do that any more than I attempt to analyze every name I am called and every name I call.

chapter seven

Style

In the first part of this chapter I attempt to apply some of the concepts we have been using in this book to the notion of style. In the second, I discuss two good studies of style and report briefly on a number of less ambitious but much more representative studies.

Ossorio has discussed style functions (1969). They are similar to traits and trait functions except that he considers them preemptive. That is, a style function is always present, not just excessively present. We shall modify this notion somewhat in the course of our discussion.

Style is an aspect of the performance parameter of intentional action, in Ossorio's analysis. We say that two people differ in styles when they perform the same intentional action in different ways.

For example, consider the intentional action that consists of saying, in a proper context, "Please pass the salt." P performs this intentional action with a southern accent. O performs it with a Brooklyn accent.

There is no problem here. There will be no debate whether P and O did the same thing. We will now and forever expect P to speak with a southern accent and O with a Brooklyn accent.

Consider the following two performances, both of which are descriptions of the performative aspects of (what we are here calling) the same intentional action, "showing defiance."

1. P put his thumb face up on the underside of his nose, then quickly flipped the thumb at O.

2. P said to O gravely, "I defy you."

If style is the way a person does something that other people do differently, what is this something? That is the crucial question. Here we have said it is "showing defiance."

But many people do not consider nose-thumbing an appropriate way of showing defiance. They would describe the whole behavior as "childish gesturing" or "inappropriate behavior for an adult under any circumstances."

Other people would not consider 2. a sufficiently strong performance to be considered a way of showing defiance. Such people would perhaps say, "But I'd laugh in his face."

Notice that people who reject 1. or 2. do so on the grounds that the performance is not of the sort that *could* accomplish the showing of defiance.

For these people, 1. and 2. are not stylistic variations on a theme. Recall when we discussed negotiation the problems we faced in attempting to find a rigorous operational definition of a number of concepts, e.g., *excess, substantial, situation*. We face the same situation here, although it is not a problem: We cannot give a rigorous operational definition of *the same intentional action*.

But it is clear that in some cases two people will agree that a behavior was carried out in two different ways by two other people. The example of speaking with an accent is close to a model case.

So let us allow that *in the appropriate circumstances* nose-thumbing is an appropriate performance of showing defiance, and in appropriate circumstances so is saying, "I defy you."

The circumstances must be appropriate. For example, it is not showing defiance to thumb one's nose at a cop who has caught you going 100 mph. That is because one of the criterial attributes of defiance must be that the defier must be more right than the person he defies.

Let us change the descriptions somewhat:

1. He showed defiance by making a rude, obscene gesture.

2. He showed defiance by a stately, firm, and powerful but almost gentle verbal gesture.

In what sense are 1. and 2. the same intentional action? They are described as instances of showing defiance. But isn't that like saying that diamonds and skyscrapers are both things?

Clearly not. *Things* is not a generic term for diamonds and skyscrapers, although diamonds and skyscrapers *can* be described as things. Recall that generic terms must have some degree of reality.

So perhaps we may be willing to say two actions are the same if the intentional action description, in this case *showing defiance,* has some degree of reality, i.e., if the performative aspects are not so strong as to wrest all reality from the generic description. By putting it this way, we codify and incorporate individual differences. If *you* don't think *showing defiance* has sufficient reality, then 1. and 2. are not the same actions. Not for *you.*

Following Ossorio, note that describing a behavior as B is a special case of treating that behavior as B. Behaviors are differentiated by differential responses to them (We treat different behaviors differently. Of course. That is a tautology).

Do we treat 1. and 2. differently? Do we show that we take them to be different descriptions by reacting to them differently?

In other words, to put the question in more classical terms, is the difference between 1. and 2. one of style or one of content?

A crucial test: If you are willing to let the generic term *(showing defiance)* stand alone, it is a difference of style. If you think the performance must be specified, the difference is one of content. Of course, there will be many borderline cases here.

If the performance is highly appropriate to the situation, we are more likely to pay attention to the content, i.e., to the fact that defiance has been shown. That is logical. If it is a normal, appropriate way of showing defiance, there is, tautologically, nothing remarkable about the performance and so we are not likely to make comments about style. For example, if one is a P.O.W. requested to give information, thumbing one's nose is highly appropriate, since one knows the dignity of one's person will not be respected. If it were a war in the grand old style (if there were such wars), then it would have been appropriate to say, "I defy you." One's captors would treat this as an expression of courage and bravery and would leave one alone. Today it would be a sign that one was a bit of a fool who had no doubt been reading old romantic war novels, and thus an easy case to crack. In other words, the inappropriate, or not so appropriate, performance attracts attention to itself, and some use of style functions is to be expected, e.g., "He's got an old fashioned concept of war. We can get him with the thumbscrews."

Performance is always part of behavior. If the performance is appropriate to the intentional action, no style attributions will be made. But style, conceived of here as an aspect of the performative parameter of intentional action, is of necessity present in all behavior. It may attract attention, in which case we are likely to make style attributions. That is, we are likely to say something about the person. In such cases, both the intentional action and the performance of it have reality.

If we make a content distinction, we will treat the situations differently: We treat defiance differently than we treat throwing in the towel. If we make a stylistic distinction, we treat the people differently. But if we have two different people, we will treat them differently. If a P.O.W. thumbs his nose at us, we will treat him differently than the P.O.W. who says, "I defy you"—although a case could be made that we would simply adopt two different approaches to breaking down defiance.

But we face the same problem: In what sense are they different treatments of the same thing?

On the other hand, consider a clear content difference (defiance versus surrender). We will treat the two people differently. We won't treat a person who shows defiance in the same way we will treat someone who gives up. So content distinctions lead to differential treatments *and* statements of people. (It looks as if we have another case of LSA IV.)

While there are model cases of stylistic differences and of content differences, these are model cases somewhat different than we have been dealing with previously. For any behavior, we *can* focus on what the person did or on how he did it.

In so-called model cases of content, i.e., where content is of major importance, usually we don't focus on style. For example, consider a newspaper account of a mugging. If A tells B, "I just read this article about a mugging," and B replies, "Oh yeh, how was it written?" we have a case of focusing on style when content seems more appropriate or at least more normal and typical. Why would someone ask about the style in such a case? B must be interested in the style of mugging accounts.

Or consider: A: "Oh, he writes the most beautiful poetry." B: "Oh, yeh? What's he say?" Here B is focusing on content when A implies that style is the important feature of the poetry. Some people are "literal-minded"; I am, for example. Unless a poet has something to say, he bores me, with the exception of poets such as James Joyce, who have studied or are involved in music and whose poetry is musical. There are people who want to know what a symphony is "about." Their question seems strange to me, but then my wanting to know what Yeats is "about" strikes some people as strange.

It is difficult to separate style from content, it has often been said. As we look at the problem here, the difficulty is partially explicated. If any behavior is performed in a certain way, and if we identify style with the performative aspects of behavior, then we must also point out that there is more to behavior than the performative aspect. *Showing defiance,* the intentional action, involves the behaver's knowing what it is to show defiance, wanting to, and being able to. (This approach is borrowed from Ossorio.) Traditionally psychology has been broken up into areas, each of which studies one aspect of behavior. So we have the psychological study of motivation, for example.

"P showed defiance" is what Ossorio would call an achievement description. That is, it focuses on what P accomplished and deletes how he did it, what he thought he was doing, the abilities he brought to the task, what he was trying to do. If that description has reality, style and content are integrated completely for that behavior.

If there is to be any disintegration, then people will be the ones who do it. That is, they will demand a more complete description. They may ask, "But why did he want to do that?" Such a question would be understandable if there was something strange about showing defiance in that context (e.g., why would he want to defy his parents who love him so?), *or* if there was something strange about the person asking the question (e.g., if he were a very submissive, passive person who could never understand defiance).

Or people may ask, "Well, how did he do it?" Such a question would be understandable from someone who was interested in style or who wanted to know something about the person who showed defiance, or if the situation was one in which it would take a very good performance to successfully show defiance.

In other words, style is an aspect of behavior we can (and often do) attend to. So is content. Sometimes it seems a little silly to attend to one or the other. Often we accept achievement descriptions, which may be looked at not as content descriptions, nor as style descriptions, but style-content descriptions. Under normal circumstances, the separation of style and content is unnecessary, queer, or something people do with an unusual aim in mind, e.g., the study of style.

An important analogy here: Recall that the Hopi cannot refer to space and time independently, and that we very often don't either. Usually space is time and time is space; we make space-time statements. Sometimes it is necessary to play a language game that requires that we speak of space without reference to time, but that doesn't make space and time independent or separate. Nor does it make them dependent and together, for to speak that way is to imply that there are two separate entities. We as people do separate them when necessary; when necessary or convenient we don't separate them.

This analogy provides another clue as to when we will separate style from content. Style and content can be congruent with each other, or they may be incongruent. When they are incongruent, then we are likely to notice style.

A schizophrenic sends incongruent messages to avoid or deny relationships with other people. That is, his incongruence helps him to say nothing. But Haley uses incongruence, in the essay discussed in Chapter One, to say something that couldn't be said with a congruent message. In the next section, we will explore incongruence further.

The Uses of Incongruence of Style

Incongruence (opposition) of style and content allows a writer or a speaker to say things that could not be said with a literal utterance (or a combination of them). By literal utterance we shall mean one where style and content are harmonious, and where the style is, in addition, inobtrusive. I do not consider the style and content of James Joyce or William Faulkner incongruent but both authors have very strong styles and do not speak literally.

Hemingway is a good example of a writer whose style and content are at odds with each other. Hemingway is a romantic. His books are famous for their love affairs; his most famous books involve famous love affairs, and his less famous books do not have central love affairs (I consider his famous books to be *The Sun Also Rises, A Farewell to Arms,* and *For Whom the Bell Tolls;* I omit *The Old Man and the Sea,* because I cannot bring myself to believe Hemingway wrote it).

His content, considered here in the rather naked sense of his plots, is sentimental and loaded with love. He has an equally sentimental insistence that suffering, imposed from outside by war or bad people, is necessary for love to exist. Love is beautiful, but it ends, again because of the outside world. Love has beautiful and very significant sex (*The Sun Also Rises* is an exception), tenderness, intense awareness of the other, beautiful settings, truth, and good wine. It is not the love of today's movies and novels, flawed by selfishness, insanity, or degeneracy. It is not possessive and grasping, as marriage is so often portrayed today. And it is certainly not dull, stolid, contented, complacent, or happy. The lovers never have time to relax and get into a rut (or groove, to balance the negative term with a positive term). (In fact, in *The Sun Also Rises,* Jake and Lady Brett have literally no time, which makes it the most romantic of Hemingway's romantic novels.) I think it is fair to say that there is no other love in American literature, movies, or legend that is as unflawed as Hemingway's.

Yet, Hemingway heroes and heroines, the people who are eligible for this kind of love, are hardly sentimental types. They are seldom permitted to say tender nothings (and never permitted to say tender somethings); if possible they refer to their feelings so obliquely that it sounds as if they are talking about the weather. They follow certain rules: one doesn't discuss one's relationship. Men must not show emotions directly, and if one is to die tomorrow, one must be silent about it—and, more important—without everyone within miles hearing the silence. One's passions are rather cool. One would hardly grunt and groan. Generally speaking, one doesn't talk too much.

The non-heroes are the talkers. They are people who would go on all night to their loved one or confidant about how deep and profound their love is, who would show panic and agony if danger was near or if their loved one had to leave for a time. They are people who would discourse on the nature of love, who would write love poems in letters, who would write sonnets to Love. In short, they are the kind of people who fall in love easily. The heroes have more important things on their minds and no time.

But here's the rub: Hemingway writes sentimental novels about unrealistic love. Hemingway is the culture's model case of a *man,* a man who spent much of his life in "manly" pursuits (war, hunting, fishing). His heroes do the same.

There is an incongruent message here, for his novels are read for their love interest. This love interest is not "thrown in" as a subplot to keep those who like such things happy; it is central to his three most famous novels.

So we have on the one hand the notion that what counts is being a man and on the other the notion that what counts is love. But one cannot focus on love and be a man. A man (and Hemingway's best women too) must have something better than mere personal love to focus on. A man doesn't seek his own gratification—that would be childish and self-indulgent. A man does what he has to do; usually that is not sitting around writing love poetry. Which is what Hemingway did, making him incongruent, a lie unto himself, a man who refused to recognize the childish, dependent, love- and security-starved romantic that he really was.

But this is of course completely unfair. The above account neglects style, and we shall have to examine what that means before we can attempt a translation of Hemingway.

Ernest Jones wrote perhaps the best known psychoanalytic interpretation of a work of literature, *Hamlet and Oedipus.* Hamlet, it seems, had an Oedipus complex. How dull. I have over-simplified Jones' argument, but I will show later why that is unimportant. If you reduce *Hamlet* to the most complex Oedipal Drama, what is all the poetry for? Why the apparent complexity of the language and the metaphor, why the richness and profusion of ideas? Why did Shakespeare go to all that trouble if all he wanted to talk about was an Oedipal complex, even a complex one? Why this icing on the cake?

Psychoanalysis has an answer. We dream of forbidden things. We are allowed to if and only if we agree to disguise our forbidden wishes. All that is not Oedipal in *Hamlet* is this kind of disguise—ideas to distract the attention from the central idea (sleeping with mother), poetry to lull the censor to sleep, and other such rot.

Literary critics look down on psychoanalytic interpretations because they cannot deal with the unique way that a certain work of art expresses whatever it has to express. That is, they ignore style. They treat all works dealing with mothers and sons as variations on the Oedipal theme, as if we had in this culture a myth (which is no more than a plot) told by various myth-tellers, each of whom has his individual *(non-essential)* idiosyncracies. Such interpretations do not take style into account. This failure is particularly dangerous when one attempts to apply psychoanalytic interpretation to the content of a writer who has a style that contradicts the content.

Psychoanalysis attempts to find a "reality" that is inappropriately significant. Golf isn't really hitting a ball around any more than *Hamlet* is really just about Oedipal complexes.

Compare "hitting a white ball around" with "flogging a helpless little white ball around a cow pasture with first one stick and then another." Both are insignificant descriptions, although the second sounds like a more complete description. Similarly, no matter how complex Jones' psychoanalytic interpretation of *Hamlet*, it won't be adequately significant. The differences between *Hamlet* and similar "Oedipal" works of art are not non-essential quirks of style. One cannot understand *Hamlet* unless one deals with all its aspects.

It is also true that writers often look down on literary critics, and for similar reasons. To a certain extent this is unavoidable: if one of the jobs of a critic is to try to figure out what the writer is trying to say, no matter how well he does it, he couldn't say what Hemingway said because he wouldn't be saying it in Hemingway's style.

What *did* Hemingway say? He said *The Sun Also Rises, A Farewell to Arms, For Whom the Bell Tolls.* Nothing more, nothing less. If he had had more to say he would have said it. If he had had less to say, he wouldn't have said all he did. Given this argument, the question of what Hemingway said seems less felicitous than: Why did he say these books *this* way?

There are a number of things Hemingway is studiously not saying. He is not saying that love won't come to you if you look for it (or rave over an iota of it). But love comes in his best novels only to those who don't look for it. We can see the insincerity and incongruity of those who do look for it. Being in love with Love precludes loving a person.

Why didn't Hemingway come right out and say that? If he had, he would have shown himself to be the kind of person who is serious about love and Love, and he therefore wouldn't be eligible to write about love, since people who write about love can never understand love.

Hemingway also is not saying that love comes only to those who have larger purposes in life. He is not saying that people who are weak and dependent can't love or be loved. This is certainly *the case* in his novels and stories. Love seems to be something some people are lucky enough to have if they are strong enough and if they are not squalid and degenerate and not spending their time enjoying themselves. What could love be or mean for one who lives in luxury and for nothing? Love comes as a contrast to war. It cannot exist, we see, in a time of peace and comfort.

Why couldn't he come out and say *that*? What would have been the case then?

It would have sounded as if he valued love, and love is clearly nothing to value but to have and to hold as long as you can and not a minute longer. And it would hardly have done to place love above war or war above love or make any sort of calibration of that sort. Both were simply there.

In order for me to say the things I am saying now, pointing out these things that seem to be true about love that Hemingway said, although he didn't, he had to send just the incongruent message he did send. Without the romantic overtones it wouldn't have been love. Without the somewhat contradictory cool attitude towards love by those who truly love it wouldn't have been love.

Hemingway also didn't say a number of things about war, very similar to the things he didn't say about love; in Hemingway's work love and war are related in much the same way that style and content or time and space are related.

In Chapter One I demonstrated that Jay Haley was able to say something that couldn't be said otherwise by using an incongruent style. In this chapter I have attempted to demonstrate that Hemingway has said something that couldn't be said literally. Let me close this section of the chapter with a more mundane example.

Sarcasm is not uncommon. It often is mistaken for nastiness, and it may in truth hurt people's feelings. It is also indirect. Why aren't people more direct and honest?

A teacher tells his high school or college class that they did very well on a test on which they obviously did poorly. He takes a rather sarcastic tone when he says it. In other words he says one thing and means the opposite.

But does he mean the opposite? What is the opposite of, "You did very well on this test."? It is hard to say. It could be that the class did very poorly. Or perhaps they did somewhat less well than the teacher thought they should, although very well compared to most classes.

The teacher does not have to commit himself in this respect. While humans do not always assume the worst, the worst is a possibility if no degree is specified. So the class might be motivated a good deal more than if the teacher had told them "the truth," e.g., "You didn't do as well as I expected you to do, given that you are very bright and I am a great teacher, so I am saddened, but you did better than most classes could." Or if the class did very badly, sarcasm might help the teacher express his frustration without hurting the students' feelings, since the teacher is, after all, only joking around. Thus sarcasm has its very good uses.

Sarcasm has another great value within the framework of this example. It is not appropriate, and is probably not productive, for a teacher to show hostility to a class. After all, to a certain extent whatever the class does is his doing. Sarcasm allows the teacher to release some hostility and at the same time deny that he is doing so. The hostility may help to motivate the students, and they will not be able to hate the teacher, since he is, after all, only joking around (assuming he is in sufficient control to keep his sarcasm from being vicious).

I will conclude this section with a brief and partially facetious discussion of the values of indirect communication to two of our most notorious and beloved occupational groups. Doctors act cold and lawyers act like crooks. I think a doctor would have good reason to act cold. Patients are overly dependent. Probably if they weren't, they wouldn't be coming down with so many psychosomatic diseases. Coldness helps patients learn independence (even if this comes at the price of hating doctors and refusing to go to them) and allows the doctor some release from having to play Dr. Welby to everyone. Dr. Welby has only one patient at a time. This is not true of all doctors, they tell me. Lawyers have to earn a living helping dishonest, lying, cheating, nogoods. Acting somewhat crooked (while of course denying it) reminds the clients that they are dealing with an expert at tricks, and thus may keep clients from trying to pull fast ones on their lawyers. It also allows the lawyer release from his own sorrow at being a lawyer rather than the very clever crook he could have been (the comparison between his cleverness and that of his clients pains him daily).

Empirical Work on Style

If style is to be studied empirically, quantification is required, and also some operational definitions of style. Typically, "indices" of style have been employed, e.g., the number of nouns per 100 words, the ratio of different words used to total number of words used.

I will discuss the general issue of the use of indices to study style, as there are many problems.

Style is not perceived or described in quantitative terms. While an art critic might speak of "extreme use of dark colors," a literary critic does not speak of "extreme use of adjectives." Literary style is described in more global concepts.

Furthermore, if writers and literary critics reject psychoanalytic interpretations of literature, they surely should reject quantitative interpretations of style. The statement, "What makes Hemingway different from Faulkner is that he uses more verbs, more active constructions, and he has a low type-token ratio," will not be taken as an adequate differentiation of the styles of the two authors, any more than the following statement will be taken as an adequate differentiation of the writers' content: "Hemingway writes of the castration complex, while Faulkner's major theme is incest." (Although, as an amateur psychoanalyst, I like the latter statement.)

Content is ignored by most quantitative indices of style, just as style is ignored by psychoanalytic interpretations of literature. Given that it makes little or no sense to study one independently of the other, the usual quantitative indices may never prove of value. Furthermore, unless the ordinary language meaning of *style* is preserved to some extent in the indices, the studies will not be studies of style, although they will indeed be studies of the percentage of adjectives or the number of active constructions.

Carroll's study, discussed in detail below, gives additional grounds for pessimism. He compared objective, numerical, word-count indices of prose passages with judgmental ratings of the passages on a number of semantic differential scales which he thought had some relevance to style, e.g., *intimate-remote, natural-affected, emotional-rational*. He found little relationship between the two types of measures.

In defense of the objective indices, however, the judgmental measures do not get at the essence of style any more than do the objective measures. A writer or critic would object—I hope—to the statement, "What makes Hemingway's style different from Faulkner's is that it is more remote, more affected, and more rational." The objection to the statement would probably center around its total avoidance of substantive matters (e.g., the world view often said to be mirrored in style). The objective measures also ignore content, but they are straightforwardly measures of performance.

Perhaps more distressing is another of Carroll's findings. He factor analyzed a matrix of correlations between a large number of measures of style. The first and most important factor was called General Stylistic Evaluation. That is, the main thing about style that people perceive is whether they like it or not. The implication is that style may "ultimately be found to" consist of a mixed bag of popularity contest guidelines, and I find this implication distressing. It is always unpleasant to find the evaluative factor lurking around accounting for most of the variance, but particularly so when it lurks around the finest achievement of humanity (or so it is often called)—literature and the use of language to its fullest capacity.

The above are general problems. For more specific problems, let us discuss the Adjective-Verb Quotient (AVQ), used in 1940 by Boder and now a staple of studies of style.

The AVQ is the number of adjectives per 100 verbs. Boder feels that verbs can be considered neutral in import, or at least necessary: They are necessary for the construction of simple grammatical sentences, while adjectives are not. An AVQ of 50 would indicate that the author had used 50 adjectives for every 100 verbs.

Boder related the mean AVQs of types of writing to their characteristics and requirements. For example, plays had a low AVQ (11.2). This "makes sense," since plays consist of dialogue, which probably has fewer adjectives than written language. Scientific language had a high AVQ (75.5). This makes sense for descriptive sciences but not for highly mathematical sciences such as physics. Business letters were low (18.5), as befits the prescription for their style that they get directly and tersely to the point. H. L. Mencken's writing was high (72.2), as would be expected from a writer of bombastic, complex thoughts.

Boder's results do fit perceived or known differences between types of writing. They do not tell us anything we do not already know, however. Nor do they explain anything we already know.

This is true of most indices of style; criticisms of the AVQ apply generally.

Maher (1966) has reviewed studies of the language of schizophrenics and other varieties of mental illness. He suggests that a low AVQ indicates low qualification as compared to action, which seems reasonable and tautological enough. Anxiety patients have a low AVQ, which has been interpreted as reflective of their active fantasies. An equally plausible explanation is that anxiety neurotics are in too much of a hurry for elaboration, and must get to the point quickly. Conversion hysterics have a high AVQ, which could be considered reflective of their lower manifest anxiety and well known tendencies for drama and hyperbole. Two studies have shown that schizophrenics have lower than normal AVQs, which could be reflective of their supposed lack of contact with or interest in reality, i.e., they do not care enough to bother with elaboration, description, or qualification, which are common chores of adjectives.

These studies are of no more scientific value than Boder's. Known features of a group are reflected by the AVQ. However, all of the above explanations relating AVQ to mental condition except the first are my own. They are therefore speculative. I do not know, for example, if the group of hysterics showed the textbook tendencies for drama and hyperbole. It should also be pointed out that I related the AVQ to just one "symptom" belonging to a diagnostic category, and that the symptom I picked for relating to the AVQ was whichever one I could think of that I could so relate. That is, the selection was done on a purely *ad hoc* basis. That the interpretation of these findings is more problematical than the interpretation of Boder's reflects the state of confusion that reigns over mental illness and diagnostic categorization.

In addition, there is a basic ambiguity in the index that makes it difficult to use even as a simple "reflection" of known characteristics. A high AVQ may mean few adjectives or many verbs. This ambiguity leads to more substantive ones. It cannot be determined if a low AVQ indicates a highly active, dynamic style (many verbs) or a hurried, anxious, uninformative style (few adjectives). Furthermore, it cannot be determined if a high AVQ indicates a style which reflects the complexity of the world, is deliberate, informative, and sensitive to shades of meaning; or whether it indicates a style that is pointlessly ornate; or one that elaborates to occupy space or to stave off anxiety. These last three styles could be very different, but all would have a high AVQ.

Thus a given numerical value of an AVQ is subject to multiple interpretations, many of which are likely to be contradictory. We can't decide which to use unless we already know the material. We choose one interpretation for the hysteric's high AVQ, but another for Mencken, because of what we know about hysterics and Mencken.

Even worse, we do not choose from several possible interpretations. We make up interpretations as we go along. Why should a high AVQ indicate hysteria? Hysterics are dramatic. So AVQs should be high for dramatic writings. But they are low for plays. This is because plays consist of dialogue. And so on, in meaningless circles. The whole process is totally *ad hoc.* The AVQ is too crude.

But let us consider whether it does indeed even do such a simple thing as measure degree of qualification. The number of adjectives is compared to the number of verbs because the verb is a neutral part of speech. But verbs have just as descriptive a function as adjectives and are used to make as many and as fine discriminations as adjectives. In a sense, we may view the use of many adjectives as reflective of an inability to come up with the right noun. If you used the right noun, you wouldn't need adjectives. Thus a choice of the perfect verb may represent a great degree of discriminating thinking.

In addition, there is no limit on the number of verbs that may occur in a simple sentence. If we wish to say many things about an object, we can put many adjectives before the noun. But if we wish to say many things about what an object is doing, we may use a string of verbs. Most damning is the consideration that the use of many verbs may in itself be of psychological significance.

There is no part of speech that can be considered neutral or as an adequate anchoring point for making statements about the usage of various other parts of speech.

(Technically speaking, any part of speech used in the divisor should not be considered a constant, as in the case of the AVQ, but as a random variable. The AVQ is more similar to a ratio mean than it is to a mean. This same criticism applies to an alternative approach to the construction of indices: the categorization of words into parts of speech, after which each part is compared with the total number of words used. This method gives many more points at which to analyze a style or compare two styles; but the divisor is still best considered a random variable, although it should have a lower standard deviation.)

Indices such as the AVQ can be used most accurately for comparing a small number of styles with each other. Perhaps our major concern with style is with the case history. For example, what is unique about Shakespeare? What's that essential nugget that makes him Shakespeare? And it is this analysis of a single style that will be impossible without some kind of comparison or normative data.

It is unlikely that completely satisfactory normative data will ever be collected, since there is no paradigm case of normal writing, nor is there such a concept. However, if styles of the same genre are compared, part of the problem of multiple interpretations of an index result is removed. If differences are found between the styles of contemporary comic novels, variations in index figures can with more validity be explained as variations on one dimension.

Some (completely or nearly) objective, nonjudgmental indices have been employed which combine the virtues of both objective and non-objective indices. For example, Carroll used percentage of Latinate verbs and action verbs. These indices are not subject to much error, and get at more "global" concepts. For example, Latinate words are considered to be less direct and more abstract than Anglo-Saxon words; the above qualities have been used by Carroll as non-objective, judmental dimensions; there is some evidence that Latinate words have the effect he attributes to them.

With this background concerning problems of measurement of style, two of the most ambitious studies in this area will be discussed.

Carroll has done a study he entitles "Vectors of Prose Style." The implication of the title is that the study will indicate along what dimensions style varies, i.e., the nature of the differences between styles.

Unfortunately, Carroll took an extremely varied sample of styles, ranging over two centuries, and including American and English sermons, biographies, scientific papers, letters, legal documents, speeches, textbooks, etc. One would not be surprised to find genre-specific factors, and nearly as many factors as there are genres in the study. Content is difficult to empirically distinguish from style; if style is the object of study, it would appear best to keep genre or content variation at a minimum. Unless this is done, we are likely to arrive at a conclusion no more significant than that styles vary according to genre, e.g., that poetry has a different style than prose.

Aside from the triviality of conclusions of this sort, they say nothing about style itself. That is, we can say that this style is different than that one, but not what this style is like and how it is different from that one.

A better approach would be to separately factor analyze variables taken from various kinds of writing, particularly if the variables for each genre were hand-picked (because there is no reason to expect the dimensions of style to be the same for all kinds of writing). Then indices of factorial similarity could be applied. However, Carroll did not find genre-specific factors, and his measures appear relatively content-free, so perhaps his results are not all trivial. However, his shotgun approach resembles Osgood's, and it does appear that he is getting at something like the connotations of style rather than style itself, just as Osgood gets at the connotative meanings of words rather than at what they mean.

In Carroll's study, judges rated 150 passages of prose on

scales considered to be relevant to style, e.g., *intimate-remote, natural-affected, subtle-obvious, precise-vague.* Some of the scales are not so obviously appropriate to style, if the attempt is to isolate style from content: *good-bad, pleasant-unpleasant, profound-superficial, interesting-boring.*

Objective measures of the prose were also obtained, e.g., percentage of indefinite articles, sentence length, number of clauses, percentage of action verbs.

All measures were correlated, and the resulting matrix was factor analyzed. Orthogonal factors were extracted by verimax rotation.

The factors are arranged in order of variance accounted for, i.e., in importance.

The first factor, General Stylistic Evaluation, accounted for the most variance. No objective measure had a high loading on this factor. So word counts of various sorts do not predict the most important dimension along which styles vary, goodness of style.

But goodness of style is not style. This factor is not a dimension of style, but rather a dimension of observer-style interaction. Styles do of course differ in the extent to which people like them, but this is a black box that must be opened rather than an interesting fact about style. That is, we would like to know what exactly it is about a style that makes it good. Such trivial findings are what you get if you ask people to rate style on dimensions that are not dimensions of style. You cannot expect to find the vectors of prose style if you ask people to rate a passage's content, as you most certainly do when you ask them whether it is profound or superficial or interesting or boring.

The second factor was called Personal Affect. Judgmental variables defining this factor included *intimate-remote* and *emotional-rational.* Percentage of Latin verbs loaded $-.33$, giving empirical support to the notion that Latin words sound impersonal or dry.

However, this loading may be an artifact of the fact that scientific writing tends to try to sound objective, rational, and impersonal, and tends therefore to use Latinate words. Latin verbs may not have an impersonal feel except in scientific and other professional writings, which are impersonal in a larger sense (and also due to other "tricks").

A problem with factor analysis of a heterogeneous sample of materials is that a strong correlation between variables in a subset of the sample may cause a loading that would have been much lower if the subset had been left out. So if science is impersonal and uses Latinate words, little of significance is demonstrated about Latinate words, since science would remain impersonal if it used Anglo-Saxon words.

Other objective measures loading on this factor were number of personal pronouns (.60); one usually expresses personal affect with personal pronouns; and percentage of cognitive verbs (.46); readers should find thought more personal than action. Other objective measures that did load made less obvious sense.

This factor is more of a dimension of style than is General Stylistic Evaluation, but it is partially observer-style-content interaction, and as such is not unlike the evaluative factor, in that people like personal interaction, even if with a book. (Technically speaking, if oblique factors had been selected, I would expect Personal Affect to correlate highly with General Stylistic Evaluation.)

Furthermore, it is unlikely that legal writers or scientists have any desire to sound cold and impersonal. The impersonality is an artifact of the formal requirements for style in these areas. Since it is expected, it is doubtful that a reader would feel any impersonality. Therefore, it is not clear what kind of impersonality this factor represents. Impersonality is not a stylistic variable if it is entirely appropriate to the situation; only if it is optional. Again, this difficulty of interpretation arises due to the heterogeneity of the sample of prose passages.

The third factor was called Ornamentation, defined by such judgmental variables as *wordy-succinct, lush-austere, elegant-uncouth, affected-natural, opinionated-impartial, complex-simple,* and *florid-plain.* Note that some of the variables defining this factor are highly evaluative, but that ornamentation is not clearly bad or good. For example, ornamentation is correlated with elegance, but also with affectation; with wordiness, but also with lushness. Thus this is a dimension of style in a sense that the first two are not. People can agree that a style has ornamentation but disagree on how good it is. Similarly, people can agree that the animal standing in front of them is a dog but disagree on how much they like it. Such a state of affairs gives us some confidence that a feature of style has been isolated. Furthermore, ornamentation is a concept that is often used to describe styles, which is not the case with the first two factors.

Several of the objective measure loadings make sense. Sentence length loads .54; ornamentation implies addition and proliferation. *Number* of clauses loads $-.60$; since the prose passages were of equal length, clause *length,* like sentence length, should have a positive loading, as it obviously does. Number of action verbs loads $-.40$; an ornamental style is not characterized by fast paced movement of events. Descriptive adjectives load .38; proliferation of description is part of what is meant by an ornamental style. The loadings of these objective measures are not surprising or revealing. If they weren't as they are, we would doubt if the factor was correctly named.

As with Personal Affect, there is some problem in identifying the nature of the ornamentation the factor represents. It could be a rich, romantic, lush view of the world, a stylistic requirement of a genre such as sermons, or flourishes for no purpose (such as might be expected from hysterics). However, while ornamentation undoubtedly plays a different role in different language games, it seems much more likely in this case that the various forms of ornamentation could appropriately be described as having a family resemblance.

The fourth factor was Abstractness, which was defined by such judgmental variables as *profound-superficial, subtle-obvious, abstract-concrete, hazy-clear, vague-precise,* and *complex-simple.* This seems to be clearly a content factor, although the loadings of *hazy-clear, vague-precise,* and *original-trite* tend to indicate the attitude people have towards abstract discourse. Again, it could be the abstractness of a philosophical theory or of a schizophrenic.

The fifth factor was called Seriousness. Its only really strong loading was, unsurprisingly, by *serious-humorous*. As was the case with Abstractness, none of the few moderately high loadings by objective indices makes much sense. This is a content factor or a genre factor or perhaps even an author factor, but it is not a stylistic factor (Not that it wouldn't be interesting to know what makes for what we call a humorous style).

The sixth factor was called Characterization. The justification for this name is not clear to me. This factor was composed almost entirely of the objective measures, showing the segregation of the judgmental and the objective measures. As a technical aside, this probably resulted from high intercorrelations between objective measures. Such correlations could be spuriously high, since they are not independent measures. If the percentage of nouns is 60%, the percentage of verbs can't be higher than 40%.

The factors which are mainly defined by judgmental measures are not purely stylistic, i.e., they are also (either entirely or in part) content, personality, genre, or observer-style interaction factors. For this reason, it is not surprising that the objective measures, which for the most part *cannot* reflect such "extraneous" aspects of written prose, did not show much relation to the non-objective measures. It is interesting in this regard that the factor with the most loadings over .20 (absolute value) by objective measures is the one that is most purely stylistic in nature (Ornamentation). This suggests that there is some hope in finding word count correlates of global judgments of style, if one can but find the proper variables.

The objective measures had, in many cases, quite respectable split-half reliabilities, although the significance of this is mitigated somewhat by the fact that the passages were continuous. Even so, it suggests that writers use the language in a consistent fashion and that this consistency is measurable. The use of objective indices may prove fruitful. If there were no such reliability, e.g., if Joe the Lawyer didn't use about the same number of noun clauses per 100 words all the time, the objective study of style would be impossible. A great deal of work is based on this assumption of reliability, e.g., studies purporting to show proof of authorship.

Objective measures, for all their flaws, do measure aspects of the technique of language use and therefore are not infected with anything else. If there is any style to be isolated from everything else, it will be done only with objective indices.

Gilman and Brown, in an excellent and imaginative comparison of the styles of Emerson and Thoreau, asked, "Is it possible to distinguish the styles of two writers living in the same time and place, educated at the same school, writing in the same genre, on the same topic, voicing the same opinion, with nothing but their personalities to keep them apart?" As they point out, it is not only the topics and opinions that match, but the arguments and philosophies of life and living. Furthermore, they make a distinction between style as "purpose" (prescriptions and proscriptions on how to write) and style as "personality." Thoreau and Emerson had the same stylistic ideal, i.e., "compression, vitality, and straightline direction." This is yet another variable held constant. All that is left to vary is that portion of verbal behavior which is uniquely bound up with personality. That is, here we have a situation where two people are doing the same thing. Whatever differences we find are bound to be stylistic differences, in the context set forth early in this chapter. Since the two people are very similar in background features, the stylistic differences will be those associated with personality—as distinct from differences produced by or associated with unessential features of human beings such as school and geographical location.

In Carroll's study, we would be more likely to ascribe content differences. Writing a legal brief is not the same as writing poems. Here there are no content differences.

According to the reports of friends and the writers (Thoreau and Emerson) themselves, Thoreau tended to be more aggressive, in the senses of combative and vigorous, than was Emerson, and was analytical and concrete, while Emerson tended to abstraction and synthesis. These were considered the major personality differences between the two.

Thus a study is even more controlled: We will not merely find "personality differences" reflected in stylistic differences, but very specific personality differences. Therefore, it should be possible to tie down the relationship between verbal behavior and non-verbal behavior, in this case personality, much more specifically. We should know, for example, how aggressiveness is expressed in language.

Gilman and Brown found thirty-two matched pairs of topics according to the following criterion: "Passages were judged to constitute a matched pair when it seemed to us that a single proposition would convey the main point of both." The passages were considered "banal" when reduced to propositions. (This illustrates my contention that to reduce a statement to its literal form is to change the significance of the statement, and to do so by robbing it of its [often] most important element, style, which may be at odds with the content as literally stated. Thus it is fortunate that neither Thoreau nor Emerson was an incongruent writer.)

Gilman and Brown give examples from the pairs of topics of differences in styles. But this method depends upon the reader's ability to grasp the concept of style. The crux of the study is a series of sign tests comparing the writers on objective measures hypothesized to be predictive of the differences in personalities. (Technical note: The sign test, of course, does not allow the particularly strong presence of a variable in one or two passages to affect the significance of the comparison.)

Thoreau used more first person pronouns, more *no*'s, *none*'s, and *not*'s, and more instances of *I* combined with a *no, none,* or *not.* Gilman and Brown interpret this to mean that Thoreau is combating ideas he feels are being pushed at him. Thoreau also shows this combativeness by his greater use of conjunctives such as *yet, but,* and *though.* Such conjunctives tend to violate expectations, and as such are combating the reader, or show that the writer is throwing out ideas to fight with.

Thoreau's concreteness compared to Emerson's abstractness is reflected by Thoreau's lower ratio of abstract to concrete nouns, as well as by his greater use of sensory and motor verbs. Emerson often used such verbs, but usually as metaphorical extensions of their concrete meaning.

There were other expectations that were not confirmed at a statistically significant level, but which were in the expected direction. Emerson used more "elevated diction," indicative of his abstraction and withdrawal. Thoreau used more superlatives, all-or-nothing words, exclamation points, and italics, indicative of his vigor and combativeness. (Tehcnical note: The authors point out that using a sign test with 32 passages, and often less, due to ties, requires strong effects for significance, so that these results may be considered weaker real effects, especially since there is no question of replication. However, when one attempts to weasel out of proper use of statistics, one also makes it difficult to generalize to style in general. Unfortunately, the perfect content match between Thoreau and Emerson is so rare as to make generalization pointless. Such matches occur once in a thousand years.)

Thoreau used more direct constructions (e.g., subject-verb-object), while Emerson used more indirect constructions (e.g., "Centrality he has, and penetration"). This is indicative of aggressiveness and directness on Thoreau's part and the lack of these on Emerson's part. Emerson used more archaisms, indicative of lack of directness, abstraction, and withdrawal.

Summing up, Gilman and Brown both say, "When indirection, abstraction, impersonality, and archaisms come together, we have Emerson's extreme manner, the stately, 'composed' style that is farthest removed from Thoreau's tart, personal, concrete manner."

Gilman and Brown have discovered quite objective indices of style that meaningfully correlate with known features of the personalities of two writers. What makes their results especially striking is that these differences were found over 32 passages, which covered a variety of topics. That is, it doesn't seem that Thoreau is more combative stylistically only when combativeness is called for by the content. However, many of the indices of style were not free of the taint of content; the indices were *ad hoc;* and the possibility of replication is limited. While superb, the study cannot be said to advance the study of style.

Representative Studies

In this concluding section I will briefly present the results of a few more representative studies of style, lest the reader be left with the false impression that the empirical, quantitative study of style is, if flawed, quite ambitious and hopeful. The studies of Carroll and of Gilman and Brown have these characteristics, but they are the best two I have seen and head and shoulders above the rest.

All of the following studies come from a relatively recent anthology of quantitative studies of style (Dolezel & Bailey, 1969). The editors have selected the "best efforts" (p. vii) in this area, and I in turn have selected the studies that are the best or at least the most comprehensible. The studies described are therefore not strictly speaking representative, but they do indicate the general level of ambitiousness and conceptual precision prevalent in this area.

Winter (1969) found that word length was longer for scientific writing than for written dialogue. Using this and similarly simple indices of style, he found that in Russian scientific writing was much different from written dialogue and fictional prose, which were highly similar. In German, fiction was not as close to dialogue as in Russian. It was in between scientific writing and dialogue. Winter explains that the spoken language of Russia had a great deal to do with the development of literature, which was not the case in Germany. That's as far as he went.

Bennett (1969) compared Shakespeare's two very different plays *Julius Caesar* and *As You Like It* on one variable: the repetitiousness of common nouns. He finds that the two plays are very similar on this index, which, I take it, implies either that Shakespeare wrote them both or/and writers are reliable in word count measure aspects of their style. Other writers differ a good deal from Shakespeare but have a good deal of cross-passage reliability. The value of the index varies according to the act in *Julius*

Caesar. In an act in which Caesar is killed and not much else happens there is more repetition than in an act with many characters doing many things.

Muller (1969) found a new mathematical formula that is better than Zipf's formula involving the number of times a word is used in a passage. The number of words used once is greater than the number of words used twice. The fascinating question is: How much greater? Muller applies a formula (not his own) and finds it predicts how much greater with more mathematical accuracy than Zipf's formula. I am not sure what one could do with such a formula.

Antosch (1969) employed a measure called the Verb-Adjective Ratio (VAR). It is the number of verbs divided by the number of adjectives. The reader will recognize that this is the reciprocal of the AVQ, so no time will be spent discussing it. Antosch found that the VAR is higher in drama than in epic writing and in theoretical writing. Recall that Boder found that scientific writing was quite high on the AVQ, while drama was quite low. Hence these results should not be surprising. Short speeches delivered with spirit are higher than monologues or longer speeches; novels and stories are higher than scientific and critical works. The VAR is higher in emotional speeches. Boder's work, reported 13 years earlier, was not even cited.

Hayes (1969) found that Gibbon had a more complex style than Hemingway. Gibbon's sentences have been transformed more times from the base structure, have more embedded structures such as relative clauses, nested structures, and expanded structures within them. Gibbon prefers the passive voice, while Hemingway prefers the active. Why anyone would compare the styles of Hemingway and Gibbon is beyond me. Hayes was attempting to show that generative-transformational grammer "has the power to differentiate different styles" (p. 90). And it no doubt does, especially if one compares two very different writers.

Finally, Dreher and Young (1969) found they could tell one Chinese writer from another on the basis of their average phrase lengths. When a particular Chinese writer became a disciple of

Mao, who wished people to write short sentences, he wrote shorter phrases. Thus we have conclusive proof that Mao had some influence in China.

It is clear to me that most of the quantitative work on style, and there has been a good deal of it, is as bad as it is because of the almost total lack of conceptual or theoretical influence on the work. On the other hand, the statements on style by the famous writers and humanists who have commented on it are vague and unsystematic. (Well, if I were a great writer I wouldn't be concerned with developing a rigorous conceptual account of style, so I would toss off such comments as, "the style is the man.") If anybody wants to learn anything new about style, mindless application of indices should stop and some attempt should be made to deal with the theoretical and conceptual problems involved before jumping in with mathematical formulas and computers. I think this chapter has succeeded in making an attempt to integrate the qualitative and the quantitative approaches to style thus far so separate from each other.

chapter eight

Explanations and
Their Vicissitudes

In this chapter we shall examine some of the ways man responds to the question, "Why?" First, let us examine the concept of a question.

Must a question have a question mark after it? Or, in speech, a rise in intonation? Let us say paradigm cases of questions do; let us further say almost all statements may be described as functions of questions and therefore similar to questions, in the specific sense that almost all statements can be challenged.

Finding the question in a statement is similar to finding the meaning of dreams: somewhat absurd but worthwhile. Consider, "I'm going to the store now to pick up some food." Where is the question? The person to whom this statement is delivered might refuse permission, i.e., might act as if a question had been asked. This is often done by people in authority. A child makes a simple declarative statement, and an adult pounces on it. Therefore children often make such seemingly paradigmatic declarative statements in a questioning tone. So simple statements may be treated as questions, and in that sense they are questions.

Consider the domain of terms which include, among others, *explanation, description, rationalization, justification,* and *excuse.* This domain is characterized by LSA IV, incomplete differentiation. Recall that one way of measuring the completeness of differentiation was to give people examples to name. Incomplete differentiation would be found if people disagreed with each other (or with themselves at a later date), were uncertain, or gave various answers.

"I hit him because he hit me."

This could be a description. If *because* had been omitted, e.g., "I hit him after he hit me," it would have been a more model case of a description, since getting hit is taken to be such a sufficient reason for retaliation that *because* is redundant. So why is the *because* in there? Perhaps the speaker is a rather violent sort, but is afraid of his own violence, and so, perhaps, to him it sounds like a rationalization. He may be trying to justify his behavior when an outside observer wouldn't see the need for justification. The statement seems to be an explanation, since model cases of (what we take to be) explanations have a word like *because.* We can't be sure what this statement is without context, and the context would not necessarily clear up the uncertainty. For who can say (and how could anyone find out) if a person has violent tendencies if he is only afraid of them? If we determine that the speaker doesn't have violent tendencies, but if he still feels that his statement is a rationalization, for him it is one.

The differentiation is not as incomplete here as in the area of comedy. There are if not model at least something like paradigmatic cases. A rationalization is an explanation that attempts to make something rather seamy look good. But if you disapprove of a behavior, almost any explanation will seem like a rationalization; while if you approve you won't even require an explanation —even from someone who is so ashamed he is trying to offer you an explanation that to him is a rationalization.

As with comedy, much depends on the reaction of the recipient of the explanation–rationalization. One man's explanation is another's rationalization. If I offer you an explanation, you may take it to be one or you may not, which allows for the possibility of at least two valid descriptions of what it was.

Most statements that we *take to be* descriptions (and that is the ultimate as well as the only criterion for determining what a statement is) lack explicit mention of motivation. But if a (statement that takes the paradigmatic form of a) description is challenged, it may be turned into an explanation, i.e., the speaker may supply the previously deleted motivational aspects.

Therefore, I will not make much of a distinction between descriptions, explanations, rationalizations, justifications, and excuses in this chapter.

Generally, descriptions are distinguished from the other terms in that they are not attempts to explain behavior. In this context they are the kind of explanation that is given when no explanation is needed; or, conversely, an explanation is the kind of description given when explicit mention of motivation is called for.

The other common distinction in this domain is between explanations on one hand and rationalizations, justifications, and excuses on another. The latter are not satisfactory. This distinction is an attempt to force order on chaos. There are many statements that are both explanations and rationalizations. A complete description of the state of affairs will have to replace truth.

Why Ask Why?

Man is always asking "why?" Why? In this chapter we explore various kinds of answers given to questions and attempt a conditional, speculative, metaphysical, and, in the long run, tautological answer to the question of why man asks "why."

Perhaps it seems natural and normal for man to ask "why?" all the time, for man, it is often said, is curious. But curiosity is something we would expect from a beast that asked "why?" and "why?" is the kind of question we would expect a curious beast to ask. So that explanation is a tautology; one aspect of the concept is explained by referring to another aspect of the concept. In terms introduced in Chapter Five, we have substantial or almost complete conceptual overlap here, much more than the overlap of *warm* and *generous.* So we will reject this explanation because it tells us nothing.

Animals do not ask "why," although they do act puzzled. Do humans, simply because they have language, have to ask "why?" Probably not. Imagine a society where everything is programmed and ritualized, for example, the Zuni, as described by Ruth Benedict in *Patterns of Culture.* Much of Zuni life is extremely ritualized, and a good deal of freedom, tolerance, and acceptance characterizes behavior and attitudes towards behavior that is not controlled by ritual. There should be little need to ask "why?" if everything is a social practice, a done thing.

There are exceptions to this statement. Adolescents typically ask a large scale "why?" that not even a highly programmed society could expect to escape completely. Adolescents tend to question the whole setup. However, even in a society such as our own, where "why?" is invited by so many aspects of life, the vast majority of our youth grow up into socialized adults who at least act as if they accepted things the way they are. In less complex and more stable cultures, particularly in cultures where adolescence doesn't exist (i.e., where a child becomes an adult directly), "why?" should be much less common.

Always there are misfits, people who don't act right and in a sense ask (or cause others to ask) "why?" by unnatural, undone behavior. They are puzzled, or they puzzle us. Even in civilized societies such as our own we remove misfits from society and put them in prisons and insane asylums. "Primitive" Indian tribes have medicine men and other roles into which misfits can fit—making them no longer misfits. But in other cases misfits are killed or banished. In our culture we have so many misfits (from the point of view of any one person) that we invent verbal categories for them, e.g., creeps, undesirables or hippies. This banishes them in a word magical but comforting way, and it relieves us of the necessity of putting a majority of the population away. That these categories function as banishers can be seen by the illogical move under stress to real banishment of such types.

"That's the way things are; that's the way things are done." Let us take this as an explanation or answer to the question "why?" that might be given by a member of a tribe where behavior was well programmed, i.e., where everybody knew what to do at what time and did it. This is a highly unsatisfactory answer for those of us who are versed in Western civilization. It is an empty explanation, the kind children often give when asked why they did something or why something is the way it is and they don't know, e.g., *Because.* It is similar to other explanations offered in our society, e.g., "I just felt like it," "I'm that sort of person," "Why the hell not?" or "I don't know."

However, as I have suggested, there are still some questions left in Western civilization to which it sounds silly to ask "why?" Eating is one of these. So is sleeping. So, while even so simple a matter as washing clothes may no longer be a done thing (a social practice), we recognize that there are areas where it makes little sense to ask "why?" So we should be able to accept that for some people in some cultures there could be a good many more activities that go unquestioned. So that if you, a curious Westerner, arrived with your endless questions ("Why do you do that dance now?" "Why is divorce so easy in your culture?" "Why does the sun come up on this side and go down on that one?"), you would be greeted with the same curiosity you would get wandering through a restaurant asking diners why they were eating—or perhaps with the same hostility you would receive if you woke up American sleepers to ask them what they were doing and why.

Perhaps when we get our explanations into the form of the above empty ones we are satisfied. That is, we are satisfied when our explanations have no content and are merely tautologies. In other words, we seek to make behaviors into social practices. Let me take the position that asking why is the precursor to a search for a body of knowledge that makes an otherwise strange or "loose" behavior into a social practice, a done thing.

A boss comes in and starts snapping at people, something he never does. Everyone wants to know why. A gossip knows: the boss's son has been picked up on charges of selling heroin to junior high school kids. Ah Ha! No wonder. People who are very upset tend to have short tempers. It is a done thing. It is not any more surprising than eating dinner and going to bed. It is no more surprising than a Zuni's whole life.

All that is different is that we need an explanation tailored to the individual case. So while in a very simple and programmed culture, it is sufficient to say, "That is how it is done," in our more complex culture it is necessary to add particulars, e.g., "That is how it is done *by that person*," or, "That is how it is done *in that situation*." We have met these two examples before in the guise of personality and situation descriptions. Another common empty explanation is a situation-personality description, "that is how it is done by that person in that situation." This is an interactive description.

A situation description describes the behavior as a function of the situation. The general form of the empty situation description is given above: That is the way people in that situation act. A personality description describes behavior as a function of the person. The general form of the empty personality description is given above: that is the way that person does it. There are other, derivative forms of empty explanations, e.g., "That is the way a member of that group does it," which is a combination of a personality and situation description: Often people who belong to a group do so because they are a certain kind of person, but belonging to a group may force, emphasize, or reinforce certain kinds of behavior. Since we can't be sure which is the case (or which mixture is the case), we avoid the problem by giving a group description.

There is also a certain kind of description we give when we

can't understand the behavior or the person and the person's behavior is upsetting. That is, these are the two criterial attributes: both must be present to some extent, although the strong presence of one can make up for the weak presence of the other. This is a deviance description. People who receive deviance descriptions are misfits and are handled accordingly.

We give a deviance description when we can't come up with an acceptable description of another sort. Generally, we accept some situation and personality descriptions, but not others. Consider, "He killed those seven people because he had a lousy childhood." This is an unacceptable situation description (at least for most of us). We may say it is unacceptable because childhood is too far away in time to be a causal agent so much later in life, but in addition a behavior must be sufficiently similar to existing social practices or done things if we are to accept *any* situation descriptions. On the other hand, there are situations so extreme that we are willing to accept explanations for behaviors that are not so close to existing social practices or done things. Hence we accept brutal killing if one is doing it in defense of his home and family—we might even allow the killer a tiny bit of sadism if his victim had hurt or killed a member of his family.

So far, then, we have found two criterial attributes for an acceptable explanation: the behavior must be close to an existing social practice, or the situation must be seen as extremely provoking. As is the case with criterial attributes, if something is lacking in one, extremity in the other can compensate; but a little bit of each must be present. Let me illustrate this by example and introduce another criterial attribute in the process.

One day I was driving up Riverside Drive in New York City around 140th Street. This is not a very safe or nice neighborhood. Four young men were harassing the traffic, pretending to be bullfighters. They were around 14, an age that terrifies New Yorkers, since these young warriors have no fear nor impulse control. I thought briefly of speeding up and running over a couple of them. Instead I slowed somewhat and they got out of the way. I thought, "I could have run over them and said to the police, 'I thought they were trying to stop the car, and they might have robbed me and killed me.' " And indeed they might have, even though it was broad daylight and there were quite a few cars on the road.

But the police wouldn't have believed me. I might have gone free, but they would have known, as would anyone who talks to me for a few mintues, that I was lying. In the first place, I am young, not small, and not weak. In the second, my hatred of harassment is stronger than my fear, and it would be very hard for me to play the part of a frightened, slightly hysterical, respectable young man beset by vicious young punks. People who know me would know I had been just as vicious as those punks could have been.

But there are many people who would quite rightfully be able to take refuge in the explanation that they had panicked. Thus the personality has to be right too.

If a person's behavior can't be explained, i.e., if it isn't sufficiently close to an existing social practice or done thing, if it isn't called for by the situation, and/or if it isn't called for by the personality (or some balance of these conditions, with the condition that there must be some of all three criterial attributes), we give a deviance description and drum the person out of society—which is perfectly logical. If we can't make him do social practices (i.e., if we can't make up an acceptable explanation for his behavior), he's not part of society.

It is not this cut and dried of course. For example, our "ability" to make behaviors social practices via the invention of an acceptable explanation is dependent upon our desire to do so. If we hate someone, we may find our inventive abilities temporarily out of service.

Explanations: Wearing Out

Explanations serve to make done things. Usually the accomplishment is magical and illusory. Furthermore, explanations do not always stop questioning. They wear out their welcome. In the discussion of this proposition, we shall first examine some explanations offered by social science and philosophy. These, along with other fields of learning, have been attempting for centuries to give us usable explanations. Science and philosophy have attempted to take over some functions that ordinary man performed himself in that mythical "state of nature." That they exist is further testimony to man's restless search for explanations. A few examples will illustrate some of the reasons why their explanations wear out their welcome.

Psychology used to explain behavior by saying that for a behavior B there was an instinct I_B, which caused that behavior. If man seemed to like company, then he had an instinct for affiliation. If man seemed to feel better if he brushed his teeth after every meal, then he had an instinct for clean teeth. This mode of explanation was quite respectable for some years.

But eventually some spoilsport pointed out that well over 8,000 instincts had been "discovered." People became suspicious. It seemed as if any time a new behavior was brought up for discussion an instinct was proposed to explain it and thus to make it a done thing. If you explain something by itself, that is a tautology, and it began to appear that the discovery of instincts was nothing more than an abuse of tautology. Saying "Instinct did it" began to sound equivalent to saying, "I did it because I wanted to," which is acceptable if and only if the behavior is.

Once an explanatory concept is invoked, it seems as if social scientists order the concept to be fruitful and multiply. Another example is provided by the history of intelligence as an explanatory concept (my brief history is much oversimplified). In the beginning there was IQ, a single solitary variable along which everyone could be placed and compared. Thus many previously difficult tasks were made easy: "Let's admit Joe. He's got a higher IQ than Fred." IQ may not have predicted job or even college success extremely well, but it did a job.

Perhaps because it didn't do a really great job, or perhaps

because social scientists felt matters shouldn't be that simple, or perhaps because the concept of intelligence as measured by IQ ignored a very important aspect of the ordinary language meaning of the concept (intelligent in the ways of the world), the Faustian spirit took over and in the 1940s Thurstone was talking about seven "primary abilities," among which were verbal comprehension, word fluency, memory, reasoning, and numerical ability. They were supposed to be (although they are not always) independent. That is, Joe should, on the average, be better than Fred on 3-1/2 of these abilities and worse on the other 3-1/2. This made comparison of Joe and Fred more difficult, although in some cases it could make the comparison more helpful than a simple IQ comparison. For example, if you want a clerk to do numerical calculations, you might hire Fred over Joe if Fred is higher than Joe on numerical ability, even if Fred is much lower on the other six abilities.

But in the 1960s Guilford's model came into prominence. Guilford postulated 120 factors (many of which he has evidence for). His so-called "structure of intellect" model takes the form of a cube. Along the edges are five operations, six products, and four contents, yielding $5x6x4 = 120$ abilities, such as Evaluation (operation) of Semantic (content) Systems (product). These 120 factors are presumed to be orthogonal, so that now Joe and Fred have to be compared on 120 different dimensions, and on the averege Joe should be better than Fred on 60 and worse on 60.

Guilford's model illustrates another problem with scientific explanations. They tend towards complexity. This complexity reduces and may destroy their usefulness. We would not know how to use Guilford's model to decide whether to pick Joe or Fred for the clerk's job unless we had a detailed analysis of the job so as to know precisely which of the 120 abilities were important in the performance of the job. Probably several factors would be important, and so unless Joe was clearly better on a substantial majority of the important factors, we would be no better off than we were when we started, and we might as well decide on the basis of neatness of dress. The complexity does not only make practical application difficult. In day-to-day life we do not want to have to think about 120 different abilities, nor do we need to. Nor does it seem possible that a good knowledge of Guilford's model *could* help us in any important way. Finally, intelligence is but one aspect of a person, so unless we are professionals in the field of intelligence we are likely to find such attention somewhat excessive. After all, Guilford's model doesn't have a neatness-of-dress factor.

Similarly, Stimulus-Response psychology began, like Adam and Eve, with S and R. Soon, however, little Ss and Rs were spawned and there were many different kinds of Ss and Rs, much as Adam and Eve produced children of many colors. Now there are fractional responses, anticipatory responses, mediated responses, conditioned responses, unconditioned responses, and on and on. The model is of no use to anyone except its professional keepers, the psychologists who devote a life to it. And one must devote a life to it to keep up with all the new twists and wrinkles. It seems as if every time a new behavior is brought up for discussion, a new kind of S or R is "discovered" (although stalwart efforts are made to make do with what is already around). Even for a psychologist such as myself, who has read a good deal of the theory in this area, Stimulus-Response psychology is like a foreign language.

So scientific explanations wear out their welcome to laymen and even to members of the same science by becoming too complicated for anyone except a devotee to understand and worthless from a practical or everyday life point of view.

Let us now examine another typology of explanations: Religious, Reductionistic, Tautological. We shall examine how these wear out their welcome.

A religious explanation invokes some supra-organismic entity, something bigger than man. A good example is "God." However, the most common religious explanatory agent throughout the history of Europe and America has been the devil. This is natural enough. Behavior that is normal, normative, acceptable, or even good is not the sort of behavior we feel any need to explain.

Behavior that is bad, disturbing, upsetting, provoking, or harmful is the kind we need to *take care of.* It calls for explanation.

Let us see why the devil, as an explanatory agent, might get to be a bit tiresome. Consider a member of the Inquisition. He has a bad day at the office and gets mad at his wife and kills her. This, perhaps, was not a terrible crime in those days, at least for a man in his position. He comes to the office a little bit late the next day and says, "This devil—the most godawful big devil I've seen in twenty years in the business—got into me last night and killed my wife. Fortunately I was able to exorcise it in a couple minutes."

His colleagues may accept this at face value, but only because women weren't very powerful in those days. But too many more devils, no matter how successfully exorcised, and the man would be in trouble.

A wife comes home with a new dress and amuses her husband by telling him the devil made her buy it. Encouraged, she buys twenty more the next day, but when he comes home she finds that her explanation has already worn out its welcome. Even the most vain devil wouldn't insist on twenty-one dresses in two days.

There are smart people about, and they listen in and pick up on the fads. They don't over-use their explanations, as the wife did; they save them until they need them, unlike the boy who cried wolf. However, the boy who cried wolf didn't have an entirely bad idea. It is well to prepare the way for your explanation. If you plan to plead temporary insanity, it would be well to have a history of slightly bizarre behavior.

But there are lots of smart people about, and soon society tires of members of the Inquisition who have momentary lapses and kill their wives. And so a perfectly good explanatory concept gets a bad name through association with behaviors that people refuse to accept for any length of time.

But religious explanations are essentially similar, and the devil is alive today working in his mysterious ways, only now, as Szasz has pointed out, he has taken on the guise of "temporary insanity." At first, temporary insanity seemed a humane idea. But by now many people are getting sick and tired of it. Too many people are pleading insanity and getting away with murder. Insanity is now a business, and it is giving the non-criminally insane (the vast majority) a bad name. So temporary insanity is on the way out.

A more recent plea is poverty and discrimination. In the beginning that seemed to be a good and humane idea too. Now many people are getting sick of this plea, and it is giving the non-criminal poor and oppressed a bad name.

Thus we see the greatest flaw of religious explanations. They do not explain why this particular person did this particular thing at this particular time. Not all poor people steal. Not all youths who grew up in the harsh environment of the ghetto turn to violence. If your baby is "taken from you" and you are told that it is the will of some supra-organismic entity who does all for a reason, to preserve the order of the universe, perhaps, you may with justice ask this entity if the next-door neighbor's baby wouldn't have done just as well.

Naturally everyone wants a piece of the action, and there is no reason to expect (nor any hope in asking) a person who murdered someone to refrain from saying he went nuts for a few minutes just because he didn't feel all *that* crazy. Nor is there reason to expect the poor to refuse the explanation of poverty— especially since they *are* poor, and poverty isn't pleasant and can't be done away with simply by having the proper moral fiber. But the deviant behaviors, especially the crimes, soon wear out society, and a new religious explanation must be found.

It is worth emphasizing that it is the behaviors that make the explanations unsatisfactory, rather than a fault in the explanations themselves. Many religious explanations have a good deal of validity.

I have an inkling what the next religious explanation may be, and it is a good one, available to everyone (unlike poverty) and carrying no other stigma (unlike insanity): it is the pace and pressure or the fear, pollution, and noise of modern life. The devil, long associated with dirt and excrement, now has taken the form of the human excrement found along our beaches and the filthy soot found in our air. The devil is everywhere.

I haven't denied that people can get into situations in which they behave in a manner very much unlike their normal selves; nor have I denied that growing up in poverty and slums with no hope will have an effect on young boys and girls. Nor will I deny that smog and noise can have an effect on tempers.

I have used this excuse upon occasion. (I call it an excuse because I don't like to think of myself as the kind of person who will allow a little air, noise, etc., to control me.) But because the smog is always with us, we can't tell if the anger we feel is due to the smog, the situation, or the kind of person we are. I happen to be a rather angry person and I can't deny it, so I have a hard time blaming much of anything on the atmosphere. But there is a choice of explanatory agents, and given that nobody can *tell for sure* (although anyone can judge) which is "really" the explanatory agent in effect, there is a temptation, and I have chosen to yield to it upon occasion.

Soon it will be too late to use this one. It is, logically speaking, not very good. Since in a given locale the various sources of pollution descend equally on everyone, excess relative to the norm of the locale cannot be explained away for any period of time. Soon people will be commenting that not every Tom, Dick, and Harry blows his stack because of the smog, and all will be over. I don't know what will follow, but history suggest we may have faith in human ingenuity. (Since this was first written, Watergate has arrived. People are already explaining immoral behavior as being caused by Watergate.)

There are various scientific explanatory concepts that have a distinctive religious flavor. For example, Rogers and Maslow talk about self-actualization. People have a tendency to actualize themselves, i.e., to develop and recognize their potential and to become what in some sense they were meant to be. The problem here is that the principle of self-actualization explains exactly nothing, since it explains everything. This is characteristic of more positive religious explanations, such as "God." If God doesn't do everything, then He is indifferent or impotent, and that is ungodlike. So God does everything, but therefore He does nothing in particular.

Similarly, Rogers, Maslow, and other social scientists do not like to believe that man is basically evil, so they postulate a principle that explains everything, attempting magically to remove evil, and as a result explain nothing *in particular* and paradoxically add to the sum total of evil in the world, allowing the murderer to leer at the psychologically competent judge and say, "But Your Honor, I was merely actualizing myself."

S-R theory is similarly religious, depending, as it does, on a deterministic view of the universe. If we behave because of the stimuli of the environment, then everything that has happened was determined and everything that will happen is determined. Once you start an S-R universe, everything is settled.

S-R philosophy can be an opiate for the passive. But what of human striving? It is determined. So why should we try to do things better? Why should Skinner want to program society to make it better? This dilemma, as it is usually called, is not new: Calvinism stressed both determinism and the value of positive striving.

Thus we are in a position to point out yet another failing of religious explanations: They are incongruent. On the one hand, here is a man telling you the devil or his childhood or the smog or the stimulus pattern of the environment made him do it, but on the other hand you have a strong feeling that *he* did it (and you have a strong suspicion that he knows he did it too). So how can you punish him? But equally, how can you excuse him?

Religious explanations are incongruent for the same reason as schizophrenic messages—they are attempts to deny. In the case of the religious explanation, responsibility is denied. In the case of the schizophrenic, relationships are denied and responsibility for one's statements is denied. In this context, we can see one of the major uses and purposes of explanations, and we can see how far from a truth-seeking or curiosity-driven use and purpose it is. Ask not what the truth is. Ask only what the person is trying to pull on you by advancing the explanation he chooses.

We have already discussed reductionistic explanations and criticized them from a formal and scientific standpoint. They explain an organism's behavior by invoking sub-organismic explanatory agents. By a sub-organismic agent I mean the following: one that can operate without a paradigmatic organism (a human being) and whose paradigmatic operation is on sub-organismic objects. For example, a molecule can exist without an organism. Furthermore, we don't think of molecules as operating *directly* on humans. Molecules of oxygen operate on molecules in our bodies and on the molecules in a hunk of iron. A cell, on the other hand, can't exist except as part of an organism (although we have single-celled organisms), but non-humans have cells. Furthermore, cells don't operate *directly* on human beings.

The flaws of reductionistic explanations in an interpersonal context are the same as those of religious explanations. Saying, "My atoms made me do it," is an attempt to evade responsibility, doesn't explain why what happened happened specifically as it did (although there is an illusion of specificity because atoms are smaller than humans), and is an incongruent message in the sense that we perceive and treat humans as humans, not as collections of atoms and molecules.

Furthermore, such explanations tend to diminish the dignity of humanity even more than religious explanations do. Are you the kind of person who is "nothing but" atoms and molecules? If so, I will have to treat you as I treat other objects that are "nothing but" atoms and molecules. There is little I treat that way: not my dog, a piece of celery, or even a twig—perhaps garbage.

Reductionistic explanations are not as common as religious explanations (although they are common among the insane, who like to say they are controlled by radio waves, for example). The most common one is sickness. We all recognize that physical sickness can affect a person's behavior; however, this explanation has been much abused, and there is a growing tendency to call most ailments psychosomatic. In other words, perhaps this explanation is wearing out its welcome in general. I am ashamed to have a common cold anymore, so I feel I must persevere no matter how bad I feel. This does me no good, nor does it help the people around me who pick up my germs. Germs *do* exist, and although they don't operate directly on humans, they produce rather noxious states in humans, sometimes letting a human feel more free to be obnoxious.

So we are left with tautology. And tautology is the proper form for explanations of human behavior. "Human behavior is intentional." That is to say no more than that humans take it that human behavior is intentional, at least much of the time. It is more accurate to say that humans act *as if* they take it that human behavior is intentional, since many humans don't know, in the sense that they haven't thought about it *in those terms,* that they take specific behaviors to be intentional, while other humans (most notably S-R psychologists) send an incongruent message: They act as if behavior were intentional, but talk as if it were determined.

To say that human behavior is intentional is to say that we take it that people intend to do things and often succeed. That is, humans have something to do with their own behavior. Thus the statement, "I did it because I wanted to," is a tautology that reflects the fact that we often *take it to be the case* that we do things because we want to, not because, e.g., something made us do it. We do not even take it that the attractiveness of doing it made us do it: *We* did it. We take it that we have a choice.

The tautological nature of many descriptions of behavior is quite legitimate, then. In fact, most of what we call descriptions are tautologies "in disguise," i.e., without a motivational statement attached. If one were added, for example, "And then he got mad," it would sound empty. If the situation is sufficiently provoking, no motivational statement need be attached. The description does not appear to be an explanation, although we can rewrite it so that it seems to be one.

Tautology explains nothing, and quite right, too; because

there is often nothing to explain. When something is done, well, it is done. And there's an end. When there is something to explain, we give other kinds of explanations. A pure situation description, a model case, leaves the person out of the causality entirely, but usually it is more legitimate to include the person in the description/explanation, making it properly tautologous. Religious and reductionistic explanations are attempts at pure model situation descriptions. What makes them (and all model situation descriptions) inaccurate is the lack of jerkiness in human behavior. We do not look as if somebody forced us to do something.

There are many cases when our motivation to leave ourselves out of the causality picture is obvious. However, it is often a very good idea to accept the blame immediately, or at least part of it. I shall now discuss a logical progression, from the framework of a relationship between husband and wife, of arguments when one person wrongs the other and does not accept any of the blame.

Let us take a time-honored deviant behavior on the part of husbands: coming home drunk. The situation has been around for years and new cartoons come out every year. The situation is probably common enough to be a good example.

The situation is one that may result in an argument, as defined in Chapter Four. That is, it is generally accepted by husbands *and* wives that husbands have some rights, one of which is the right to have a night out with the boys now and then. And it is generally accepted by wives *and* husbands that wives have some rights, one of which is that she not be forced to deal with a drunken, stumbling, stinking bum.

This argument could be resolved. As suggested in Chapter Four, social engineering is called for by this kind of state of affairs. The husband will want to drink now and again; the wife won't learn to like it. So, for example, the couple could decide that the man may come home drunk now and then. Not too often, but with no limit: he must be expected and allowed to use his own judgment. But he must come home late enough that the kids are in bed, and he must quietly sneak down to the basement, to sleep on the old sofa down there, and he must wash and brush his teeth before appearing in the morning. In return for this debasement, the husband will not be given any sort of punishment. If more couples did this, a few cartoonists, bartenders, and marriage counselors would be out of business.

A slightly different example should be set forth to illustrate other aspects of refusing to take responsibility. Suppose a wife has been talking to a man other than her husband during the afternoons. He happens to be unemployed. At first the conversations are nothing but a way of passing the boring afternoons of a housewife, but they get to be something more, although not yet a physical relationship. The husband finds out.

There can be no engineering here. A wife is not usually given the right to expect her husband to accept this kind of behavior without question. Nor are husbands always given freedom to have friends of the opposite sex. We shall return to this example.

P, the person who has done the wrong thing, would like to say that it is the situation only that is responsible for his behavior. To the extent that P is successful, he has evaded responsibility. The situation should be described as a once in a lifetime thing. If it may be expected to recur, so may the behavior, *given* that it has the power P *has to claim it has.* (Already P is paying for what he gets.) For example, the husband coming home drunk may claim, and quite correctly, that an old friend he hadn't seen in many years came into town. But if old friends come into town often, and if the husband gets drunk each time, the situation description will be less and less acceptable. The value of the pure situation description is not in its truth value but in its ability to convince O, the wronged one, that the behavior was not P's, and so was not directed at O, and in addition won't happen again.

After all, if a man has old friends dropping in all the time and if he always gets drunk with them, then this is a fact about *him.* In other words, he has an *excessive* (in the sense discussed in Chapter One) number of old friends who are former drinking partners, and so a personality description is quite logical.

The wife who is becoming involved has a difficult task from the beginning. Suppose she agrees she should stop seeing the other man and denies that she is involved. This little lie seems acceptable under the circumstances, since sexual relationships are the usual signal and symbol of involvement. But the husband is likely to be suspicious. Even if she promises not to do it again, claims lack of involvement, and says she recognizes the impropriety even while denying that there was any real impropriety, he is likely to ask why she did it in the first place. This is usually *taken to be* a more serious breach of the relationship than drunkenness, which is less directly a potential threat to the relationship.

He shouldn't ask why. Let us assume that she tells the truth and says she was bored and found talking to this other man more entertaining that watching soap operas and game shows on television, even though she knows her husband believes he has a right to expect that she not put herself in a position where she *might* get involved with other men, and even though she may have been socialized to believe this also. She has a right not to be bored, too, but getting involved with other men is not an appropriate performative aspect of the intentional action of avoiding boredom.

This quite legitimate situation description is very poor as a container and remover of the behavior. She is likely to continue to be bored. Women who believe that they lead lives of quiet desperation are a major social problem for which there is no obvious solution (getting involved with other men or with many men is not a real solution). It would be nice if women didn't believe this, but many of them do, and it looks like more will.

And that is precisely what will frustrate the husband about this situation description. There are no easy solutions, e.g., "OK, so I'll take you out more often." Or, "I'll bring you home some interesting books." Or, "Let's have another baby." Or, "Why don't you do some volunteer work at the hospital?" Or, "Why don't you and Janet get together anymore?"

This illustrates another reason why situation descriptions wear out their welcome. Even if a situation description hints at a chronic situation, there are solutions. When the first wife to become bored with her lot told her husband something had to be done, no doubt he had lots of bright ideas about how to solve the problem, such as the ones quoted above. And no doubt she thought they had great promise too. But over the years we have found that these solutions don't work, and we haven't found any that do.

The same is true of personality descriptions. Whenever a behavior is redescribed, the possibility of new solutions is presented. For example, "We might as well face it. I have a drinking problem," says the husband eventually. That he says this is a tacit admission that he, like his wife, is tired of the descriptions he's been trying, since the solutions they suggest don't work. And the cries of joy on the part of the wife and the relief felt by the husband on the occasion of such an "admission" will not last long unless the husband starts dealing with the problem, i.e., *unless he begins to take responsibility for his own behavior.* Since we are dealing with systematic attempts to avoid responsibility, his admission will be only (as such admissions often are) a temporary stopgap to keep his wife from the door.

Situation descriptions do not always go bad for this reason. Perhaps the husband tries a new situation description each time he comes home drunk. Perhaps they are all very good indeed, i.e., it does appear as if an extremely improbable chain of events has led to this drunkenness which is so unlike him normally. But recall from Chapter One the notion that we are likely to ascribe personality traits if a behavior takes place *too often,* even if the situation calls for it each time and even if the behavior is not disproportionate. If the husband succumbs *every time* to the (admittedly) incredible temptation, the wife can quite correctly assume that he never has anything to keep him from getting drunk. That is, he may get drunk only on command, but he never resists a command. In other words, the only behavior the wife has seen is drunken behavior.

If a behavior cannot be located in the situation, logically one would look to the person. Where else? And thus personality descriptions are generated. As I have indicated, descriptions which take both situation and personality into account are best. Situation-personality descriptions often sound tautologous, but that they do reflects the unity of situation and personality under normal circumstances, in much the same way that style and content and space and time are usually united. To focus on the content of a writer to the exclusion of his style may often lead to inappropriately significant descriptions of what he is saying, and to focus on the style to the exclusion of content is also to do the writer an injustice. Similarly, to focus on a person's personality to the exclusion of the situation in which he finds himself is to do him an injustice.

However, by attempting to avoid responsibility, we *use up* our situation descriptions, and *only personality is left.* In more concrete terms, if the husband has used many different situation descriptions and his wife goes to a personality description, he has run out of excuses. If the husband has been so foolish and dishonest as to continually attempt to absolve himself of blame, he has left himself more exposed than he need be, for, just as an absence of content makes style excessively visible, an absence of situational determinants of behavior makes personality excessively visible.

Put somewhat differently, I have suggested that tautological situation-personality descriptions are the proper form for explanations of human behavior. As they say in psychology, behavior is a function of the person and the environment. If the husband emphasizes the situation to the exclusion of the environment, eventually the wife will balance the equation by emphasizing personality to the exclusion of the situation. Overall, the balance between situation and personality must be maintained. Given that the situation has been rather bad, in the sense that it has produced bad behaviors, the personality will have to shoulder all the blame. In a sense it will then shoulder more than it should, from the point of view of a scientifically neutral observer. That is, the personality description will be excessively harsh, but only because the husband made his situation seem excessively demanding in the first place.

The necessity for situation-personality descriptions can be further illustrated by looking at what happens if a person accepts *too much* blame. He may be apologetic and say it's all his fault and generally show what a wonderfully brave person he is to accept all the blame. But this is an incongruent message. The person is saying, "I am to blame," in a context where he is attempting to escape punishment. Really to accept blame is to accept the punishment that goes with it, even if that is only a feeling of guilt. If our nearly adulterous wife were to apologize profusely and even promise it would never happen again, the husband could get the impression that she was trying to keep his eyes off the *situation* by making her personality excessively visible.

Furthermore, such explanations quickly become unacceptable; if the behavior recurs, the complainer can with justice say, "I don't give a damn how sorry you are or how completely you accept all blame, what you did makes me mad."

Thus the husband who says, "I am drunk but I didn't do it," sends an incongruent message and receives for it, eventually, "You are a drunk." This latter statement disqualifies *post facto* all previous situation descriptions. He can no longer claim the situation had *anything* to do with his behavior (or so his wife is claiming). The personality descriptions at this stage are likely to be disproportionately harsh.

Since all the blame must rest on only one of the usual two causal agents, the one that receives it has more to shoulder, so we are likely to slide down the emotive conjugation as the situation is unable to serve as a support, e.g., "I'm a person who drinks too much, you have a drinking problem, he's an alcoholic."

Consequently, such personality descriptions are likely to be rejected. The man who has suddenly become in the eyes of his wife nothing more than "a drunk" can with some justice feel that he is more than just a drunk and that she is focusing too extensively upon the performative aspect of his behavior. But he deserves it. Similarly, a wife will not be happy with his description of her as "a nag." There is (or was) certainly more to her actions: initially at least she was trying to make the relationship a good one.

Personality descriptions do not need to be negative, although in this context they usually are. If they aren't, if the behavior continues along with arguments as to which personality description is appropriate, they will become unacceptable, at least in the context of an interpersonal relationship.

Recall the discussion of negotiation. Negotiation can end with P giving a description of O which explains why O gives the kind of behavior description he does, and with O giving a similar descrption of P. That is, negotiation can end with personality descriptions.

However, within the context of interpersonal relationships, personality has more significance than it has in other contexts. Drunks, nags, sluts, and bores can be borne unless you have to live with them.

A behavior or a personality trait that a husband or wife doesn't like may be described by the injured party as the performative aspect of the intentional action, "hurting me." If the husband is a drunk, he is drunk to his wife. And she can rightfully take it that the behavior is directed at her.

He may deny that his drunkenness has anything to do with her. He is certainly not getting drunk to hurt her, whatever his reasons are. And it need not be *deliberate* in that sense to still be *intentional* (to use Ossorio's distinction). For if a person continues in an interpersonal relationship to behave in a way that the partner doesn't like, he is doing so intentionally. Thus the injured party will, appealing to the rights that accrue to one who is in an interpersonal relationship of this sort, give a damage description, in which the personality trait or behavior is taken to be the performative aspect of a behavior that is described as "causing damage that you have no right to cause." (One can also give damage descriptions of the other's personality descriptions, e.g., "It hurts me so when you call me a nag.")

Thus personality descriptions, given in the context of an interpersonal relationship, lead inevitably to damage descriptions —unless something is done to stop the progression.

Note that the progression is harder and harder to stop: A behavior in a situation description is a single behavior, and, hopefully, *not even P's.* In the context of a personality description it is one of many other behaviors (the past and future manifestations of the trait), and it has been assigned, along with all the other manifestations, to P and to P alone (no situational determinants need apply). And once a damage description has been given, the personality description becomes merely the performative aspect of a much more significant behavior, intentionally hurting one's partner.

If the couple had dealt with their problems initially, e.g., by setting up rules about the husband's drunkenness, resolution would have been relatively easy. But if they now were to attempt a resolution, there would be more problems and they would be more significant. It is clearly more significant to the relationship intentionally to hurt the other than it is to get drunk.

Damage descriptions are not welcome. It is impossible for a relationship to continue as the same relationship if one person is intentionally damaging his partner. If the problems are not remedied, the damaged party or parties will have nothing more to bargain with but the existence of the relationship, and the next step is to threaten it. "Threatening the relationship" ("Do this or else") is no longer something we would call a description or explanation. So, in the context of interpersonal relationships, explanations are offered and rejected, until finally the relationship ends.

As I have indicated, the couple may at any time resolve their problems by dealing with them directly rather than attempting to deal with them in a (merely and purely) verbal way. Explaining is of no value unless something hinges on which explanation it is; the process I have outlined here involves no change in the relationship to accommodate the behavior that violated it, but merely verbal maneuvering to escape blame.

As I indicated earlier, there are several criterial attributes of an "acceptable explanation." Some explanations will work for some people but not for others. If our nearly adulterous wife is a very warm and passionate person, she will probably not get away with saying that her relationship with the other man was insignificant, unless her husband is a very trusting person. What seems to be clear is that an initial denial of responsibility leads to a more and more serious situation as more and more explanations wear themselves out. The initial denial of personality means that when personality outs, as it will, it will be overemphasized. Being thus overemphasized, the intentional hurting of the other person by that personality will be overemphasized, i.e., it is *you* (not this series of events, of which you were a part) who is hurting me.

In the next section I discuss an approach to changing oneself that involves what seems to be a rationalization, i.e., an attempt to evade responsibility for a slightly shabby performance. However, this kind of description always involves the locution, "I did B." It is the acceptance of responsibility for one's own behavior that makes the "method" plausible.

Why, in the last analysis, do situation and personality descriptions fail to make a behavior a done thing? Perhaps it is because situations do not cause behavior. Nor do people: They don't *cause behavior,* they *behave.* People are not puppets, which is to say we don't usually take them to be. Nor are people *simply* or *merely* drunks or nags or sluts or bores (i.e., merely personalities), although if they deprive themselves of their context, they are, as we have seen. There are few or no done things or social practices that are done by situations or by one person in isolation of all context. So situation and personality descriptions are formally inadequate.

In fact, damage descriptions state that what has been done "isn't done" (in the sense of the British usage, e.g., "That kind of thing just isn't done around here, old boy"). They deny that it is possible that the personality traits that have been ascribed can be acceptable within the context of the relationship, i.e., that they can ever be "done" personality traits.

Perhaps more important, a damage description supplies the missing situation for the personality descriptions of arguments. As I said, such personality descriptions are not quite fair in that they leave out all situational context. Damage descriptions can be seen as a logical filling of the void left by the removal of the normal situational determinants of behavior: "This personality trait exists in the context of the relationship, and it is hurting me."

Clearly, this is not the kind of situational context P would have liked in the beginning.

Finally, let us be fair and point out that the denial of responsibility that begins the process described here is not solely the responsibility or even always initiated by the person who has behaved badly. For every person who wants to escape being seen by his or her mate in a negative light there is a person who wants to escape seeing his or her mate in a negative light.

Beyond Rationalization and Explanation

In Chapter One, a particular interpersonal move was discussed: redescribing a behavior with excessive emphasis upon its performative aspect, with the result being an inappropriately insignificant description. As discussed, it is also possible to pay *insufficient* attention to the performative aspect of behavior and come up with a description that is inappropriately significant. In these cases it is accurate to say the description was excessively significant. To say that getting drunk is making a moral statement about the boredom and stupidity of the social world is making a little much of getting drunk. To say that robbing a bank is showing the evils of modern society is making a bit much of robbing a bank.

These are clearly rationalizations. They are attempts to evade responsibility. However, they contain tacit recognition of the fact that an *I* performed the act, rather than a devil or a particle of smog. And they are commitments. If one wishes to stick with them, one may have to modify the performative aspect of the intentional action one is claiming in order to make it the kind of performance that could be the performative aspect of the said intentional action. In Chapter Seven I discussed the relationship between an intentional action and its performative aspect. In this section I shall suggest that people might attempt to change their behavior and themselves by redescribing their behavior in a more dignified manner, specifically by claiming their behavior is merely the performative aspect of a larger, more significant behavior.

Humans don't think very highly of themselves. Situation descriptions, including religious and reductionistic descriptions, may be seen as attempts to obtain or retain one's dignity and place a positive (or at least not a negative) evaluation on one's behavior. They may also be seen as self-degradations. It is hardly flattering to portray oneself as a helpless puppet or nothing but hormones or atoms. In effect, one is saying, "Don't blame me, I'm not a human being, or if I am there are forces larger than myself." If you want to escape the responsibility human beings must assume, you also avoid being a human being.

But what kind of objective, scientific language is this, talking about how humans *must* assume responsibility for their behavior?

Again, the fact of the matter is that we take it to be the case that humans must assume responsibility for their own behavior. It is a criterial attribute for the attribution of the concept of "human being." And nowhere is this so clear as in the degradation involved in the process of evading responsibility described in the previous section. If we dehumanize ourselves when we evade responsibility, we are acting *as if* human beings must accept responsibility. And what other criterion could we want to require?

We send ourselves an incongruent message when we attempt to evade responsibility: In order to maintain our human dignity we must describe ourselves as puppets or atoms or hormones, none of which need or are eligible for dignity. The person who does something to maintain dignity because of oppression, something anti-social and undignified, claims to be in need of human dignity, but acts as if oppression has forced him to scurry like a rat into illicit behavior. Rats scurry but humans have a choice. So, even when our own behavior is involved, we show that we take it that we must assume responsibility because we have choices by treating ourselves as if we have acted in some non-paradigmatically human way.

Why does man think poorly of himself? In other words, can

we describe the state of affairs in such a way that man's tendency to think poorly of himself does not seem at odds with what we take to be the case in general? That is, can we make it into a done thing?

Man is particularly suspicious of his own motives. This is not surprising. Model cases of doing things to satisfy ourselves abound. Much of what we do we do to satisfy ourselves. However, there are few model cases of doing things for another's satisfaction. In order to do something for someone else, it has to be something we don't want to do. Otherwise, we would be *uncertain* whether we did it for ourselves or for the other person. Since there are so many cases of doing things for our own satisfaction, given a choice between assuming we did it for someone else and assuming we did it for ourselves, we take the more common case. Particularly since to choose otherwise we have to prove to ourselves that we really hated it. Since masochism was "discovered," even doing things we hate can come under the heading of doing something for our own gratification.

Recently studies of "altruistic" behavior have become a rage in social psychology, and several of my students have attempted to do a conceptual analysis of altruism, with the aim of criticizing the conceptual accuracy of experiments in this area. They universally can't come up with a model case. They do not heed Wilson's (1966) dictum that you should allow a concept to do some work. If altruism is so rigidly and rigorously defined that nothing qualifies as altruism, then we are not letting the concept do any work. Wilson and Wittgenstein too would suggest that we look at the use of the term, and perhaps we would find that in day-to-day life people use such terms as *altruism, unselfish,* and *charitable* without as much rigor.

But people don't. We accept various kinds of behavior with no personal gain only up to a point. Let us take a well-storied example. Consider the husband who puts up with a wife who plays around, taunts him, and downgrades him. He says he stays with her because he "loves her." But we are likely to reject this and to believe he is afraid of breaking up with her because then he would be alone and would have difficulty starting another relationship. The man cannot put up with so much and say he does it because he loves her, because if he loved her (which is to say, if he used the word appropriately), he would not treat her as a child. He would not consistently let her get away with behaviors we might allow children to get away with for a year or two. He is assisting in her own degradation if he allows her to act the bitch, and no doubt in many cases it would be appropriate to describe her as doing it on purpose in the hopes of being stopped. But that is as incongruent as his saying, "I love you even though you treat me like a worm." But part of loving someone is trying to break through their incongruent messages. Finally, a man who accepts much bad treatment is not the type who can be said to love someone. He is too neurotic.

In general, we are suspicious of other people if they do things that it would appear they should hate. It is possible to do rather sacrificial things—if one is a very strong person, etc., one can do many things. But then one isn't doing anything one should hate, since one is strong enough to take it without much pain. But who would one do such things?

To take a rather petty example, I have let a child hit me many times as hard as he could, because I knew he was mad (at me or something else), and I thought it would calm him down somewhat. That was neither altruistic nor selfish in any senses of either term. Why did I do it? I wanted the child to be calm. Why did I want the child to be calm? To make life easier for myself.

So by continually, even if inappropriately, asking why, one can eventually find an ulterior motive. This is taken to be damning; but, putting another construction on it, it simply indicates that man behaves intentionally, i.e., that he doesn't do things for no reason and that he usually doesn't do things he doesn't want to do. Or, as Ossorio would point out, if a man does something he doesn't want to, he must logically have a stronger reason to do it (this is the way humans think about behavior). And usually we can find this stronger reason. A man doesn't want to join the army, but if he doesn't he may be drafted and get a worse deal. He may therefore join, but that does not mean that he likes joining the army.

The important distinction here that is often missed is between wanting to do something and getting personal profit and satisfaction out of it. Humans do things out of a sense of duty or responsibility. Such behavior is neither altruistic nor non-altruistic. It is, from the standpoint of the behaver, a done thing, something which he does without requiring an explanation from himself. It makes no more sense to ask a person who does something out of a sense of duty what's in it for him than it makes to ask the diner why he's eating. Any answer will be given out of politeness and will be solely for the benefit of the (rather strange) questioner.

This distinction is hard to maintain, however, since humans tend to look at senses of duty with some suspicion. It is always hard—in fact it is usually impossible—to tell if you do something for someone else (or for a sense of duty) or for yourself. It often seems as if we prefer the certainty of self-degradation to the uncertainty that comes with trying to say something good about ourselves.

In most cases, this tendency is not harmful. But literature is filled with people who have been ruined by self-doubts when a cynic casts doubts on the motivational bases of their idealism. Even more important, the world is full of people and groups who have accepted degrading descriptions of themselves. Women and various "color groups" are good examples. The so-called mentally ill are first persecuted for their deviant behavior and later for being mentally ill. Drinkers can either stop drinking or be treated as alcoholics.

But no group of people have been oppressed without cooperation, and the groups mentioned above have accepted their labels and believed in them. Society does not allow some people or groups to have situation descriptions. They will have to create them themselves, against the opposition of society and the uncertainty in their own minds whether what they are doing is a rationalization or an explanation.

When it comes to rationalization versus explanation, the decision cannot be made until all the votes are in. It is incumbent upon the woman, the black, the drunk, or the nut to *make* it an explanation, or even better, a description, rather than keep the rationalization society favors.

Let us examine some of the problems a person who attempts such a difficult course of action can expect to face. In the process it will become clearer what I mean by changing a rationalization into an explanation. This is a process that can take place in an individual, and in an individual who is not part of a supportive group. The reasons for this will be made clear later through the examples.

Something similar to an existential decision is involved. Man may choose what he wishes to be, and he may initiate being what he wishes to be by redescribing his behavior.

The first problem a person faces is one of ability. One cannot choose to be what one can't be. If I choose to be a major league baseball player, I will be frustrated. I could be like Kierkegaard's Knight of Faith (in *Fear and Trembling*), who believes the impossible and thus embraces the absurd, but heroes of existential works have a much easier life than most of us. So I had better choose something I can do.

Suppose P finds that at parties he sometimes gets drunkenly rude and obnoxious. But suppose he refuses to accept that he is a drunk with a drinking problem. Perhaps his rudeness takes the form of making rather pointed remarks at people—in a very friendly way—to show them how they are shallow liars when they could be fine people. P could decide that he got drunk so that he could say the things that need to be said before people can be open and honest with each other and remove the nail polish veneer of over-civilization. In other words, P describes his drunkenness as the performative aspect of the intentional action, "Attempting intimacy with people by probing through their masks."

His description doesn't sound all that far-fetched, since it is well known that drinking allows people to loosen up with each other and that people go to bars to escape loneliness. But what if

P is not a very friendly person in the rest of his life? Suppose P is generally suspicious in real life of attempts at intimacy. Then it does not make much sense to say P is seeking intimacy. The explanation doesn't fit the facts, since P avoids intimacy, true or false, most of the time. Therefore, his explanation would seem to have been rendered worthless. At least he will have a hard time making this an explanation. He will have to change himself to become less nasty and more intimate.

This is no game. P's future depends upon the outcome. Perhaps P will try and succeed in being an intimate type of person; but perhaps that is so contrary to what he is now that the intimacy will always be a bit suspect and he will always be a bit uncomfortable about it. If so, he has made the wrong decision, and that can happen.

Perhaps, however, he finds this description, although flattering, too foreign to his nature, so he restlessly looks for another. Perhaps, he thinks, in getting drunk he is making a moral statement; he does hate polite society and its hypocrisy, and yet he likes interaction with honest and relaxed people sufficiently that he doesn't wish to leave society. This is hard to swallow. Getting drunk is a rather clumsy, offensive, and shallow (not to mention ineffective) way of making a moral statement. For many people, and no doubt for P, it probably is not the kind of performance that can be the performative aspect of the intentional action, "making a moral statement." In fact, to the extent that P is a moral person, he will take drunkenness to be a pretty lousy way of making a moral statement.

Suppose P is somewhat defensive, in addition to being moral, and says, "If I may make a moral statement, I think the same may be said of adultery and other sexual behaviors if it is taken to be the performative aspect of the intentional action, 'being free from old-fashioned clinging morality and possessiveness.' I don't care if people want to swap each other around, but I do object if people attempt to dignify such disgusting displays by claiming they are making a proclamation of emancipation, as they so often and so piously do these days."

It is now clear that P is the sort of person who doesn't mind making moral statements, and, to boot, moral statements in the old-fashioned style, with words like *disgusting*. So it appears that this explanation is better suited to his personality.

However, P will have to give up drinking. Getting abusively drunk is too far from the concept of morality to expect anyone to allow P to claim he is in that manner making moral statements. Furthermore, a person who makes moral statements must make them himself. He cannot stand behind liquor and he as well as his listeners must be able to be sure it is he and not his liquor speaking.

Thus from several points of view P must discontinue drinking. Furthermore, he must become a moral person in general and make moral statements in various contexts: we ascribe traits if and only if the behavior occurs in a variety of circumstances. In fact, it would seem that to the extent that P has been a worthless drunk he must become moral. The more of a drunk, the more moral. In this sense the morality of his later life is his rationalization for his earlier drunkenness. He has more to compensate for and more to prove to himself and to the rest of the world. He spends his life proving he *never was* (just) a heavy, abusive drinker (shades of *1984*).

Why, given all the trouble P will have to go through, shouldn't he just give up drinking and forget turning into a moralist?

Part and parcel of taking responsibility for your own behavior—in fact, what you get by paying in the currency of responsibility—is that you also get to take yourself and your behavior seriously. If you drink, you drink for a reason, because you are trying to accomplish something by it, albeit awkwardly. You are not *just* a drunk. And you haven't wasted all those months or years being a drunk. It was a stage along life's way.

You do not have to throw out your own behaviors any more than you throw out your own children if they act anti-socially. If you take responsibility for your own behavior you take responsibility for all your behavior, get to know all of it, and accept all of it as equal in the sense that it's all yours. You don't have to follow society and keep only those behaviors that are socially acceptable any more than you get to keep only those of your children society will let you keep. Drinking or insanity or whatever other deviant behavior you have been emitting becomes part of you, not an "illness" encrusted on the real.

Many of our great men and women have been great because they have taken themselves seriously and attempted to get others to do so also. If William Blake had decided he was *simply* crazy we would have been without his proverb, "The road of excess leads to the palace of wisdom."

And often it does. If you assume responsibility you may also assume credit, although there is the risk of blame. Thus minority groups that give situation descriptions of their plight and get them accepted by society at large and who then therefore receive various special favors can never really take credit for what they achieve. Ultimately they are dependent upon the larger society. I do not mean to suggest that minority groups shouldn't seek or have equal rights. But what applies to people in interpersonal relationships applies to groups in the relationship imposed by society. If the oppressing part of society gets all the blame, it gets any credit that is due too.

Dishonesty is the disorder of the day, however, despite the possibility of change if one is willing to accept responsibility. In the final section of this chapter I will discuss a number of forms of verbal dishonesty and their effects.

Verbal Rationalizations

And speaking *Personally* and if a man speak any other way we might as well start looking for his Protoplasm Daddy or Mother Cell.

William S. Burroughs, *Naked Lunch*

This book is a serious, scholarly book. I think I have made

some original contributions and I think I have applied a few central concepts and Ossorio's approach to several areas with some consequent integration of these areas. And I think the book serves as a good introduction to the social psychology of language use. In other words, it is a scholarly book rather than a popularization, a summary, or an entertainment. And yet I have written much of it in the first person singular, which is not appropriate for a scholarly book.

In scholarly books and articles *I* is replaced by such circumlocutions as *the present author, this writer,* or *the author.* Sometimes even more elaborate precautions are taken, and instead of saying, "the writer thought," the author says, "It was thought that."

From the context of this chapter, it appears (see, there it is) that this kind of locution *could* be used to evade responsibility. For example, if a writer says, "It was thought that X is the case," it is not quite clear who thought it, and the writer has a possible out—he can say, if challenged, that the janitor thought it. It is not even clear *when* it was thought.

It is of course true that authors can't *really* (in the sense of real names) evade responsibility in this manner, but it looks like another word magical attempt to do something that can't be done otherwise.

Often, when an article or book is written by more than one person, the authors employ *we.* I have seen this usage slip out when an article has been written by one person, and it is common usage by social scientists giving talks. Presumably these latter are referring to their graduate student assistants, who helped them with their research. But often they don't mention these assistants either by name or by implication. This looks like a classic case of diffusion of responsibility: if ten people said it, then each person can only receive one-tenth of the blame. (But, as I made clear in the last section, each person can only receive one-tenth of the credit.)

As I am flying in the face of the style manuals, I had better examine the official reasons for such locutions before leveling such a charge at all the thousands of respectable people who have used them. Probably many of them use such locutions because they are required, and required with an authoritarian righteousness. I recall having some graduate student assistant when I was in college crossing out all the *I*'s in a long and, if I may say so, brilliant essay on the romantic poets, but making no comments on the essay itself. He was giving excessive attention to style—and not even to style: to a symbol of style. I felt as if I had left myself exposed and had been wounded.

Yet perhaps the high point of my teaching career came, after I had berated a class for these various verbal ways of avoiding responsibility, when a student told me I had taught her how to write. She had never been able to write college papers, although she wrote good poetry. She felt the relief that comes when many inhibitions are suddenly removed. However, I am sure if she wrote a relaxed paper for an English class she was sharply criticized and felt guilty again. The use of the pronoun I is taken to be self-exposure by the guardians of proper style, and they can make you feel as if you have exposed yourself.

But why should being forced to use a few circumlocutions cause anyone any trouble? I think it is like trying to say something original, profound, or difficult in a language you don't know very well. You have to direct a great deal of attention to how you say it, so you can't pay proper or full attention to what you are saying. You are forced to pay excessive attention to a symbol of style.

In other terms, it is simply not natural. In ordinary discourse we don't refer to ourselves as *the speaker*. A schizophrenic might, as another attempt to avoid a relationship. Saying, "The speaker feels that the food is lousy," is a partial denial that the speaker is the one who feels the food is lousy. But it is not a very effective denial. More imaginative schizophrenics would claim that Jesus was the one who thought the food was lousy. Writers can't go that far. But at least this way of looking at it gives us an insight into why social scientific writing is said to be cold, impersonal, and *difficult to understand.* Perhaps the coldness and impersonality and difficulty are intentional. Perhaps the writer is attempting to deny a relationship between himself and the reader, much as a schizophrenic tries to deny a relationship between himself and his therapist.

The motive? Many critics of the social sciences have said that we attempt to write so that nobody can understand us, because if anybody could they would know that we say nothing new when we say anything, which is rare. The critics are equally guilty of evasion of responsibility, though: social science isn't that bad, and one has to give it a chance—if one pretends to be a critic. The critic who says, "I can't stand this jargon," is admitting he'd rather not try to understand it.

So the person forced to write in the elliptical style favored by the guardians may either ignore the proscriptions and feel exposed (as I suspect many schizophrenics feel), or they may accept the style with, it appears, the feeling of being somewhat schizophrenic. But surely there are good reasons for such proscriptions, especially if they do cause pain, so let us examine some of them.

Science, social science, journalism, literary criticism—all are (supposed to be) objective things, while human beings are subjective things. *I*'s that think, however, are presumably objective.

Clearly, objectivity cannot be accomplished simply by verbal tricks. But, it is possible, once one pays the proper lip service to objectivity through style, he can go ahead and be *excessively* subjective. The objective-subjective distinction is another one of those many we have met in this book where we have a unity that can be split by a focus on one aspect. We noted that if too much attention was paid to situational determinants of behavior, eventually too much would be paid to personal determinants to balance the scales. Perhaps a verbal homage to objectivity will allow the subjective to come out in an insidious manner. Recall the husband who killed his wife symbolically.

Another common locution will illustrate this possibility nicely. It is common for writers to say, "It might be that X is the case." This shows a proper regard for the fallibility of human judgment, and takes care of any possible subjectivity that might be lurking about. But note that X can be anything. "It could be that Hitler had the right idea." Challenge the writer and he need only say,

"Well, it *could* be. Part of science is that we never rule out anything in advance without empirical test."

It is hard to imagine that a writer would be allowed off the hook here, because this is such an extreme case. So perhaps he should have said, "It is thought by some that Hitler had the right idea." This is true, but unless the writer is pointing this out, rather than advancing an argument, he is trying to absolve himself of responsibility for the idea, and yet he is using it in advancing an argument; furthermore, he is lending it his name and authority. Who remembers the specifics of locutions? Any politician knows the terrible harm rumors can do to a career. If one politician says, "It has come to my attention that some people believe that Politician Z has been cheating on his income tax," Politician Z will be effectively put in the position one is placed in by the question, "And when did you stop beating your wife?" That is, one is forced to deny what one probably has no need to deny. Thus vicious slander may creep in under the cloak of language that is symbolically objective but in fact criminally subjective.

Not all writers who use these locutions are doing any real harm, and not all of them are even trying to evade responsibility. But no writer becomes objective simply by using the prescribed style. I would think, in fact, that if one is trying to be objective, it will be harder if he has to pay a good deal of attention to symbols of style. People can be objective. Any judgment is a person's judgment, of course, but we can tell one that tries to take all relevant considerations into account from one that is self-serving, narrow, or uninformed. Ordinarily, we expect people to try to render as good a judgment as they are capable of, but we recognize that they must judge from their own perspective. They have no other, after all.

Another common reason given for avoiding, e.g., the first person singular, is that the writer should not intrude his personality between the reader and his material. This is fair enough, although there is some implicit assumption that computers or *it*s write.

Norman Mailer seems often to be intruding irrelevant personal facts into his books, and this can be irritating. You may object, "I want to read about the moon shot, not about Norman's problems with his wife." Well, then, you should read an account of the moon shot by someone else, because Mailer considers his personal life quite relevant to the moon shot and vice versa. Nevertheless, we may have a sneaking suspicion that Mailer is up to something. In *Advertisements For Myself* he (using the first person) admits that he altered the first sentence of *The Deer Park* to slow the reader down by a slight irregularity of style. Perhaps he is trying to intrude. But why?

Style allows a writer to say something he couldn't say literally. We have discussed incongruent styles; Mailer's is interruptive. I think his interruptions may be read as follows: He is trying to say that individual human beings are being squashed by society, and that they should not be assimilated and swallowed by society to become automatic emitters of social practices. He is simply not going to let you relax with him. He has asked readers to please not understand him too quickly. He uses silly devices for referring to himself, e.g., Aquarius and PW, which stands for, among other things, Prisoner of Wedlock. He refuses even to say *I*, for *I* is common enough that it doesn't draw that much attention to the writer.

Why couldn't he come right out and say that society is killing us individuals? In the first place, he has said so *(Advertisements For Myself)*. But as he says it literally ("The shits are killing us") it sounds passive, silly, empty, and adolescent. In his recent writing, which could be called over-stylistic, he is showing that he refuses to be killed by attempting to bring himself to everything he writes about.

Exceptions such as Mailer aside, however, we do have a legitimate right not to be bothered by irrelevancies. That is, you have a legitimate right to not have to read the following paragraph (skip it if you want your rights):

As I write this, I am still recovering from a migraine headache that started three days ago on a Saturday. I don't know why it came, and I am ashamed of it because men aren't supposed to have migraines. They're supposed to get ulcers. I guess I'd rather have migraines, though, even if they aren't manly. They don't cause the damage that ulcers do, and they don't cost as much.

Now that is *real* interruption. But using *I* isn't.

You may have noticed that I used *I* rather freely, however, and your concentration may have been jolted time and time again as I used this common form. You may even have decided that I am a foolish egomaniac, since I don't have Norman Mailer's name.

Fortunately, we have the conceptual resources to deal with this problem. We ascribe traits when the behavior is excessive. Saying *I* is excessive in the context of a serious scholarly book, which I claim this is, but it is not excessive in the context of a conversation. I believe that scholarly books and articles are bad to the extent that they depart from the style and content of a conversation, and using *I* is sort of my way of saying this—it is also the way of writing that comes naturally to me because I have been using *I* all my life.

I strongly recommend directness. As I have indicated throughout this book, it doesn't seem to be the case that changing verbal behavior necessarily involves changing anything else. But the dangers I have mentioned are present and *may be* avoided by avoiding the verbal locutions that promote the potential for the dangers. If you refuse to stand behind euphemisms for *I* (and they may aptly be so described), you may have to take real precautions rather than just verbal ones.

Furthermore, saying "might" stops thinking. If you say, "It might be the case that X," you have codified all the possibilities—it might be and then again it might not, and your job as a thinker is done. On the other hand, if you make a direct statement of what you believe is the case, then you or someone else can be challenged, and your thinking can become more complex. In general, there are few propositions that are entirely true or false, and it is the specification of the exceptions to a proposition that is difficult, rare, and an important job of the social sciences.

Ossorio's cardinal principle is that every utterance is a person's utterance. The stylistic devices I have discussed here can legitimately be described as attempts to act as if utterances can be made by such things as *it*s. In the concluding section of this chapter I will discuss a pseudo-technique for ridding oneself of harmful prejudices against oneself by asking the simple question, Who says? (and accepting no *it*s or *Society*s). In other words, the technique involves trying to bring oneself to recognize that there are no truths: There are only statements by people, and all such statements can be challenged. Thus in the first part of this section I recommended that you speak personally. In the second I recommend you require statements to get themselves to a person.

The Source of Explanations

I have suggested that minority groups make the wrong move if they blame the oppressing class. By doing so they admit that the oppressing class has power. It may have, but acting as if it has only perpetuates the power structure. Furthermore, blaming someone else, like all situation descriptions, involves self-degradation. It is admitting you are the kind of person who can be and is pushed around. You don't have to act as if this is the case. If you do and everyone else does, then, for all practical purposes, you *are* pushed around. If you don't act as if this is the case, then there is at least one valid human statement to the effect that you are not the kind of person who can be pushed around.

I also believe that minority groups make the wrong move when they act as groups. In numbers is strength, to be sure, but what happens when you are alone again speaking with the oppressor? What you do with a group, including the sentiments you voice, may or may not be things you can or will do when you are without the rest of your group. You can't be sure until you do the same things alone, because you can't be sure if you did what you did (told someone off, beat up an oppressor, etc.) because of how you feel and are or because of the way the group helps or even forces you to feel. Thus several times I have received complaint visits from contingents of black students, who, I tell them, must be afraid to come in by themselves. Furthermore, while they say they are coming to complain about their grades or the work load, I tell them that the fact that they have come as a group of blacks makes it hard for me to ignore the implication that they feel that whatever is wrong results from my bigotry, and this, I inform them, irritates and insults me, and I refuse to do anything.

Groups can't speak personally, nor can they be spoken personally to. They are undifferentiated blobs of protoplasm— Mother Cells or Protoplasm Daddies.

The main reason, from the standpoint of this section, that blaming the oppressors as a group is not a good move is that the state of affairs thus represented is inaccurate. I have talked with college women many times about the problems they have as females who wish to be something else in addition. They often say that they are discriminated against because they are considered inferior; it is said that they are not aggressive enough, are emotionally unstable, and belong in the home. If they want a man's job they are castrating, ball-busting bitches, lesbians, or sexual cripples compensating for missing that most beautiful anatomical feature ever invented, the penis. They are thought of as sexual objects rather than human beings. Society believes they aren't smart in the ways of the world, they are physically weak, they can't stand pressure, they are dull and have nothing to say, they have no sense of humor or playfulness, they are slaves to ritual and symbols of joy they can't possess non-symbolically, they go for style and care little for substance, and they are likely at any moment to break down, give up the job (just as the new formula for a brand new laundry soap is about to be discovered) and have a baby.

Who Sez?

I want to become famous so that I can be on Johnny Carson and Dick Cavett and other such organs. I want these outlets so I can make pronouncements, like Norman Mailer, John Wayne, and football players, whose opinions on everything under the sun or on the ground are news. My fantasy headlines: KELLING SAYS GENE VINCENT GREATEST ROCK STAR EVER!!! IT'S NOT

THE HEAT THAT HURTS, IT'S THE HUMIDITY, CLAIMS
PSYCHOLOGIST.

I think the only way I can get to this position is to continue
to do research and to think about the two things I understand
least, interpersonal relationships and language, because I think I
have a good deal of ability in these areas.

Not everyone agrees. One person who doesn't is me. When
I am depressed or get another rejection letter or don't have any
pronouncements to make even if I could, I think I am pretty
worthless and ugly too and I've done some pretty rotten things
and why didn't mom and dad love me? One of the best ways to
get me depressed is to tell me I have no talent as a thinker/
researcher.

Women believe those things I mentioned above when they
are depressed, and, if my experience is any guide, they believe
them most strongly when somebody is saying them to them.
Thus, when they most need their defensive and offensive resources, they are likely to be most dispirited.

It is not easy to stop believing those things, but one can try
to believe them as little as possible, and even if one believes them
one can act as if one does not. One thing is sure: it doesn't help
to believe them. Surely a whole half of the human race can't have
been oppressed for centuries without some cooperation.

First I will ask *Who Sez?* of the women and then of the men.

What kind of woman would believe that a woman's place
was in the home? A weak, passive little thing who knew no
better? A brainwashed yeswoman for her husband? Perhaps. It is
this kind of woman who would think these things, *sez* woman's
lib.

But what of a woman who somewhere in the depths of her
soul recognizes that woman's liberation will mean an end to the
sheltered life of the housewife? Or what of a woman who didn't
want to take care of herself if she didn't want to and who would
like to be able to say to her husband, "I just can't cope anymore,
you'll have to take care of the whole thing," knowing full well
that unless he can and does his masculinity is impugned? Or a

woman who thinks that bringing children up is really more interesting than figuring out how to sell more toothpaste. Such might think these things too, *sez me.*

At any rate, if a woman has any of these feelings I have mentioned, she would do well to be aware of them and perhaps, if she takes herself seriously (which you can do if you take responsibility for all your behavior and feelings), she will take these feelings seriously and modify somewhat her goals for the future.

From another point of view: When would a woman say such things, say, to another woman? If P is a woman who feels rather poorly about herself, inferior, etc., and O is a friend who is trying to beat her own feelings of inferiority and do something with her life, P will have a reason for bringing forth the platitudes about women to keep O down on the farm so that O can keep her (P) company in misery. So the next time a woman tries to put you down, ask her why she's doing it and advance some speculative hypotheses.

But now to the oppressors. What kind of man would say such things about or to a woman? A depressed man, just like P above, who comes home from the office every day feeling just a little bit more defeated and who can hardly be expected to face a wife who is happy about all the wonderful things that happened to her that day (and if she fails it's because she's a woman; if he fails it's because he's *not* a man). Or a man who is plagued by a general inferiority and wants to have at least one person around to feel paternally superior to. Or a very stupid person, the kind who picks up a few slogans and devotes his life to them and is understandably perturbed, upset, angry, or outraged if his few cherished but very poorly defended beliefs are challenged. Or the father of the bridegroom, who wants his son to make good and knows he will be hindered if his wife starts acting uppity. Or the father of the bride, who hopes his little darling won't mess up her chances of being the wife of a famous man by trying to do things herself. Or the bride, who doesn't want to hurt her husband's feelings by being better than he, or who has tried and failed to make it on her own. And other specific human beings.

And nobody else. But so what? What if we do know that people who are chronically or temporarily weak and/or inferior, and only such people, believe these stereotypes with any intensity?

In the first place, we can begin to believe that no huge monolithic "society" is saying them, although this is not strictly true—when a number of people act in concert, it makes sense to talk about society doing something. But it doesn't help to feel that the whole world has it in for you and to attempt to attack the world as a whole. One can take each of the people aside and attack them separately: "Listen, you dried up old prune, just because you never liked sex or anything else either doesn't make you a fountain of wisdom on the conduct of marriage. Now you shut your yapper or I'll tell everyone about your joyless existence and why you feel the way you do."

This example illustrates that speaking personally has the advantage that you can tailor your attacks to the person. This makes them more effective, and it also avoids offending people for no reason. For example, many whites object to being told they can't help being prejudiced—they take part in institutional racism just by being born into this society. Such gross undifferentiated attacks do little good—and, even if you aren't interested in doing good but in doing damage, the personal attack is always best.

So requesting large entities such as "society" to speak personally may allow you the comfort of knowing that the labels pinned on you are pinned on for reasons other than their appropriateness, although one should never fail to examine each and every label for possible applicability. You will learn that all men are brothers in their need to step on each other. Perhaps more important, you can tailor your attacks to be effective: to tell a weak little man that his refusal to let you take a job is a sign that he is a male chauvinist oppressor will do nothing but inflate his ego (which may make him strong enough to let you take a job).

The aim of speaking personally, in the context of this section, is to make yourself independent of society for your definition of yourself. That is the problem for most deviant or minority groups (women, blacks and other colors, homosexuals, drunks, nuts, and criminals): they accept the labels they have been given.

Oddly enough, the group that seems most willing and able to verbally and violently reject society's names and labels are the so-called criminals. It strikes me as ludicrous, obscene, and obnoxious when a jailed criminal, having engaged in a riot which killed guards and cost people money in damage to state or federal property, and having done something against the law to begin with, speaks to the television camera with righteous indignation about the quality of the food and lodging. So it is odd that of those groups mentioned above the only one that has freely and vigorously without self-doubt complained is the only one that has done something to deserve what it got.

Perhaps the explanation is simple enough. Perhaps criminals are rugged individualists, or perhaps their punishment is so direct and non-incongruent that they can give a single solitary message in reply. But I tend to describe it differently. Unlike the other groups, the criminal needs the oppressing class, and he needs it to stay exactly as it is. He has a stake in the status quo. If the "establishment" were to change he would be without status, and his existence would have no rationale. The goal of speaking personally is to be a person, separate and individual. The criminal, by virtue of the nature of his occupation, can't be separate and individual. Hence, paradoxically, he is part of the society and feels free to complain, just as a child does.

Thus this book concludes with a bit of practical application. But the "advice" isn't very helpful. It is like the advice columnist who advises a shy person to go out and get a date (psychologists sneer at the simplicity of such advice).

Social science must be straightforwardly and intentionally applied, or it will be misused and abused (as we have seen in many cases, neglect of an important aspect of something allows it out later in a rather bad form, e.g., personality descriptions in arguments). The kind of application I offer here is about all social science can or should give. That that is the case follows almost directly from a major theme of this book: people aren't puppets.

So social science will not be able to come up with legitimate advice which is the kind that sounds as if it could be applied to puppets, e.g., "Do X and Y will happen."

As long as social science dreams of planning things so that everything will be nice regardless of the wishes of people who want things rotten or don't like what other people call nice, it will not be applied social science. But it will be applied, with, perhaps, great harm, as in the case of the man who couldn't kill his wife and killed her more effectively symbolically. So watch your language.

Bibliography

Bibliography I: Producers of Paradigms and Concepts

Brown, R. *Social Psychology*. Glencoe, Ill.: Free Press, 1965.

Haley, J. *Strategies of Psychotherapy*. New York: Grune & Stratton, 1963.

————. *The Power Tactics of Jesus Christ*. New York: Avon, 1969.

Ossorio, P. *Persons*. Los Angeles: Linguistic Research Institute, 1966 (a).

————. *Outline of Behavior Description*. Los Angeles: Linguistic Research Institute, 1966 (b).

————. *Notes on Behavior Description*. Los Angeles: Linguistic Research Institute, 1969.

————. *Meaning and Symbolism*. Los Angeles: Linguistic Research Institute, 1971.

————. Never smile at a crocodile. *Journal for the Theory of Social Behavior*, 1973, **3**, 121–40.

————. *What Actually Happens: The Representation of Real World Phenomena in Behavioral Science*. Descriptive Psychology Monographs, Volume 1. Boulder, Colo.: Linguistic Research Institute, 1974.

Whorf, B. L. *Language, Thought, and Reality* (edited and with an introduction by J. B. Carroll). Cambridge, Mass.: M.I.T. Press & New York: John Wiley & Sons, 1956.

Wittgenstein, L. *Philosophical Investigations* (trans. G.E.M. Anscombe). New York: Macmillan, 1953.

Bibliography

Bibliography II: References

Alston, W. P. *Philosophy of Language.* Englewood Cliffs, N.J.: Prentice-Hall, 1964.

Antosch, F. The diagnosis of literary style with the verb-adjective ratio. In L. Dolezel and R. W. Bailey (eds.), *Statistics and Style.* New York: American Elsevier Publishing Company, 1969.

Barron, F. The psychology of creativity. In *New Directions in Psychology II.* New York: Holt, Rinehart & Winston, 1965.

Bem, D. J. Self-perception: An alternative interpretation of cognitive dissonance phenomena. *Psychological Review,* 1967, 74, 183–200.

Benedict, R. *Patterns of Culture.* New York: Penguin Books, 1946.

Bennett, P. E. The statistical measurement of a stylistic trait in *Julius Caesar* and *As You Like It.* In L. Dolezel and R. W. Bailey (eds.), *Statistics and Style.* New York: American Elsevier Publishing Company, 1969.

Berko, J. The child's learning of English morphology. *Word,* 1958, 14, 150–77.

Berlyne, D. E. Laughter, humor, and play. In G. Lindzey and E. Aronson (eds.), *The Handbook of Social Psychology.* Reading, Mass.: Addison Wesley, 1969.

Boder, D. P. The adjective-verb quotient; a contribution to the psychology of language. *Psychological Record, 1940,* 3, 309–43.

Bolinger, D. *Aspects of Language.* New York: Harcourt, Brace, & World, 1968.

Bibliography

Brown, R. *Words and Things.* Glencoe, Ill.: Free Press, 1958.

———. *Social Psychology.* Glencoe, Ill.: Free Press, 1965.

Brown, R., and M. Ford. Address in American English. *Journal of Abnormal and Social Psychology,* 1961, **62,** 375–85.

Brown, R., and C. Fraser. The acquisition of syntax. In C. N. Cofer and B. S. Musgrave (eds.), *Verbal Behavior and Learning: Problems and Processes.* New York: McGraw-Hill, 1963.

Brown, R., and A. Gilman. The pronouns of power and solidarity. In T. A. Sebeok (ed.), *Style in Language.* Cambridge, Mass.: M. I. T. Press, 1960.

Brown, R., and E. H. Lenneberg. A study in language and cognition. *Journal of Abnormal and Social Psychology,* 1954, **49,** 454–62.

Brown, R. W. Language and categories. In J. S. Bruner, J. J. Goodnow, and G. A. Austin, *A Study of Thinking.* New York: John Wiley & Sons, 1956.

Bull, W. E. *Time, Tense, and the Verb.* Berkeley: University of California Press, 1960.

Burroughs, W. S. *Naked Lunch.* New York: Grove Press, 1959.

———. *The Ticket That Exploded.* New York: Grove Press, 1962.

Carmichael, L.; H. P. Hogan; and A. A. Walter. An experimental study of the effect of language on the representation of visually perceived form. *Journal of Experimental Psychology,* 1932, **15,** 73–86.

Carroll, J. B. Review of "The Measurement of Meaning." *Language,* 1959, **35,** 58–77.

———. Vectors of prose style. In T. A. Sebeok (ed.), *Style in Language.* Cambridge, Mass.: M. I. T. Press, 1960.

———. *Language and Thought.* Englewood Cliffs, N.J.: Prentice-Hall, 1964.

Carroll, J. B., and J. B. Casagrande. The function of language classification. In E. E. Maccoby et al. (eds.), *Readings in Social Psychology* (3d ed.). New York: Holt, Rinehart & Winston, 1958.

Chomsky, N. *Language and Mind.* New York: Harcourt Brace Jovanovich, 1968.

Cliff, N. Adverbs as multipliers. *Psychological Review,* 1959, **66,** 27–44.

Deese, J. On the structure of associative meaning. *Psychological Review,* 1962, **69,** 161–75.

————. *Psycholinguistics.* Boston: Allyn & Bacon, 1970.

Dreher, J. J., and E. L. Young. Chinese author identification by segment distribution. In L. Dolezel and R. W. Bailey (eds.), *Statistics and Style.* New York: American Elsevier Publishing Company, 1969.

Fishman, J. A. A systematization of the Whorfian hypothesis. *Behavioral Science,* 1960, **5,** 1–29.

Flavell, J. H. A test of the Whorfian theory. *Psychological Reports,* 1958, **4,** 455–62.

Fodor, J. A., and T. Bever. The psychological reality of linguistic segments. *Journal of Verbal Learning and Verbal Behavior,* 1965, **4,** 414–20.

Garrett, M.; T. Bever; and J. A. Fodor. The active use of grammar in speech perception. *Perception and Psychophysics,* 1966, **1,** 30–32.

Gilman, A., and R. Brown. Emerson and Thoreau: Personality and style in Concord. In M. Simon and T. Parsons (eds.), *The Legacy of Transcendentalism.* Ann Arbor: University of Michigan Press, 1966.

Greenberg, J. H. Some universals of grammar with particular reference to the order of meaningful elements. In J. H. Greenberg (ed.), *Universals of Language.* Cambridge, Mass.: M. I. T. Press, 1962.

Gross, M. L. *The Brain Watchers.* New York: New American Library of World Literature, 1962.

Haley, J. *Strategies of Psychotherapy.* New York: Grune & Stratton, 1963.

————. *The Power Tactics of Jesus Christ.* New York: Avon, 1969.

Hall, E. T. *The Silent Language.* Garden City, N.Y.: Doubleday, 1959.

Hall, R. A., Jr. *Linguistics and Your Language.* New York: Anchor, 1960.

Bibliography

Hayes, C. W. A study in prose styles: Edward Gibbon and Ernest Hemingway. In L. Dolezel and R. W. Bailey (eds.), *Statistics and Style.* New York: American Elsevier Publishing Company, 1969.

Jenkins, J. J. Commonality of association as an indicator of more general patterns of verbal behavior. In T. A. Sebeok (ed.), *Style in Language.* Cambridge, Mass.: M. I. T. Press, 1960.

Johnson, M. G. Syntactic position and rated meaning. *Journal of Verbal Learning and Verbal Behavior,* 1967, **6.**

Jones, E. *Hamlet and Oedipus.* New York: Doubleday, 1963.

Kelling, G. W. The personality of the creative person. Unpublished manuscript, 1967.

Kierkegaard, S. *Fear and Trembling.* Garden City, N.Y. Doubleday, 1954.

Kolers, P. A. It loses something in the translation. *Psychology Today,* 1969, **2, 32–35.**

Kuhn, T. S. *The Structure of Scientific Revolutions.* Chicago: University of Chicago Press, 1962.

Kumata, H., and W. Schramm. A pilot study of cross-cultural meaning. *Public Opinion Quarterly,* 1956, **20,** 229–38.

Lantz, D. L., and V. Stefflre. Language and cognition revisited. *Journal of Abnormal and Social Psychology,* 1964, **69,** 472–81.

Lee, D. D. Lineal and non-lineal codifications of reality. *Psychosomatic Medicine,* 1950, **12,** 89–97.

Lenneberg, E. H. Cognition and ethnolinguistics. *Language,* 1953, **29,** 463–71.

———. Color naming, color recognition, color discrimination: A reappraisal. *Perceptual and Motor Skills,* 1961, **12,** 375–82.

Lenneberg, E. H., and J. M. Roberts. The language of experience. *International Journal of American Linguistics,* 1956, **22,** No. 2.

Livant, W. P. A comparison of noun and verb forms of the semantic differential. *Journal of Verbal Learning and Verbal Behavior,* 1963, **1,** 357–60.

Luce, G. G. *Body Time.* New York: Pantheon Books, 1971.

Bibliography

MacKinnon, D. W. The nature and nurture of creative talent. *American Psychologist,* 1962, **17,** 484–95.

Maclay, H. An experimental study of language and non-linguistic behavior. *Southwestern Journal of Anthropology,* 1958, **14,** 220–29.

Maclay, H., and E. E. Ware. Cross-cultural use of the semantic differential. *Behavioral Science,* 1961, **6,** 185–90.

Maher, B. A. *Principles of Psychopathology.* New York: McGraw-Hill, 1966.

Mailer, N. *Advertisements For Myself.* New York: Signet, 1960.

Miller, G. A., and D. McNeill. Psycholinguistics. In G. Lindzey and E. Aronson (eds.), *The Handbook of Social Psychology.* Reading, Mass.: Addison Wesley, 1969.

Muller, C. Lexical distribution reconsidered: The Waring-Herdan formula. In L. Dolezel and R. W. Bailey (eds.), *Statistics and Style.* New York: American Elsevier Publishing Company, 1969.

Pavy, D. Verbal behavior in schizophrenia. *Psychological Bulletin,* 1968, **70,** 455–62.

Piaget, J. *The Child's Conception of Physical Causality.* Totowa, N.J.: Littlefield, Adams & Company, 1969.

Robinson, W. P. *Language and Social Behavior.* Harmondsworth, Middlesex, England: Penguin Books, 1972.

Rosenberg, S. *Directions in Psycholinguistics.* New York: Macmillan, 1965.

Slobin, D. I. *Psycholinguistics.* Glenview, Ill.: Scott, Foresman & Company, 1971.

Suci, G. J. A comparison of semantic structures in American Southwest culture groups. *Journal of Abnormal and Social Psychology,* 1960, **62,** 25–30.

Triandis, H. C., and C. E. Osgood. A comparative factorial analysis of semantic structures in monolingual Greek and American college students. *Journal of Abnormal and Social Psychology,* 1958, **57,** 187–96.

Van De Geer, J. P. Studies in codability: I. Identification and recognition of colors. *Psychological Institute,* State University of Leyden, The Netherlands, Report No. E001–60, 1960.

Bibliography

Van De Geer, J. P., and N. H. Frijda. Studies in codability: II. Identification and recognition of facial expressions. *Psychological Institute,* State University of Leyden, The Netherlands, Report No. E002–60, 1960.

Wells, W.D.; F. J. Goi; and S. A. Seader. A change in product image. *Journal of Applied Psychology,* 1958, **42,** 120–21.

Wentworth, H., and S. B. Flexner. *Dictionary of American Slang.* New York: Thomas Crowell, 1960.

Whorf, B. L. *Language, Thought, and Reality* (edited and with an introduction by J. B. Carroll). Cambridge, Mass.: M. I. T. Press & New York: John Wiley & Sons, 1956.

Wilson, J. *Thinking With Concepts.* Cambridge: Cambridge University Press, 1966.

Winter, W. Styles as dialects. In L. Dolezel and R. W. Bailey (eds.), *Statistics and Style.* New York: American Elsevier Publishing Company, 1969.

Wittgenstein, L. *Philosophical Investigations* (trans. by G. E. M. Anscombe). New York: Macmillan, 1953.

Zipf, G. K. *The Psycho-Biology of Language.* Boston: Houghton Mifflin, 1935

Bibliography

Bibliography III: A Brief, Incomplete Annotated Bibliography of Similar Works

Alston, William P. *Philosophy of Language.* Englewood Cliffs, N.J. Prentice-Hall, 1964. An excellent discussion of the problem of meaning, well worth the difficulty of the material.

Bolinger, D. *Aspects of Language.* New York: Harcourt, Brace & World, 1968. A highly readable and literate introduction to linguistics. While it is not quite a popularization, it is perhaps the best of the books in this area for the lay reader.

Brown, R. *Words and Things.* Glencoe, Ill.: Free Press, 1958. Anything by Brown is highly recommended. This deals with animal communication, meaning, linguistic relativity, and many other subjects. A good book, although I recommend his 1965 textbook for a more complete and up-to-date coverage of many of the topics in this book.

Carroll, J. B. *Language and Thought.* Englewood Cliffs, N.J.: Prentice-Hall, 1964. Short and too broad, but with occasional fine passages. Developmental emphasis.

Chomsky, N. *Language and Mind.* New York: Harcourt Brace Jovanovich, 1968. The best and least technical introduction to the theory and especially the social implications of the theory of the man who I am almost alone among non-behavioristic social scientists in thinking is not responsible for one of the most revolutionary conceptions in intellectual and scientific history.

Deese, J. *Psycholinguistics.* Boston: Allyn & Bacon, 1970. Quite technical, but contains material not often covered in such books.

Hall, E. T. *The Silent Language.* Garden City, N.Y.: Doubleday, 1959. A sometimes interesting discussion of non-verbal communication, with particular attention to personal distance. If you feel trespassed on when someone gets too close to you (or if you feel that you must have B.O. or Bad Breath despite the protestations of your best friends), you should read all about how we like people to keep a certain distance from us.

Hall, Robert A., Jr. *Linguistics and Your Language.* New York: Anchor, 1960. A brief introduction to linguistics, with a good deal of discussion of the issue of correctness. If you feel inferior (or superior) about your accent or syntax or even about your language, this book might help you.

Robinson, W. P. *Language and Social Behavior.* Harmondsworth, Middlesex, England: Penguin Books, 1972. Interesting and generally well written, covering subjects not often covered in American books. Unlike most books in this area (Bolinger's is the other major exception), Robinson adds something of his own.

Rosenberg, Sheldon. *Directions in Psycholinguistics.* New York: Macmillan, 1965. A collection of articles on a rather unintegrated variety of topics, with heavy emphasis on verbal learning. Technical.

Slobin, Dan I. *Psycholinguistics.* Glenview, Ill.: Scott, Foresman & Company, 1971. A brief introduction to various topics in psycholinguistics, including generative-transformational grammar, developmental psycholinguistics, meaning, and "Language and Cognitions" (essentially the subject matter of this book). Although almost too over-simplified to be of much value, it is well written and has good examples and illustrations.

INDEX